A Long Way From Nowhere

A Couple's Journey on the Continental Divide Trail

Matt and Julie Urbanski

Kristy,

We've been on an adventure together for almost 10 years now. I wouldn't trade a minute of it for anything else in life. You've talked about the Divide Trail for years now & this book is the first step in making that dream a reality. Thank you so very much for letting me be your partner in all these adventures. Let's go make some more adventures together!

- Love, JB

Copyright © 2014 Matt and Julie Urbanski

All rights reserved. No part of this publication may be reproduced, distributed, or transmitted in any forms or by any means, including photocopying, recording, or other electronic or mechanical methods, without the prior written permission of the publisher, except in the case of brief quotations embodied in critical reviews and certain other noncommercial uses permitted by copyright law.

A Long Way From Nowhere: A Couple's Journey on the Continental Divide Trail

Self-published by Matt and Julie Urbanski
Images and editing provided by Matt and Julie Urbanski
Front cover: A rock cairn guiding the way in New Mexico
www.urbyville.com
First Edition
ISBN: 149549540X
ISBN-13: 978-1495495403

For TJ

CONTENTS

Part 1 1

Part 2 83

Part 3 141

Part 4 251

PART 1

1
Stopwatch

Our plane landed in El Paso, Texas, at 5:00pm and Matt and I headed towards baggage claim to pick up our packs. Before reaching the carousel, we ran into Raisins and Tatu-jo, their packs already sitting loosely on their backs.

"Sam's not here," Raisins said.

My stomach fell.

"Seriously?" Matt asked.

"We've been here for hours and have walked around looking for him, but he hasn't shown up. We need another ride to Crazy Cook," Raisins confirmed.

While we were curious why Sam hadn't shown up despite our scheduled meet-up, we were more concerned about setting up a new ride to a place that was fairly far away and even more remote, the start of the Continental Divide Trail. Both Matt and I let out a heavy sigh as we put aside our anxiety over starting the trail and put on our problem-solving hats in order to figure out how to get to the trail, which was 150 miles away.

"I already called another guy and I think we have a ride tomorrow morning. I just have to call him to confirm as long as you guys are all ok with it," Joe assured us.

Thankfully, Raisins and Joe had been at the airport for so many hours that they'd already done most of the Plan B legwork.

"There are lots of hotels nearby that have shuttles from the airport. We can all share a room tonight for like a hundred bucks, and then get a ride to the start tomorrow morning," Joe continued.

The plan sounded good to us and frankly, it was all we had. People weren't exactly offering up rides, there weren't trail angels this far away from the trail, and Matt and I were so tired from a day of flying that I was ready to tag along with any group decision. Despite a rocky start to our Continental Divide Trail, we were still making forward progress, and that was something to be positive about.

As we stood there, stranded at the airport, I had to swallow the fact that the flexibility factor of the CDT, something I'd only heard about, was very real. We hadn't even made it to the start of the trail before adapting our plans to a factor outside of our control. That moment of altering the first step of our CDT journey set the tone for the rest of the trail.

The Continental Divide Trail, the CDT, is a south to north trail that spans approximately 3,000 miles from Mexico to Canada through New Mexico, Colorado, Wyoming, Idaho, and Montana. It's likened to the PhD of thru-hiking because of the many challenges it presents, along with the required skills it takes to cover the miles and deal with the many unknowns that happen along the way. The trail is long, it's often unmarked and without tread, it's dry in many sections, it's high in elevation, lightning is an ongoing threat, and it has grizzly bears. These factors differentiate it from other trails and yet it's also similar to other long trails because it is just that, a long trail that requires all the gear to live outside for several months and that involves resupplies and continuous progress from one end to the other.

My husband and I, also known as Optimist and Stopwatch on the trail, were at the tail end of a two-year hiatus from work before the start of the trail. We both worked in finance for several years in our late twenties, saving away a nest egg and finally cashing it in during the spring of 2011 for a lifestyle of traveling, running, and hiking. The CDT fit in perfectly as our final adventure before returning to a more settled lifestyle of nursing school for Matt and professional work for me. We had already hiked the Pacific Crest Trail in 2007, the Appalachian Trail in 2011, and the Colorado Trail in 2012. We felt confident in our abilities to hike the CDT. The problem was, despite the miles on our hiking resumes, the CDT still scared the hell out of me, and for good reason.

The CDT is the longest of the three major south to north trails in the US, including the AT and the PCT, also known as the "Triple Crown." Both fortunately and unfortunately, the length is perhaps the easiest aspect of the CDT. The trail itself is only about seventy percent complete, a trait that's fairly hard to fathom. In other words, there are many portions of the trail which simply aren't trail, where a map and compass at the least and ideally a GPS, are necessary to find one's way. New Mexico, along with other sections in Wyoming and Montana, is notorious for a near lack of water, including a sixty-mile stretch without a single water source. Much of Colorado is above 10,000' of continuous miles, not just peaks, passes, or high points, like on the PCT, but rather, days above tree line. Those days above tree line are threatened by the reliable, daily thunderstorms of Colorado that can easily stop a day's hike and force a hiker to descend in elevation and wait out a storm for safety. Lastly, in addition to the typical assortment of wildlife, including bears and mountain lions, two animals I prefer to avoid, the CDT adds in the grizzly bear, a creature that knows it's at the top of the food chain.

As if all those aspects weren't enough to scare me into the urban jungle for the rest of my life, the final icing on the cake as I prepared for the CDT was that there were few good planning resources for the trail. There were many resources, just none that spanned all aspects of the CDT, which made it a daunting task to prepare for the trail. There were several different route choices, including three starting points in New Mexico and two endpoints in Canada. There wasn't just one set of maps, but rather several sets from different sources, all varying in quality, cost, and detail. There were several different guidebooks, in addition to free resources here and there that kind souls had put together in their free time. Information was scattered about and even sometimes obtained through word of mouth. There were in fact popular guidebooks published by hikers from previous years, but because I'd been spoiled on previous trails by a single book that was a one-stop shop for my route, my resupplies, and logistical aspects of the trail, I didn't find the CDT books useful enough. Admittedly, I'd never carried or even needed maps on any previous hikes, I had never learned how to use a compass or read a map, and I certainly never did much research beyond buying a small, compact data book for the trail and picking out future resupply points. There would be a lot of "firsts" on the CDT, these aspects included.

I dubbed the CDT, "The Mystery Trail," before we started hiking. I likened its preparations to that of a video game from my childhood, "The Legend of Zelda." I was in grade school when we first purchased the game for our Nintendo system and our family was hooked on it for several months. The game was a mixture of action, puzzles, adventure, exploration, and questing. There were hidden passages, secret doors, useful tokens…I loved it.

Preparing for the CDT was a little like playing Zelda. Nothing was really set in stone, finding information on it was like discovering a secret passage, and there were a lot of rumors about it based on others' opinions. The CDT was shrouded in mystery and it took me months of research, preparation, and spreadsheet building before I felt comfortable about the journey we were embarking on. I wanted to leave no stone unturned as I tried to uncover each and every aspect of trail preparation, including the big pieces like route choices, resupply strategies, food choices, and gear updates. The smaller pieces included park permits, blog preparations, and instructions for family members to mail our food on time and to the right addresses. It was nearly a full-time job to prepare for the trail and I embraced every part of it, hoping every moment spent preparing translated to a moment spent enjoying the trail. The less I had to hassle with logistics on-trail, the better.

Matt's preparations were a little different than mine. He's not a researcher, he doesn't naturally gravitate towards spreadsheets, and he refuses to waste energy on worrying. In fact, one of his few preparations included counting out toilet paper squares, one of the jobs I assigned to him as I packed our resupply boxes before leaving. In case you're interested, we allotted ourselves twenty squares a day; quite a generous number in the thru-hiker world, but absolutely necessary, as you'll soon learn.

Matt is known as Optimist for a reason and that reason is because he always finds the bright side of a situation, no matter how difficult it might seem, and he usually does it with a smile on his face. Before the trail, every time I brought up a concern like a waterless stretch in the Black Range of New Mexico, he said something like, "Ah, forget about it. We'll be fine!"

By the time the start of the trail came around, every piece was in place that I had thought of and had control over, and I relinquished all other unknown or uncontrollable factors to the simple strategy of letting things play out as they may. Matt was ecstatic that the planning part of the trail was finally over, mainly because I could then stop worrying about it and we could simply start walking.

After all the preparations, prepared or not, we flew to El Paso on May 23rd with the intent of getting picked up by Sam Hughes, a well-known and much-loved trail angel that lived in nearby Hachita, NM. He was an older man with meager means and fairly poor health, and trying to reach him was like hitting the jackpot in the lottery. In today's tech-heavy world, he was nearly in the dark with only a landline phone to connect him to the outside world. We all hoped his lack of presence at the airport simply meant that he forgot about our plans. We had originally planned on driving to the trail that very same night.

Those plans fell by the wayside after we arrived in El Paso and learned that there was no sign of Sam. Instead of spending that first night on the trail, we agreed with Raisins and Joe to get a hotel room among the four of us. Joe had already set up a ride with a man named Roger, whose information was in a newly published trail guidebook. Roger was to pick us up at 9:30am the next morning and from there we'd begin our CDT journey, which in my mind had already begun the moment we stepped off the plane and had to make a Plan B. I tried not to let it bother me that we were already off-track and we were on a fairly tight schedule. We only had 118 days to hike 3,018 miles, as Matt had to return to Seattle before September 19th for a required nursing school meeting. If he missed the meeting, he wouldn't be allowed to start nursing school, something he spent the last year trying to get into.

That evening in El Paso with Raisins and Joe was like a big show and tell. All of us had already hiked both the PCT and AT, and yet all of us had very different hiking styles and therefore different gear, different food, different resupplies, and different routes. Raisins hiked the AT the same year as us, 2011, and though he finished just four days behind us, we never met him. He knew plenty about us after following us up the trail for a summer, seeing our names in the shelter journals along the way. We happened to cross paths with him in a post on the CDT Facebook page and a friendship was born from there. Over the course of months of preparation, Raisins was my spreadsheet buddy and go-to resource as we prepared for the trip. He researched every aspect of the trail to such minute details that even me, who took pride in my ability to gather hard-to-find information, never found half the information he provided so effortlessly on gear, routes, food, weather, etc. Raisins had just finished his junior year of college in Maine and had hiked the PCT and AT in the summers between spring and fall semesters, meaning he could hike fast, given those breaks barely lasted over 100 days.

Joe was somewhat of a hikeaholic, especially since he lived so close to trails in his Southern California home, having hiked the PCT several times, at one point holding the speed record for it, and having hiked thousands of other miles compounded over years of hiking. He worked construction projects in the off-season, oftentimes building up his calorie reserves, only to take time off to hike and burn it all off again. We met him six years prior on the PCT as he was on his way to a speed record. The PCT was my first experience in long distance backpacking and I felt like a different person since the last time we saw him. He knew us as trail newbies with heavy packs and poor planning skills, and there we were with ten pound packs, thousands of miles under our belts, and impeccable plans. I would have never guessed that our lives would have taken us all full-circle to start the CDT together, as it was the final piece of the triple crown for all of us. Being in that hotel room with such unique, talented people felt like an appropriate start to such an epic adventure and it created a tangible buzz of excitement.

It was a case of opposites attract with Raisins and Joe, who were similarly successful at thru-hiking and yet incredibly different in personality. Raisins was of Korean descent, with a reserved personality, a witty sense of humor, and a little bit of college-student softness to his figure. Joe (Tatu-jo was his trail name, but we just called him Joe) was a middle-aged Southern Californian with an overweight, bronzed physique and a loud, social personality. Even though their demeanors were different, they both had magnetic personalities that demanded attention. We were happy to be in their company. Both of them combined had plenty of hiking experience and the stories to back up any of their claims. The one glaring thing they had in common was that they both hiked light and fast. Their packs weighed well under ten pounds and each could easily cover thirty miles a day without taxing themselves too much. We spent all night comparing notes, talking gear, swapping stories, and discussing future plans.

The next morning, my plan was to simply go with the flow and accept the changes to the plan. I could see that we were not in control of the situation and I was happy that Plan B had been a fairly easy option.

At 9:30am on the dot, our Plan B showed up and we all exhaled a sigh of relief that we didn't need to resort to Plan C, which didn't even exist. Roger pulled up to the curb in front of the hotel and all four of us slung our clean, well-organized packs into the bed of his truck. I would need to get used to throwing my pack in the back of a stranger's car if I hoped to get to some of the remote trail towns along the way.

After Roger picked us up, we spent the better part of the day getting to Crazy Cook, the official southern terminus of the CDT, located in the Bootheel of New Mexico. From El Paso we drove through Deming, NM, a small town with a grocery store, where all of us loaded up on gallon jugs of water, Gatorade, and snacks.

From the moment we started driving, I gathered two things about the surrounding environment. It was hot and it was desolate. We saw flat, open expanses of sun-baked land for miles in each direction. Everything was brown, there were no trees to offer shade or even a different color in the landscape, and gusts of wind kicked up small tornadoes of dust off the ground. Since I'd seen photos of New Mexico, I had an idea of what it looked like, but I could have never guessed what it felt like. It truly felt like a final frontier of the US, where few people boldly went and where mistakes were not easily forgiven by the terrain. I imagined Alaska had similar feelings of being a final frontier, only colder. The area felt incredibly lonely as Roger's truck drove along the one sign of civilization in such abyss-like surroundings, the strip of highway asphalt cutting through the desert like a single black thread sewn across a light brown quilt.

I didn't have much hope of running into any hikers other than Raisins or Joe, as the majority of northbounders, approximately 100 total, had left Crazy Cook long ago, about a month ahead of us. Raisins couldn't start any earlier because his school semester had ended two days prior and none of us wanted to start any earlier because of snow in Colorado. Most northbounders ahead of us avoided the furnace of heat we were about to enter in New Mexico but they also had to deal with the challenges of snow, which had yet to melt in many parts of Colorado.

The scenery never changed for the entire trip as I stared out the window. There was some small talk among everyone in the truck, but for the most part there was a nervous silence. The reality was setting in as we all looked out the window and peered into our future landscape for the next 700 miles.

Before heading to the southern terminus, we stopped at three different road crossings to cache water for ourselves. There weren't any water sources for the first several days so we bought and cached our own gallon jugs of water, hiding them off the side of the trail, behind bushes and out of sight. The last thing I wanted was to reach those spots over the next couple of days, only to find empty jugs that someone else had discovered because I hadn't hid them well enough. It seemed like a counter-intuitive thought, based on how empty the surroundings felt, but I wasn't taking any chances with my water.

Each time we exited the truck to put out water, the temperature seemed higher and the air seemed drier. Though it wasn't humid, the heat still felt suffocating, like I was in a dry sauna, breathing in the thick, hot air. The southern portion of the PCT was similarly lacking in many water sources but it had been six years since I had worried about water, so I had a hard time remembering just how bad it had been. I didn't try to remember for long because my present situation in New Mexico was at the forefront of my mind.

After caching water, we had just one more road to drive before reaching Crazy Cook.

For the next twenty miles, Roger's sturdy truck and trusty GPS guided us over bumpy, rutted, unmaintained dirt roads. It took the next two and half hours to traverse those miles, a speed which Matt could run faster. None of us had any idea that the ride was that rough or that slow. While Raisins was lulled into sleep by the rocking of the truck, Matt bounced along in the middle-back seat and I watched the minutes on the clock tick by. I gave up any hope of hiking much that day. It would be another day that we'd have to relinquish to the flexibility factor of the CDT.

My trail name is Stopwatch and that day explained why. I'm the type of person that can't help but run numbers through my head, calculating time and mileage, sometimes letting anxiety over those numbers get the better of me, sometimes not. While I wasn't upset over the loss of another hiking day, as I knew plans were destined to change, it was still in my nature to think about how a change in plans affected those numbers. I did a lot of mental calculations in the car ride that day.

Each time one of us asked Roger for an update, he pointed to a hillside far off into the distance and replied, "Oh, just a couple more miles to go." It all looked the same to me. I just hoped we never actually hiked deeply into the hills alongside the dirt road, as the rocky, barren hillsides looked unforgiving and rugged. I already knew none of them had any water.

Finally, Roger came to a stop within a few feet of a flimsy barbed wire fence, the border between Mexico and the United States. All my memories from the first day on the PCT came flooding back to me, as we'd started midday in mid-May, just as we were here. It was 3:30pm, nearly 100 degrees outside, and there was nothing out there but us five human beings, the sun, and the wind. We walked over to the monument that marked the spot as Crazy Cook, only to find a small piece of stone lying in the dirt. One line of sloppy handwriting was etched into the stone, marking the location as a place where a man was murdered in cold blood in 1907 by a crazy cook. There was also a CDT monolith, its concrete base marking it as the Southernmost Point of the CDT, with a kiosk nearby with information on the trail and even a pavilion to offer shade. I wondered just how many people in the world had actually seen this spot, miles from civilization but still claimed by humans.

We took pictures, dusted off our packs, topped off water bottles, and said goodbye to Roger.

Before Roger climbed into his truck, his parting words to all of us were, "Good luck, because from here, you're a long way from nowhere."

2
Optimist

Roger's big white truck headed off into the distance kicking up dust. It seemed we could see him for miles as he slowly headed back toward civilization, leaving us, all smiles in the middle of nowhere.

As we stood alongside the US/Mexico border, literally a sagging little barbed wire fence, it was now just the four of us. We found the journal near the monument under a pavilion set up alongside the border, we wrote our names and start times, and we got our packs ready to go. I was so eager to get started! I had patiently endured all the logistical work that needed to be done to get here, handled my part in the responsibilities of caching water along the first sixty miles of trail, and endured the bumpy, wild road to Crazy Cook. I was bursting and couldn't wait any longer.

It was 3:30 in the afternoon, it was hot, and it was dry. Julie and I were wearing matching red running t-shirts and short running shorts along with trail running shoes. This was a normal look for us, having been runners for decades. Joe and Raisins looked decked out for a trip to the moon. They had shorts and shirts that were normal enough but then came their sun gear which included various white coverings for their legs and arms along with shiny silver umbrellas to provide them with shade as they walked. We were quite the crew.

We started with five to six liters of water each and knew that the next available water was twenty-five miles up the trail where we left it, hidden among prickly bushes. It must have been the buzz of starting a new trail because though the temperatures were over ninety degrees, I didn't seem to care or notice it much. It was time to get walking!

It's a funny thing looking back at how eager I was to start, hardly able to wait another moment before getting going because a thru-hike is such a long and slow activity. Therefore, a sense of urgency and a strong desire to get going seem as if they shouldn't be important but I always get so excited to be back on the trail, to be moving, to be living the trail life.

When planning for thru-hikes, we tend to break the trail up into sections based on our resupply strategy. We first figure out our route and then we figure out where along that route we can reasonably go to pick up more food. Julie was the wizard with this sort of business and she derived great pleasure from this aspect of thru-hiking; she has loads of spreadsheets as proof. The resupply points along the way served as the backbone of our plan. Once we had the list of town targets, we next figured out a mileage estimate of how far we'd hike each day in order to estimate how long it would take to get from town to town. That way, we would know how much food to pack. Our ambitious plan was to average thirty miles per day from start to finish.

Our first section took us eighty-one miles from Crazy Cook to the little town of Lordsburg, New Mexico along Interstate 10. Our route kept us at fairly low elevation, starting a little over 4,000' and not straying too far from that elevation. We would be traversing mainly desert landscape and eventually walking right into and through the town of Lordsburg.

We'd originally planned to mail ourselves food to Lordsburg, meaning that with our thirty mile per day mileage estimates, we'd only need to be carrying a little less than three days' worth of food. With an estimated two pounds of food per day along with our base pack weights of around ten pounds each, that would mean we should only be starting with about sixteen pounds on our backs minus water weight. However, with our May 24th start date, this had us arriving in Lordsburg on Memorial Day weekend and with post office hours being limited, we opted to carry food for 150 miles and go all the way to the next town of Silver City to avoid post office hour conflicts.

We weren't too concerned with the heavy food carry knowing how eager and fresh we were. We failed to fully factor in just how much water we'd be carrying and just how heavy that additional water would be. Six liters of water weighed over twelve pounds, more than all my gear combined.

And then we walked. If the story of our CDT hike were simply about our day to day actions, the story could potentially be quite boring because we literally walked for hours and hours every day and much of the time was spent grinding it out on the trail, putting one foot in front of the other.

But somehow, nearly every day on the trail seemed special. That first day, not only were we eager to get started, but we were also hiking with other people. Over the years, we've learned that we're a bit different, even in the hiking world. While we're social and love meeting other people on our adventures, we often don't stay around others very long as we inevitably go faster than the majority of hikers out there. We're not speedsters in the sense that we cover ground very quickly. We walk a comfortable pace and when we're in shape, we tend to cover roughly three miles per hour. What separates us is we often prefer hiking longer days, with more hours on trail, and less hours in camp. We like pushing ourselves and we love the feeling of lying down in our tent in the evening after a hard day's work, and for us, seasoned hikers and long distance runners, it takes a lot to tire us out. We also tend to spend much of our time on trail opposed to in towns and as a result, we tend to leave other hikers behind.

This time around though, it felt like we were starting with legends. Joe has some fame in the hiking community for being a speedster. He hikes huge days and does it day in and day out. Raisins is also fast, and he is also really into hiking. He and Julie made a great team as we planned this trip because they were both really into this aspect of the trail and if it was said on the web, Raisins had probably read it.

While it was generally known amongst the four of us that there were no firm commitments for staying together, it seemed pretty likely based on our hiking resumes that we'd all be together for the first 150 miles to Silver City, where we would likely split as Julie and I took the Bear Creek route heading into the Black Range while the other two planned on doing the Gila River route. Nonetheless, during the late afternoon on that first day while walking with Raisins, I said to him, "No strings attached. If for some reason we split earlier than Silver City and we don't show up some evening, please don't wait for us or worry about us." We all knew we were capable hikers and that we were all used to going alone. However, the odds seemed to point to us hiking together for some time.

We got in thirteen miles that first afternoon and hiked until dark. The feelings of excitement and anticipation were with me nearly every step of those miles. It was hot and sunny and my pack was a bit too heavy with all the water weight, but I was free. Sitting down for a snack break in the dirt alongside the trail brought back rushes of good memories from past trails and the feeling of digging through my pack looking for snacks invoked a surge of nostalgia and joy that confirmed that this outdoor life in the wilderness was one I truly loved.

I first learned about the CDT while on my first big life adventure on the Appalachian Trail at age nineteen. I'd left college after my freshman year and hit the trail as a total novice, not even knowing the basics of outdoor living. I not only came away with plenty of knowledge, a stronger personal identity, and self confidence, but I also came away with a treasure trove of dreams and ideas. The CDT was one of those big dreams and after thirteen years of dreaming, thousands of additional trail miles under my belt, and plenty more adventures in between, here we were, setting out on our 3,000 mile hike into the unknown.

We finished day one by the light of a full moon, walking through a rocky, sandy, and dried-out wash. The ground was so hard that setting up the tent was not easy. It didn't seem necessary to set up our tarp tent with how dry everything was but Julie was adamant about setting up our home for the night so she piled rocks to hold the stakes to our non-freestanding tent. With Joe and Raisins sleeping on the ground in the open night air close by, and with a few minutes of pillow talk about how great it was to be living the trail life again, we were asleep, happy to finally be on the trail yet again.

The next morning started early as Joe and Raisins were up and hiking before it was light. It was a good strategy for beating the heat and we quickly followed suit. We said farewell and that we'd see them up the trail, most likely by our first water cache, now twelve miles to our north.

The trail followed the wash a little while longer and then started climbing up the side of a hill. We thought we knew where we were going as we followed a lightly used path, but eventually the trail died out and we were left wondering if we were going the right direction.

This was what we expected from the CDT though. One of the common themes of our research pointed to there being large sections of the trail where there actually wasn't any trail. Instead, there were large swathes of open public land laid out in front of us that we needed to cross in order to get from one point to the next. We were happy and even a little bit giddy at the novelty of having to find our own way rather than simply following a path all day.

This meant it was now time to test our new route-finding skills. At first, we were able to spot wooden posts that were put out in the mountainous desert to guide us. There wasn't a tree in sight, only low prickly bushes dotting the desolate, brown hued landscape, so the six-foot tall wooden posts were pretty easy to follow. They were generally spaced a couple hundred yards apart and usually within sight, at least for a little while. Then they too disappeared. As the coolness of the early morning air began to change to warm oven temperatures I pulled out our GPS, which Julie had loaded and had figured out how to use, and we tried to find our way. Neither of us had used one before and being the eager couple on our first full day on the trail, we tore through prickly bushes, climbed in and out of dry creek beds, and got ourselves all scratched up as we attempted to go from one GPS waypoint to the next.

This was fun until about ten o'clock when the reality set in that it was getting hot out, we were almost out of water, and we were still a few miles from our first water cache. Plus, positive as we may both have been, Julie was not feeling well. She had woken up with a head cold and was sniffling all morning. Her throat was getting sore and she was already a little achy. The novelty of route-finding was quickly wearing off and we focused our efforts, intent on finding water.

Julie began lagging behind and though we usually walked together, I tried to keep up the pace knowing we needed to get to the cache. The little water we had remaining was now hot and not at all refreshing. I was also hoping to catch up with Joe and Raisins so we could talk about the morning and have their camaraderie through what were quickly becoming harsh hiking conditions. Then Julie started vomiting. She rinsed her mouth out with a little bit of hot water and then vomited again.

Things were not looking good and they were quickly getting worse. We pushed on through the now sandy, slow terrain and as we neared the road, I could see the shimmer from Joe and Raisins' shiny umbrellas. They were stationary which meant they were at the water cache and resting. It was lunchtime. I pushed the pace more hoping to catch them but when I looked back to check that Julie was still close by, I could no longer see her. I had a mini freak out thinking that maybe she'd passed out and fallen. I hurried to look for her and quickly found her as she had been behind some large cacti a hundred yards behind. She was looking really rough and barely moving as she drug her feet through the hot sand. As we hiked the last quarter mile to the water cache we sadly watched the silver umbrellas of our friends bob away as they continued up the trail.

Our friends were gone, our phone didn't work, there was absolutely no shade visible for miles to hide from the scorching sun, and it was now the heat of the early afternoon. We were at a road crossing and while there wasn't much traffic, it would be possible to flag someone down for help. Things had changed drastically for the worse. The day had begun with anticipation and excitement and now, here we were with Julie vomiting and in a fairly scary state, debating if we should bail and go for help.

Neither of us knew much about first aid and what little I'd gathered from taking nursing school pre-requisites pointed to Julie experiencing heat stroke. Her pulse and temperature were high and she couldn't hold fluids. I set up the tent for her and though it was hot inside, there was a slight breeze to cool her and she was free from the direct sun. She collapsed down in the tent, eyes closed, in a big sweaty mess. I sat out in the sun and thought through the situation, still in a bit of shock at how quickly all this had happened.

Julie didn't want to go for help yet and seemed to benefit from resting in the shade, even though the heat in the tent was stifling. We sat it out for a few hours. Eventually Julie was able to keep down fluids and she perked up a little bit. Her pulse was better but her temperature was still really high. Being known on the trail as Stopwatch, she of course had a super fancy watch that measured things like altitude, barometric pressure, and temperature. Though we knew she was warm and that it was really hot outside, we figured there had to be some error as the temperature on her wrist that afternoon reached a high of 117 degrees.

We did have some things going for us at this point though. We had three gallons of semi-warm water and we had rested for nearly three hours. Julie was mentally with it again and together we decided to keep going, leaving the safety of the road behind as we headed from the shade of our tent back into the late afternoon sun. We drank as much as we could, we filled all our bottles, and we still had a little water remaining. We carried the remaining water in gallon jugs in our hands as we walked back out into the hot sun. We used the water in the gallon jug to frequently pour over our heads and to wet our bandanas. This, along with a slight breeze, kept us from getting anymore overheated. We also put on our headphones to distract ourselves from the physical discomforts of the moment and we kept walking, heading towards the next water cache.

When the sun finally ducked behind the mountains that evening it was sweet relief. While we were still positive and happy to be on the trail again, the newness and novelty were already gone and we were both acutely focused on how to survive. After one full day on the trail, we now knew what we were up against and that the desert conditions of New Mexico were very unforgiving. We knew we needed to be more calculating and on our game if we were going to succeed.

Julie was still feeling congested and weak as we cleaned up that evening with some soap and a small amount of water. We concluded that she had probably picked up a bug on the plane trip to El Paso. She had gone from having a sore throat, to feeling achy with sinus pressure, to now being completely plugged up with heavy yellow mucus clogging her nasal passages. We hoped that with a good night's rest and more walking, she would be able to shake it. We had the carrot dangling in front of us of not only our next water cache pulling us forward, but also the town of Lordsburg, which was still over fifty-five miles away.

That night we slept in another dry creek bed, and slept soundly as we were both exhausted. The plan was to get up early in order to beat the heat.

We were up shortly after 5:00am, packed up within twenty-five minutes, and on the trail. The temperature was warm but it felt like residual heat from the previous day's oven-like sun. We only had a few short hours before the new day's oven kicked on and began roasting us again so we hurried to make miles while the getting was good.

That first day of sitting out in the sun did some damage to me. I generally am not big on wearing sunscreen but New Mexico changed that attitude very quickly. On the morning of day three little blisters began popping up on my bright red thighs, singed by the previous day's sun exposure. I now fully understood Joe's high white socks that covered his legs and was a little envious of their umbrellas.

Julie hadn't slept all that well. Her sore throat bothered her and all the mucus kept her from breathing well, continually waking her throughout the night. Upon getting up she began a new routine that would carry on for nearly the next two weeks: Every morning she spent the first couple hours of the day clearing her sinuses of nasty green and yellow snot. It was thick and disgusting. It was also necessary and a sign that she was getting better.

While we were less than two days from Lordsburg, we were not going through our food as quickly as planned so our packs felt heavier than needed. The heat had killed much of our appetites and it had melted all of our chocolate. We found ourselves craving salty foods and cold drinks. We were very cautious those first few days not to go through our water too quickly and as a result, we were in a general state of dehydration. Plus, the water wasn't very thirst quenching because it was usually hot. There was nowhere to keep us or our food and water from being baked by the sun.

This was hiking like we'd never experienced before. Yes, we'd hiked the desert of southern California on the PCT, but this trail felt so desolate and isolated. On the PCT we also had waterless stretches but we also knew we were close to civilization with all of southern California close by. Water caches were left along roads by local trail angels and there was a well-developed network for helping hikers such that while we were aware of water issues there, it never felt nearly as dire or desperate as it felt those first few days in New Mexico. It also felt so brutal and hot. There was nowhere to hide and no hope for shade until the sun finally went down. Yet, especially in the mornings and evenings, there was indeed a beauty to the scenery, and I found myself feeling a sense of appreciation for the life that was able to survive in such tough conditions.

While the evenings were often the best time for us to be hiking due to the cooler temperatures and the relief from the powerful sun, we found quickly that this was also the time that other creatures came alive. During the daytime, we'd seen plenty of little lizards, both the flat, skinny, fast ones and the slow, chubby dragon-bearded ones.

We'd seen big jackrabbits with oversized back legs and large ears, but in general, the heat of the day was void of nearly all signs of life, at least to our untrained desert eyes. On the evening of day three, as we traipsed across a flat, barren, dusty field that had obviously at some point been grazed by cattle, but now appeared incapable of supporting any life whatsoever, the desert came alive. As I followed behind Julie, lost in thought or mindlessly putting one foot in front of the other, I was suddenly overcome by sensory alarms and a major shot of adrenaline that sent me straight into the air with a leap I didn't know I was capable of, followed by a major flight response that sent me sprinting forward at full speed. The snake popped off the ground nearly as high as I did and upon landing the little rattlesnake exhibited its fight response, coiling up in ready-strike position and sounding off with that eerily familiar sound of a really angry rattlesnake. I shrieked as I ran to get away from it. I've seen snakes before on trails and I've heard the creepy sound of their tails but I'm lucky I was fairly dehydrated with an empty bladder because that snake scared the piss out of me.

We pressed on and I spent the rest of the evening eyeing my every step. It took the rest of the night for my adrenaline to come down and probably a few days for my paranoia to dissipate.

We were adapting to the desert life and upon waking on day four, we were happy to be on pace to walk through Lordsburg later that day. Even though we didn't have food waiting for us and we weren't planning on stopping for a motel room, we hadn't seen any other humans since the second morning when Joe and Raisins left camp. It was Memorial Day and we weren't even sure if any stores would be open so we were mentally prepared to walk right through town and back to the desert life that same evening. We did hold out hope that there may be a convenience store or grocery open so we could get some cold drinks and snacks.

Julie was still feeling sick but the worst of it now seemed to be behind us. We'd hiked nearly twenty-eight miles the previous day and we were now moving better, and each day we were gaining strength. My thighs ached to touch from the sunburn but we were now both vigilant to lather up in sunscreen multiple times per day. The sunscreen protected us but it also helped attract dirt to our skin. So despite our desires to live a more hygienically sound lifestyle on this trip compared to our previous hikes, we were dirty quickly. Despite the early challenges though, we could both feel ourselves transforming back into our familiar trail selves, like a chameleon coming home to familiar territory.

As we found our way from marker to marker through the expansive and shadeless desert through thickly covered terrain of mesquite and creosote, Julie coined a new name for the CDT: the Connect the Dots Trail. Much of our first few days on the trail were characterized by a continuous effort to find our way and to move in the general direction of the trail. We hadn't actually had much of any real trail to follow thus far and we hadn't hiked under more than a handful of trees in four days. However, we managed to find our way, all the while gaining confidence in our abilities to survive in New Mexico.

Coming into Lordsburg that afternoon felt like coming out of a battle. Give round one to the CDT but we were still standing. We had cell reception for the first time as we got closer to town. We called our parents, letting them know we were doing fine and sparing them some of the details that may cause them to worry unnecessarily. We descended down a hill which eventually turned into a dirt road, which eventually became pavement and we walked into town.

Most of the town was closed as we expected. The Family Dollar was open though and we were quick to find the shaded side of the building, drop our packs, and come up with a plan. Julie went in first and came back with cold Gatorades and a box of popsicles. All she wanted was cold and sugar. I then headed into the store for the salty food coming back with chips and canned vegetables. We ate for an hour, called more family, and then began thinking about getting back to the trail.

At this point we didn't think it was likely we'd catch Joe and Raisins, but we wanted to try. Much of the past two days were spent speculating on where they were, how they were dealing with the harsh conditions, and if we'd ever see them again on this increasingly lonely and isolated trail. We had been following their footprints over the past few days in the dry, dusty soil, so we knew they were ahead and that they were close, but we also knew how quick and unrelenting they were. We therefore knew the odds of being alone on the trail were increasing, even though we didn't yet know just how isolating the CDT could really be.

3
Stopwatch

Aside from the Family Dollar being open, Lordsburg felt completely shut down as we walked through town in the late afternoon of Memorial Day. The main grocery store was even closed, further increasing our gratitude for the Family Dollar.

We followed our maps through the quiet, small town and soon found ourselves at the underpass of a highway at the edge of town. I realized our rookie town mistake as we stood there confirming our route. I was already thirsty, I had only two liters of water, and there weren't any water sources for the rest of the day. The next day's sources were questionable. I'd failed to drink extra water in town with all the salty and sugary foods I'd consumed and my dry mouth was already punishing me. Matt felt the same. We looked around for a convenience store of some type, but no such luck in a town so small, with such definite borders.

Going back to the Family Dollar would have meant walking back over a mile, so we decided to keep moving forward. The moment we crossed under the highway, it felt like we left town for good and passed the point of no return.

Still, I was proud of us for leaving in the first place. Though we were behind in miles and not making them up any time soon, the thought of a hot shower and a bed was still tempting after five days outside. The temptation wasn't strong enough though, as we still felt driven to get in miles. What bothered us the most was that we were already so dirty from walking through such dusty, dry terrain. We were carrying Dr. Bronner's soap but it didn't do much good without plentiful water, and our daily allotment of one baby wipe wasn't enough to clean all the dirt off our legs. Personal hygiene was set aside yet again as we headed back to the trail.

It was still quite hot as we left Lordsburg in the early evening sun. We walked a few flat, exposed miles along the highway before taking a sharp right turn onto the trail, where we were faced with a large, open expanse of cracked dirt, like a dry lake bed. It extended for miles until it reached the base of mountains. To our excitement, it looked like the mountains were dotted with trees and we hoped to reach those shade-bearing wonders as soon as possible.

We walked for several miles, weaving around bleached animal bones and sagebrush, continually seeking out Raisins' and Joe's footprints while also searching for CDT signs in the distance. Sometimes we needed our GPS to find the next waypoint, only to reach a CDT sign that was on its side on the ground. So frustrating and yet so eye-opening to realize just how much maintenance the trail needed.

Our home that night was a flat spot in the middle of sagebrush that avoided nearby anthills and animal holes. We ate dinner as the sun went down, using some of our precious water that we'd so badly miscalculated, and crawled into the tent, whose zippers were starting to stick because of all the dusty ground and sand we'd been camping on. As we sat in the tent, Matt groaned as he rubbed his feet. Our feet were usually the first body part to hurt on a daily basis because they took the brunt of the impact day in and day out.

"My foot really hurts Julie, like really, really hurts," Matt said.

I was surprised to hear concern in his voice but I knew immediately where he was going with it.

"You mean, like stress-fracture hurt?" I asked.

"I don't know, but it hurts in one pin-pointed spot when I touch it, and it was really painful to walk those last few miles," he answered, still touching the top of his left foot, around his big toe.

"Well, take some ibuprofen tonight and tomorrow before we start, and we'll just see what happens," I answered calmly, though inside I was worried. A stress fracture would be the end of the hike and if we took time for it to heal, we certainly wouldn't have enough time left to complete the entire trail. We both went to sleep with the hope that it would magically feel better the next day.

The first thing Matt checked as we packed up the next morning was his foot. It was still just as painful as the night before, so he took more pain pills and said he'd try to favor the other foot and use his hiking poles to relieve some pressure. It was as good a plan as any so we continued packing up and starting walking while the morning was still cool.

I had my own problems to deal with that morning as well. I still hadn't kicked the head cold that I picked up on the flight to El Paso and my stomach wasn't right during the heat of the day, which was nearly twelve hours' worth of time in the direct sunlight. To top it off, my lips were starting to swell to noticeable proportions; I could see them as I looked down at my nose. I'd thought of sunscreen but not lip balm and since we'd just left a town, I knew I wouldn't find a solution until Silver City, still two days away.

Both of us were also thirsty. Considering we'd just left town, we were in fairly bad shape.

Our thirst continued as the morning wore on and our first three potential water sources were dry. Ten miles in and over fifteen miles after town, we reached a windmill just off the side of the trail and we crossed our fingers as we rounded a bend to look inside the tank. It was spilling over with clear water, the bottom of the tank covered in green algae, and I wanted to jump right in. The water tank was as inviting as a kid's plastic pool full of fresh, cold water in the front lawn on a hot summer's day.

We hooted and hollered with happiness as I purified the water with drops of bleach and as Matt washed clothes in a gallon-sized Ziploc, all under the watchful eye of about twenty cows on the other side of the fence that straddled the water tank. The cows were initially flustered by our boisterous presence, but it didn't take long before they heeded the call of the water and drank from the other side of the tank while I filled up our bottles.

The heat was still unrelenting that day, yet we were able to cope with it better because of the new presence of trees. We made our way into the hills, witnessing the ever-changing landscape, as we walked several miles on dirt roads lined with trees. Most of the trees stood tall with scraggly branches, bare of any leaves but still offering some shade. We took each break in the shade and even took a late afternoon nap under a large, leafy tree. By that point in the day, my nausea was at its high and I was glad for the long break in the shade to cool my body temperature.

Just after the break, as we made our way over colorful, lichen-covered rocks with little sign of a trail, I couldn't stop my nausea. The heat was getting to me yet again and in just two seconds, all the couscous and crackers from lunch came back up. Matt was leading the way and swung around just in time to see me throw up a second round of lunch onto the rocks off the side of the trail. I felt so embarrassed that I wasn't handling the heat well and was even more frustrated that I'd wasted the food.

Those first few days included some of my worst physical moments on any trail because of my head cold and nausea, but I was determined to not let it get to me. Before the trail started I had promised myself I would be better, I would be more positive, and I would improve upon the self I had been on both the AT and PCT. In my mind, both the AT and PCT were successful hikes because I finished both of them, yet unsuccessful because I had a hard time being happy during them. I suffered a lot during each trail and finished each one with the feeling that I needed to hike another one so I could redeem myself and do it better than the previous hike.

My tactic during those first few days on the trail, especially after throwing up my entire lunch in two strong heaves, was to tell myself, "Be a hero." Be better than the challenges I faced, be above illogical, emotional reactions, be the protagonist that everyone was rooting for to succeed in the end. I repeated my mantra in my head as we continued walking over uneven, rocky terrain.

Later that day, as we walked dirt roads and climbed up to 8,000', a full 3,600' higher than the morning, we noticed something in the footsteps ahead of us. Not only were we following Raisins and Joe, but we were also following a bear. Its footprints were *on top* of Raisins' and Joe's. It was the freshest footprint of all and we were about to look for a campsite.

We walked as long as we could afford in the daylight and finally gave up on the bear worries and picked a spot tucked into several bushes off the side of the trail. I hung our food in one of the many trees available and figured that in these parts of New Mexico, we weren't the only ones who preferred trees. That night the wind howled around us and our bear bag was hung fairly far from our tent, so I wouldn't have even heard a bear trying to get at it.

The next day was a town day. It felt strange to be so excited to reach town again, considering we just left one thirty-six hours prior, but this next town, Silver City, represented the first real town for us. We'd sent a box of food there, it had a large grocery store and even an outfitter, and we hoped to reach it by mid-afternoon so we'd have plenty of time to rest in town before heading back out.

Silver City was also important to us because it meant the end of Raisins' and Joe's footprints. They would be taking the Gila River route, the most popular route among hikers because it was full of water, such that it crossed the river hundreds of times, and because it was said to be a beautifully scenic route. We planned on taking the Black Range route, which was the official route, as deemed by the US Forest Service and as mapped out in our Bear Creek Survey maps.

If none of that previous sentence makes any sense to you, then that means you feel exactly how we did when we first started preparing for the CDT. There are multiple routes? Multiple sets of maps? Different mileages? What kind of trail is this? The questions abounded before we ever found solid answers.

The year we hiked, there was technically one official CDT route with a mileage of 3,018 miles, but practically no one had ever hiked it before…until Jerry Brown came into the equation. Jerry Brown's company, Bear Creek Survey Service, LLC, mapped out the entire official route and created GPS waypoints every half-mile for the entire length of the trail. Those maps were for sale online and the waypoints were free. This official route using the maps created by Jerry Brown was informally called the Bear Creek route. Those maps and the idea of a walkable official route were still fresh the year we hiked, so the idea of an actual Continental Divide Trail route versus a Continental Divide Trail corridor was relatively new, along with the effort on people's part to hike the entire official route. In addition to the maps and waypoints, a hiker by the name of Beacon created a data book that organized all the notable waypoints, such as water sources, turns, and towns, into a readable format. It was like the data books we'd used on other trails and all we had to do was download and print it, as Beacon offered it for free online.

On the other side of the coin, there was a man by the name of Jonathan Ley who created his own set of maps while preparing for his 2001 CDT thru-hike. His maps were less scientific than the Bear

Creek maps, seeing that his lines were hand-drawn, but he gathered information from hikers every year before updating the maps and provided alternates to routes in the event of droughts, lightning storms, or the need for a more direct or scenic route. These maps were distributed in the form of a free CD-ROM that hikers merely emailed him to obtain in the mail. Hikers printed the maps at their own cost; the only thing Ley asked for in return was a donation, if possible. This method of maps and route-finding was known as the Ley route.

Other than those two routes, Bear Creek and Ley, there were additional maps, guides, and waypoints that were helpful in planning for the hike, but those two particular routes, either one or a combination of the two, were used by every hiker we met on the CDT.

Before we started my head was spinning in thinking about which route or set of routes to choose. Options paralyzed me and since I'd never hiked the CDT, it was difficult to make decisions about routes so blindly. I also didn't want to just go with the herd and do what other hikers automatically did, and yet I wasn't sure I wanted to hike the routes that no one else was hiking, making the trail that much more desolate than it already was. Matt, being opposed to logistical complications, suggested we only follow the Bear Creek route since it was the most official route and because it made decision-making that much easier. We had only one route to walk, one list of towns to choose from to create a resupply plan, and therefore that much less planning rather than mixing and matching routes with two different sets of maps. I couldn't think of a better plan and since I liked the quality of the Bear Creek maps, along with the matching waypoints, I agreed to go with it.

In looking at the Bear Creek route before leaving the comfortable couch of my in-laws' home in Ohio, the Black Range of New Mexico worried me. The Black Range was much drier than the Gila River route, as some years it was void of any reliable water, it was much more remote, as we knew of only two other people who hiked the entire section, and it was longer than the Gila River route by around sixty miles. However, once Matt heard that Jerry Brown said that the Black Range was one of the wildest, most memorable and enjoyable hikes on the CDT, Matt was looking for the dotted line to sign up.

We talked a lot about routes with Raisins and Joe before splitting off from them and routes were at the forefront of our minds as we made our way to Silver City, getting closer and closer to what seemed like the entrance to the lion's mouth of the Black Range. Considering what a rough start we'd had so far with our health and route-finding, both of us were downright curious as to what other challenges were ahead of us.

Raisins' and Joe's footprints lead us over dirt roads as we descended out of the mountains and turned onto Highway 90, our trail for the next thirteen miles, all the way into Silver City. Our plan for the next several hours of road-walking was to rock out to the most energetic music we could find on our mp3 players. I pumped my arms and legs to the beats of Madonna's greatest hits while Matt nearly wiggled as he walked to Latino pop artists like Juanes. It was probably the most fun I'd had road-walking yet, despite the hot sun beating down and the cars whizzing by us.

We made it to Silver City by 2:00pm on our sixth day, nearly twenty-five miles under our legs and almost 145 miles total. Our first stop was the post office and I was shocked by my own reflection in the window as I neared the entrance. My face was burnt, my lower lip stuck out a half-inch farther than normal, my freckles had popped out on the sides of my face where my hat brim ended, and my upper arms were a deep red, signifying days of sunburn compounded on each other. Lastly, my black hat was covered in white salt crystals. Looking down, my calves were slightly swollen from the heat and scratched up from winding through sagebrush. Then I turned to Matt, assessing the damage the first several days had done to him, seeing him in a different light now that we were in the context of a town rather than the trail. He too showed battle scars, his upper thighs still red and swollen from a lack of sunscreen on the first full day, his arm and leg hair already golden, and his normally clean-shaven face now a light scruff of reddish, brown hair. We looked downright haggard from only having had a taste of New Mexico.

After picking up our boxes at the post office and snack foods at the supermarket, we found a local park with thick green grass, so soft and luxurious that it massaged our bare feet. We sat at a picnic table under a large tree while we ate chips and salsa and packed up our next round of food. It was a near perfect afternoon.

We walked out of town around 5:00pm, feeling completely recharged. The stop in Silver City went about as well as we could have planned and we were patting ourselves on the back for leaving a town feeling so fresh without actually spending the night in it.

The walk out of Silver City was a road walk for six miles before reaching trail and despite feeling fresh, we were certainly weighed down. In addition to our base weights of around ten pounds, we each had four days of food and seven liters of water, for a total of about thirty-three pounds. The next water source that was reported online as flowing was forty-four miles from town. Matt's foot had felt better and better over the last two days but the combination of a heavy pack and asphalt brought back some of the pain.

We left town with the plan of reaching the trail just before dusk and after about an hour and a half of walking the road, Matt pulled out the GPS to check the location of the upcoming turnoff for the trail. We didn't want to miss it since we knew the signage for turns could be poor, so we took off our heavy packs and sat in the dirt on the side of the road. The sun was just starting to go down.

Matt was silent as he checked the GPS and I noticed he was pushing a lot of buttons.

"How far is it?" I asked.

"Um, we have a problem," Matt said. "It says we're six miles from any waypoint."

"What?"

"I don't think this is right. There's no way we can be this far from a waypoint. Maybe the satellites are off or something," Matt reasoned.

"Well, let's get out the maps," I suggested. It occurred to me then that we hadn't checked the maps since the road walk into Silver City, meaning we hadn't checked them for the walk *out* of Silver City. We had simply looked at the data book, which said, "Left on Highway 180."

"Oh no," Matt said as he scanned the maps. "We're nowhere near the trail. We were supposed to turn on a road off of Highway 180, just after town."

My stomach dropped as I processed his words.

4
Optimist

"Holy crap, we went the wrong way!" And not just a little off as we had done numerous times on the trail thus far. We were nearly six miles from any waypoint, we'd been walking for two hours, and it was now nearly dark.

It was deflating to say the least. As we scrambled to deal with our emotions, to think of a new plan, and to figure out just how this all happened, a speeding truck came flying over the hill heading towards Silver City. We instinctively stuck out our thumbs and with screeching tires, the truck skidded to a halt right in the middle of the two lane highway.

We ran over to it and the tattoo-covered driver told us to hop in. Without hesitation we tossed our packs in the back and jumped in. Just like that, we were speeding back to Silver City. The ride would take no more than ten minutes, even though it'd just taken us two hours to walk, but at the moment, with the sun nearly down, on a highway far from our comfortable and familiar trail home, meeting Rey was exactly what we needed. Rey had the look of a tough guy but he was extremely thoughtful and he was quick to help us figure out a solution to our current predicament. As we arrived back in Silver City shortly after dark, Rey dropped us off at a nice, inexpensive motel not far from where the trail weaved through town and he wished us well.

What a turn of events. We were proudly walking out of town, refreshed and resupplied, heading into the sunset and suddenly, here we were again, back in Silver City, after dark, trying to figure out what to do next. I had this irrational, fighter urge to just walk through the night the remaining six miles back to the trail on the correct route. Julie would have none of it. She didn't want to night hike and she didn't want to potentially deal with dogs as we walked past people's property on our six mile road walk back to the trail.

The motel gave us a bargain, we were able to shower up and eat some trail food that we already had ready for the evening, and then we went straight to bed. We were worn out from the day and we were also ambitious and eager to get out early the next morning. Despite having the comforts of a hotel and town, at this point we were still all about being on the trail, having not been too long removed from the pleasures of town life.

Somewhat to our surprise, we were actually able to get up at 5:00am the next morning, pack up our bags, and begin walking out of town just as the sun was coming up. I was glad Julie had pushed for calling it a night and for getting the room. We were well rested and we had a chance to let our emotions cool a bit after admitting defeat. It was a crisp, chill morning, and we, now much more vigilant regarding our maps and turns, found where we'd gone wrong the day before. We made our way up a neighborhood street that eventually turned into a dirt road that was eventually supposed to have a turn off where we'd get back on trail.

Julie's fear of dogs as we walked out of town through neighborhoods and past private property proved reasonable and we were both glad we confronted the three energetic barking dogs in the daylight rather than at 11:00pm. There was no going around them as we walked by the property and thankfully, a stern voice accompanied by the waving of our hiking poles was enough to get them to back down so we could hike on by.

At this point we had about 105 miles to our next resupply point. This section held many mysteries for us as it meant we were heading into the mysterious Black Range. Most CDT hikers didn't take this route and much of the concern revolved around there being a lack of water. After what we'd been through thus far, it was hard to imagine it being any tougher.

As we made our way past rural homes outside of town, we finally entered forest land again. Sure enough, we managed to miss the turn for the trail, walking an extra half-mile before realizing it. It's not that each extra mile in itself was a big deal, but we were only a week into the trail and the extra miles were beginning to pile up into the double digits already, which equated to multiple hours of extra walking. In all our hiking we'd never missed turns or gotten off route as much as we did in our first week on the CDT and it didn't seem to be getting any better. We were keeping our cool though and we were trying our best to correct each situation as it occurred. However, the emotions became more and more difficult to handle with each ensuing detour, especially with the heat and scarcity of water seemingly compounding the mistake of each wrong turn.

Plus, we were now really isolated from the trail community with no hope of catching Joe or Raisins as we followed the Bear Creek route and they headed toward the Gila River. This was likely to be a big test for us and for me personally as I was the one pushing for the more remote route.

Prior to starting our hike at Crazy Cook, my understanding of the trail was that there was no real trail but instead a number of various routes that people hiked within a corridor of mountain ranges from Mexico to Canada and that was what we all collectively termed the Continental Divide Trail. Somewhere in our planning, I came to understand that there was now a collection of maps with one "official route" as designated by the US Forest Service. It was at that moment that my thoughts about how to do the hike changed.

I am a competitive runner and I like measuring myself against both myself and others. I think this plays into why I like so much the idea of there being a clearly defined Continental Divide Trail and once I learned that there were people out there trying to create an official CDT from Mexico to Canada, I jumped on the idea. However, as we communicated with Raisins, one of the most informed trail guys we've ever met, his first question to us was, "How are you going to deal with the water in the Black Range?"

"What do you mean deal with water in the Black Range?" I thought.

Julie, knowing the other guys were going the more traditional route, was leaning heavily towards going with the flow and taking the Gila River route, which was claimed to be one of the more scenic and unique parts of the entire trip. However, the idea was in my head to hike the route that our maps followed and if I wanted to do it, I had to answer the question about water.

So before we set foot on the trail, I posted the question about water in the Black Range on the CDT Facebook page. The maker of the Bear Creek Survey maps, Jerry Brown, was quick to respond. He said that the Black Range was one of his favorite sections and that it was doable, though we did need to mark our maps and be sure to not miss some key water sources along the way. We learned from reading about the route that it was one of the more remote places that any of the major US mountain trails traverse and it's home to abundant wildlife, including the rare Mexican Grey Wolf. I was quickly sold and the plan was set to head into the remote Black Range.

One other potential complication was the difficulty of resupply. While the little town of Winston was an option, it was reportedly very difficult to get to. It required a twenty-four mile hitch on a rarely used road to a town of less than 100 people. The other option was to carry 255 miles worth of food to the small town of Quemado. At that point in the hike, 255 miles was way too big of a carry, especially given the water situation and the general sense of unknown surrounding the area we were heading into. I found a blog post from some people that claimed to have resupplied in Winston the previous year, and being the optimist, I figured that we could do it too.

We were pleasantly surprised with the well-marked trail and trees that often shaded us as the day progressed. However, the water issue raised its head on that very first day out of town. Not only had we marked our maps with some key water points as Jerry Brown had suggested, but we'd also found a report online from another hiker that had hiked the route a few weeks prior. Thankfully, he'd listed all water sources he had been able to find for nearly the entire stretch of trail through this remote section. Yet, as the day wore on and our supply of water dwindled, we both started getting anxious.

After twenty miles of walking we reached a road crossing. We were both feeling a little desperate. We checked our maps and water report for probably the tenth time that day and we determined that it was time to aggressively seek out water. Julie jogged up the trail a quarter mile to where the map indicated a potential stream. It was totally dry and she came back empty-handed. Our last option was a cluster of buildings down the road a mile or two. Our maps showed some private property and with this glimmer of hope, I decided to run for it. It seemed to make the most sense to only send one of us and to only carry the necessities. So I emptied my pack except for the map and all our empty bottles.

It felt freeing to run again after being weighed down by a pack and I chugged down the road for about ten minutes before seeing a few small buildings. Thankfully, there was a man smoking a cigar sitting out in front of the first one as I ran up to it. I told him we were out of water and asked if we could have some. He said he was a guest at the rental cabin but was happy to share. I filled up twelve liters of water, and after chugging some there on the spot, I loaded up my now twenty-plus pound pack and shuffled back up the road.

I triumphantly presented the water to Julie upon getting back to the junction with the trail and the road. It felt so rewarding and I felt proud of my resourcefulness, especially since we were both getting anxious.

The trail, while getting more remote and desolate by the mile, was still fairly well marked, especially compared to the first section heading north from the border. We found a nice spot for the evening, stopping a little early for the night, as we wanted the rest and some time to look over our maps in order to plan for the next day's water. Again, water looked scarce.

Prior to starting the trail Julie had made an effort to write down the names and phone numbers of any and all trail angels. Trail angels are people that go out of their way to help out hikers. They are integral to making thru-hikes happen and they are quite possibly one of the best parts of long distance journeys. Given our predicament of not having reliable water for the next day, we decided to give the local trail angel a call. Amazingly, our phone had a signal – this ended up happening only a handful of times on the entire trail. They immediately offered to put a cache of water alongside a road crossing near the Sapillo Campground for us. If all went well, we'd arrive at the cache the following mid-afternoon, after a solid morning of hiking. They were very specific and told us exactly where to find the water jugs, hidden under some bushes out of the sun. We thanked them profusely and crossed our fingers that we could actually find the water the next day.

That evening, we also updated our blog on our iPad as well as our GPS map on our website that tracked our location. After our trip on the Colorado Trail in 2012, which had us completely cut off from the world for three weeks because we didn't carry any technology, we'd determined that we wanted to stay more connected this time around. We liked staying in touch with family and we knew there were plenty of people interested in following our journey through our blog. Julie had found a GPS app that tracked our location and we had thought this feature would be cool for those following our journey back home. We were quickly learning that it wasn't all that helpful since the map required a cell signal in order to update the website map, and we had had very little of that thus far. Nonetheless, we were able to connect with the rest of the world that night via the phone and the iPad, showing our location and assuring our loved ones that all was well.

The next morning, our eighth day on the trail, we headed out with hopes of finding our water cache from the generous trail angels. Water was on our minds most of the morning as the heat of the day seemed to come earlier and earlier. It was the last day of May and we knew it was likely to only be getting hotter. We also knew we had hundreds of miles before we reached the higher elevations of Colorado so we knew water concerns were here to stay. In this case, the cache was to be left at a road crossing near a campground so we thought that along with the potential for water, we may also have the pleasure of human interaction. Since losing Joe and Raisins on day two, we hadn't seen another human soul on the trail.

The streak of trail isolation continued. As we headed down the hill towards the campground, there were indeed picnic tables, pit toilets, and campsites, but no sign of anyone inhabiting the campground. We graciously used the toilets and we eagerly looked around for signs of life, but quickly realized that no one was spending their days in this hot, dry campground. We pushed on and were so pleased to find three gallons of water stashed under some bushes, right where we were instructed to look. We tanked up and headed back into the mountains.

Being the optimist, I was able to find some silver lining in the isolation of New Mexico. With the presence of trees here and there along the trail, we now always made an effort to find a good shade tree whenever we took breaks. As expected, we were generally hot, sweaty, hungry, and tired as we would stop for our breaks and it became my routine to completely strip down to my birthday suit, sit on my sleeping mat, and relax in the shade. I would cool down instantly, especially if there was a breeze to whisk the sweat right off my skin. The CDT was now not only the "Connect the Dots Trail," but it had also become the "Naked Trail."

Despite a complete lack of humans on the trail, bears started becoming much more prevalent. We were seeing bear prints in the dirt, scat all around, and even a few black bears here and there. We actually saw more bears than humans on the trail in New Mexico.

The trail on days eight and nine went from well-marked and easy to follow to gradually more and more overgrown. There were sections where it was obvious that trail had once existed but that it hadn't been maintained for quite some time. Bushes and branches hung over the sides of the trail in many spots and at one point we both got snagged on a blown down tree, tearing small holes in the pockets of our packs. Oftentimes, the trail would traverse ridgelines following small barbed wire fences. The trail often felt directionless as we never seemed to be going in any one direction for very long, but instead we would seemingly travel west for awhile, followed by some time heading north, then maybe head a little to the east, and sometimes even south.

We were also getting noticeably higher in elevation. This was exciting for us because higher elevations brought lower temperatures, which was a relief from the scorching desert. It was also nice to be climbing. Our legs were getting stronger and after a week on the trail, they were ready to attack some hills. We ended our ninth day atop Diamond Peak at 9,850', the highest point on the trail thus far. We had a prime camp spot on some open ground with a gorgeous view overlooking the dry desert below as the sun set.

The next morning we were out early as usual and we were cruising. We were careful not to step in the huge piles of scat littering the trail and we were also extra aware, looking for a right turn that we'd seen on our maps the night before. Within fifteen minutes of walking, our ears, and then all our senses perked up as we saw a large black bear ahead on the trail. It first looked at us and then barreled down the hill from Diamond Peak, straight down the path we were traveling.

As usual in these types of situations, our adrenaline was pumping, but once the bear was clearly out of sight, we proceeded to follow it since we were going the same direction. We talked about the bear and made plenty of noise in hopes of scaring it off should it have decided to not travel too far after seeing us.

As we walked and talked, following the path of the bear, we both began feeling that now-familiar apprehension regarding missing turns. I pulled out the GPS and our maps, and we tried to figure out where we were. Based on our assessment, we concluded that we'd missed our turn as we came down from the peak where we'd started our day, the very turn we were so adamant about not missing. We were now faced with turning around and hiking back up the mountain to the point where the turnoff should have been.

And all the calm and collectedness that we'd exhibited thus far in these situations went out the window. Julie turned back toward the hill and started slamming her poles into the ground. She screamed in a piercing tone and had a brief meltdown. She was so upset and so angry about continually getting off-trail that she lost it.

I think as a couple we often tend to balance each other out and because she was so upset, I gravitated toward the other extreme. I was nonchalant and even laughed a little at her craziness. It probably wasn't the best way to handle the situation as my seeming lack of concern juxtaposed to her extreme frustration probably only added fuel to her fire. We traveled on in silence and sure enough, we found the turn we'd missed the first time through. It wasn't marked well, but it was there, and it was right around the point where we had seen the bear a half hour earlier.

Part of the issue with getting off track on this particular day was that it was to be a town day, and it was not just any town. Today was the little town of Winston with the twenty-four mile hopeless hitch. We'd talked in the tent the night before about getting out early, making good time, and giving ourselves as much daylight as possible to get into town, get our food, and maybe even get back out if we were lucky.

That plan went out the window with the hour detour to start the day. Plus, water was being its normal, challenging self. The water report we'd been using had been fairly accurate over the past couple days but on this day the first few sources cited as still flowing were now finally dry for the season.

As we made our way that day, with partially frayed nerves and ever-building anxiety regarding our next water source, we found ourselves amidst a small herd of livestock. They seemed surprised to see us and whenever we'd get anywhere close to them they'd run. The cattle often ran in the same direction we were traveling, dropping liquid green cow crap all along the trail as they ran. The general pattern was that the cows would get ahead of us, we'd catch them, they'd freak out again and run away, and then we'd catch them again. We played this game for a couple miles as we followed a dry creek bed. We assumed that with all the cattle there must be water around, but despite our best efforts, we couldn't find it.

Twenty miles into the day and completely out of water (I was out, Julie always kept a few sips), Julie insisted on going off-trail for water. We were only four miles from the road but without knowing how quickly we'd get to town, we felt we needed to play it safe. There was reportedly a good flowing trough for livestock a few hundred yards down a hill. It was Julie's turn to run for water this time so I lay down on my mat and closed my eyes, the day wearing heavily on me.

I was beat from the heat, dehydration, and the emotion of the day. I couldn't find a comfy position on the side of the hill. The flies had increased dramatically in number during the past couple days, making life a bit more challenging. Then I heard crunching sounds.

The ground was covered with dead, dry leaves and I heard the sound of crunching leaves coming from the other side of the hill toward me. I got in an anticipatory stance and was ready for action. Three large male elk crested the hill and kept walking right toward me. They had large, impressive racks that any hunter would cherish. I don't think they noticed me as they continued getting closer. While I initially stared in awe, mouth hanging wide open, I eventually became concerned with how close the large mammals were getting to me. So I started making noise to make my presence known, and just like that, they looked at me with a casual glance and trotted off.

Not more than two minutes later, Julie returned triumphantly with water for both of us. We chugged it immediately through our emergency straws. Normally, we had to wait thirty minutes for our bleach to purify the water, but we also carried one ounce straws that filtered the water as we sucked it through the straw.

I was still sluggish as we made those last few miles to the road to Winston, lagging behind Julie quite a bit. My feet ached and I was dragging myself up the trail. We eventually made the road but not until 6:30pm. That gave us a little more than two hours to get a ride into town to make it by dark. Otherwise, we'd have to camp near the road and try again the next morning.

We were eager and ready to get to town and our spirits were high. We got organized, put on cleaner clothes to look nicer and to protect us from the new fly population, and we waited. We waited a long time. Not a single car passed us in our first hour of waiting. Then a big white pickup truck crested the hill, heading our way. They slowed but didn't stop. It was a Forest Service vehicle and it was our understanding that they're not permitted to pick up hitchhikers.

I was less vigilant than Julie at this point and I went to the other side of the road to relax in the shade. A second truck eventually came, and this time not in a Forest Service vehicle. The female driver saw Julie and began to slow down. I jumped up, excited to be getting out of there, but when the driver noticed me running towards the road, she picked up her speed and drove off. Ahh!

We were both really dejected. Shortly after 8:00pm, we both were reaching acceptance that this night may not be a town night after all. We talked about where we would set up the tent for the night. We also talked about possibly trying to walk the twenty-four miles into town rather than rely on a hitch. Over two hours and only two cars didn't give us good odds for getting a ride.

We were literally lying on the side of the road on our mats when a car, heading the opposite direction of Winston, drove by. The driver slowed as he got to us and asked us if we were all right. We told him our situation and he said he'd be happy to take us in, as he and his friend were out looking at the wildlife and would be heading back toward Winston.

We thanked them as we hurried to get our stuff in the car. As we tossed our gear in the back of the SUV, we asked if we should put our packs on top of his dry cleaning. In the back were six pairs of freshly pressed denim overalls, identical to the pair he was currently wearing. He said to toss the packs in and off we headed to the town of Winston.

All I could think about as we drove the twenty-four miles to Winston was how lucky I felt at the moment. The landscape was dry and desolate, and walking that road in the dark would have been miserable. Ken and his friend were locals, living not in Winston, but in a town another thirty miles away. They were both retired and seemed to enjoy telling us all about the major drought they'd been in and how the animals were coming down out of the mountains looking for food and water. He said that with the plants dying due to the drought, it made for lots of animal sighting and plenty of stories of desperate animals struggling to survive.

I felt like I knew what those animals were going through. We were living on generally one water source per day, with usually more than twenty miles between each source. We carried up to fourteen pounds of water at a time on our backs, along with four to five days' worth of food, while trying to keep going in the correct direction toward our next source, in order to stay alive and moving.

As with nearly every hitching experience, there were idiosyncrasies that presented themselves, and our gracious trail angels were no exception. Ken was a comedian and had jokes for every subject that came up along the way. As we were pulling into town, we all spotted a big jack rabbit and Ken burst out, "Put a saddle on that guy and you can ride him!"

It was now dark. Ken offered to take us to the larger town of Truth or Consequences, New Mexico, which was where they were headed. However, it was thirty additional miles away from the trail. Instead, we asked about hotels in Winston. They chuckled and said we weren't likely to find one. Restaurants? Nope. It was a Sunday night, after 8:30pm, in a town with no stop lights, no restaurants, and no hotels.

Ken said our best bet was to sleep under the pavilion at the Community Center located next to the post office. It seemed like the best option, so we hopped out of the car and thanked them for saving our day. We then began trying to figure out the next challenge: Where do we sleep in this small town that is safe and legal?

We looked around at the Community Center, which consisted of one large barn-like building that had a metal-roofed pavilion attached to it. There was a concrete slab under the pavilion along with old wooden seats, seemingly taken directly from an old auditorium and plopped down in the middle of this desolate little town. We'd been there for no more than three minutes when we noticed two ATVs driving down the road, heading toward us. We braced ourselves and when the two men, one older and the other younger, showed up and asked us what we were doing, we quickly told them our story.

They instantaneously went from concerned and cautious to gracious and caring, and they told us they'd be happy to have us in their town for the night. They said that with it being a small town, everyone noticed when someone new was walking around town, especially on a Sunday night, so they wanted to make sure there wasn't any trouble. They welcomed us, asked some questions about our adventure, and wished us a good evening. The old man said he lived next door and that he'd keep an eye on us, telling us to find him if we had any trouble.

We got out our bags and our sleeping mats, and without brushing our teeth or taking out my contacts, we tried to sleep. It'd been a tough day filled with emotional and physical challenges yet here we were in the little town of Winston, New Mexico, sleeping on a concrete floor under a metal pavilion, in the middle of nowhere, getting hospitality from the concerned people of the town. We had been on the trail for ten days, but our old lives seemed to be in the distant past. We were fully immersed in the trail life now, with all the ups and downs that came with it.

5
Stopwatch

My biggest concern as I woke up outside the community center in Winston was that I had to poop. Normally I just dug a hole but this morning was a little unique. When I peeked out from my sleeping bag, I finally saw my surroundings: small homes dotting the roads, chained fences surrounding dry, dusty yards, and several barking dogs behind those fences. The bottom line was that I wasn't pooping anywhere outside and I needed to find a solution fast.

Within the dirt compound of the community center, I saw a small, wooden outhouse-like structure that looked like it could be a bathroom. It looked old and worn down, the outside paint having peeled off long ago, and I feared the smell inside of years of poop and pee baking in the hot sun each day. My body didn't give me much choice and I hurried to what I hoped was a relatively clean bathroom. Thankfully it was and task number one was complete for the day.

After I picked up our resupply boxes and supportive letters from friends and family at the post office, which was merely a small trailer right next to the community center, Matt and I quickly packed up the contents. We needed to save time for hitching back to the trail, a task I assumed would be fairly difficult, given the traffic we saw the previous night.

As we packed up, the older man from last night came over to check on us, making sure we were ok. We showed our gratitude for having a place to stay and he was just as nice back to us, asking us questions about the hike, our route, and the timing of it all. He left on his four-wheeler, only to come back a few seconds later, looking like he'd forgotten something.

"Have you seen any rattlesnakes?" he asked.

"Just one," Matt said, "and it was a baby one that I nearly stuck my hiking pole into, right off the side of the trail at sunset one night in the desert."

"Oh! I could never do that trail. I'm really afraid of snakes," he admitted. "I was curious about snakes and if you saw them or not, that's all. Have a good day!"

The general store was open by then, so we perused the small inventory and dined on Ramen, canned fruit and veggies, and orange juice. It was a far cry from the fresh foods our bodies were craving, but we left feeling happily full.

After breakfast we stuck out our thumbs on the side of the road as we watched the sun climb higher, continuously losing our shade under one of the few trees along the road. After ninety minutes a woman pulled over.

"Where you headed?" she asked.

"Back to the CDT trailhead, off 59, about twenty-four miles away," I explained. It was apparent that this trail was different in the sense that few people knew what the CDT was, let alone where its trailhead was, so I always felt the need to give directions to its location.

"Oh, well I'm going to a forest road just past there. Hop on in," she answered.

Our packs were in the back of her truck before she had the chance to re-consider her decision. The woman's husband worked for the Forest Service and worked in a fire tower close to the CDT, so she knew about the trail and most importantly, she was headed right towards it.

"You guys are the first hitchhikers I've ever picked up," she admitted.

I was both shocked and thrilled that a single woman who appeared to be in her late fifties, who had never picked up a hitchhiker, thought we looked safe enough to pick up. If we could pull that off, we'd have no problem getting rides for the rest of the trail. It helped that we were wearing matching outfits and Matt attributed it to us being cleaner on this hike than previous ones, especially since we lathered Old Spice deodorant on our arm pits each morning. It was completely against thru-hiker code to carry deodorant but both of us were tired of stinking, so it was one of our few luxury items.

Back on the trail, our packs were their heaviest weight yet with a gallon of water each and five and a half days of food to get us to Quemado, almost 149 miles away.

The rest of the day was a slow and steady effort, mainly over ATV tracks with trees alongside us. Our packs were so heavy we stopped for ten minutes after each hour of walking, just to take off the packs and have a quick rest. Despite all the breaks and a slow pace, the one saving grace was the presence of real trail, which allowed us to cruise along for twenty miles until dusk.

Our trees from the day out of Winston disappeared by the next afternoon and we faced a two-tone colored landscape, blue skies sitting atop brown land that stretched for miles in front of us. Such wide open expanses made it easy to spot wildlife, including herds of cows, elk, and antelope. It was fairly amazing that elk and antelope had already become commonplace in our lives, herds of them running past us at times and many more of them visible as silhouettes on the horizon at dawn and dusk.

We didn't encounter our next water source until early afternoon that day and the source was a mile and a half from the trail. There weren't any sources for another seventeen miles and it had already been thirty miles since town.

Matt volunteered to run with an empty pack to the water source, a windmill that was reported online as a good source. As he took off running down a dirt road, in a wide open expanse with nothing but sagebrush dotting the scenery under the hot sun, I saw him stop about 200 yards later. A herd of antelope had nearly run into him and they too all stopped in unison to stare at Matt, staring right back at them. I wasn't sure if it was a standoff or a bit of astonishment from both sides and I saw Matt slowly start running once again, the opposite direction the antelope had been heading, and soon they too took off. When Matt returned from the windmill, he was thrilled to have had that moment with the antelope, when the common denominator of running brought them together. He was also thrilled with the water source and brought back enough water for drinking and for washing our clothes. We both performed the rinse, wash, and rinse cycles on our spare set of clothing in a Ziploc, including a t-shirt, running shorts, and running socks. By the time we finished, the water was dark brown.

If yesterday's trail was forgiving of our pack weight with good tread, the rest of this day seemed to punish us for enjoying it. Once we left easy dirt road walking, we cairn hunted for the rest of the day, mainly walking on the spine of the Divide over rocky, uneven terrain. From afar it looked like we traversed smooth, rolling hills, and yet up close we maneuvered over clumpy grass and patches of sharp rocks. It was hard to keep up a good pace and it took so much more effort than normal, especially in the shadeless, open expanse of windswept terrain, revealing nothing more than an occasional leaning tree or a barbed wire fence.

Looking back, I stayed amazingly positive through that section and even moved relatively fast, as Matt had a hard time keeping up. Neither of us could look around for long, for fear of falling on such technical terrain, but when I did stop to look around and take in the views, the immensity of the land around me, it's simplicity from afar and ruggedness up close, was overwhelmingly beautiful and harsh, all at the same time. I felt special for having such a unique view of New Mexico, a state I doubted was high on many tourists' lists, and yet I felt a strong respect for my surroundings, knowing how unforgiving such desolate, dry terrain could be.

We finished the day near our second water source since Winston, forty-seven miles out of town, Batton Pond. I still shiver when I say its name, picturing its lime green water, with hoof marks and cow shit surrounding the shore of the pond, and hair floating on top of the water. We had no other choice but to drink it, as we had another fifteen miles until the next water. The strangest and perhaps the grossest aspect of the water? It tasted like iced tea. I didn't like iced tea before the trail and I am strongly opposed to it now because I'm so scarred from that water source.

We walked another two miles on a dirt road after the pond, trying to distance ourselves from the water source before dusk settled in. We assumed we weren't the only creatures counting on that water source, considering a deer had been in the shadows by the pond while we were there, waiting for us to leave before taking its turn in drinking the green tea water. Just for safe measures, we hung our food in a nearby tree since we were near water and among trees once again.

Sometimes when I look back on a day on the trail I think, "Man, that was an epic day. I didn't know what was coming and I'm glad I didn't, because I would have been scared to get through it."

The next two days were such days.

Matt woke up and almost immediately had to poop. Once he had to poop, nothing else mattered and he had about thirty seconds to dig a hole because his body never waited. It released its contents no matter what he wanted; it's been an issue in the past and he's pooped in some interesting places because of it.

That morning, he kind of didn't make it. He barely got ten feet from the tent before he had to hurry and drop his pants, only to look down and see that he was pooping on his pants.

"Ah, man! I just shit all over myself!" he yelled as he continued pooping, because once he started, he also couldn't stop.

"Don't worry, we'll clean up your pants," I assured him, having no idea when we'd actually do that with the lack of water coming up.

That was strike one for Matt.

After pooping, he got back in the tent to put in his contacts and moaned in agony over all the little particles of dirt that inevitably transferred from his fingers to his contacts. Even after using a baby wipe to clean his hands, he still got dirt in his contacts.

"I'm lying back down and starting this day over," he grumbled from inside the tent.

"Ok," I said calmly. I had plenty to do with taking down the bear bag and packing up my stuff, so I just continued my morning as he tried to gather himself and get out of his grumpy mood.

The first half of the day was rough. We mainly followed the spine of the Divide, with little to no trail as we made our way up and down short, steep ascents and descents. The footing was again over clumpy grass and sharp rocks, working in and out of thick patches of trees, and we tried our best to seek out cairns in the distance and to use the GPS to locate waypoints. We were getting better at looking up to find the cairns at the same time of walking over tricky terrain, being careful to avoid falling but cognizant of the need to keep moving, feeling like open-water swimmers that had to keep swimming while sighting buoys in the water ahead. Sometimes, seemingly out of nowhere, there was a CDT sign in a tree, leaving us feeling relieved that we were on the right track. Several times we got turned around in the process, often following a cow path if we couldn't see a cairn, only to find ourselves deep in a patch of trees or thick brush, farther away from any waypoint. Rather than backtrack we'd simply head straight to the next waypoint, bushwhacking over blow downs and overgrowth in the process to find the "trail" again. It was an exhausting process and made us all the more grateful for real trail.

That afternoon, we looked down from the side of the trail to see a cabin in the distance, about a quarter mile from the trail down a steep slope. Matt went down with an empty pack to get water, only to come back up fifteen minutes later with an equally empty pack.

"No water?" I asked.

"There's water alright, but there's also lunch. RB, the guy who lives there, said that we're both invited to lunch before we leave and he wasn't taking 'No' for an answer," Matt explained.

I could tell there was no arguing so we packed up our stuff and headed back downhill towards the cabin. Once there, we were treated to a lunch of canned fruits and veggies alongside the instant hummus and pita chips we'd already packed. We sat and talked with RB for two hours about life in his cabin, which was built on private property, smack dab in the middle of the Gila National Forest. He recounted the story of seeing a mountain lion take down an elk, only to have a bear come and take the carcass away from the mountain lion, all in front of his large living room window, which he called his TV. He said he went months at a time without seeing another person. It was our thirteenth day on the trail and we had yet to see another hiker; it was hard to imagine going for months without a human connection.

After lunch we each carried out five liters from RB's water, as the next source listed was nearly twenty-nine miles away and we felt confident it was a good source. The trail always had a way of giving and taking, and that afternoon it gave a little and we had real, tree-lined trail for nearly all of the day's remaining miles. It was a continual reminder that things could change in an instant.

That evening, as we got ready for bed in the tent, Matt opened up his glasses case with a gasp.

"My glasses! They're not in the case!" he said, startled.

We looked everywhere for them but there were only so many places they could be because we carried such few belongings. With all the commotion of the morning, he must have taken his glasses off while he was packing up and he never put them in his case. They were gone forever. This was a major blow to Matt as he was nearly blind without glasses or contacts. Though he often slept with his contacts in, it was damaging to his eyes long-term. I would have to be the eyes at night in case we had any encounters with animals or people.

The next morning was chilly. We'd camped near the top of the ridge and it had been windy all night, though we found a calm spot tucked in among trees. We started early and walked quietly on the spine of the mountain that morning, walking from cairn to cairn over patchy, rocky ground.

Ten minutes into the morning, Matt turned back to me and said in an eerily calm voice, "Julie, I think there's a mountain lion bedded down right in front of us."

As he said it, I looked over his shoulder and saw a large mass of an animal jump out from the side of a bush and run to the right of us, only to circle back and head up the trail in the direction we were headed, all in a matter of less than two seconds and three strides.

Since Matt was turned towards me, he didn't see the mountain lion run. He only saw its head pop up from out of the bushes as he approached it and he knew it was a mountain lion by the way its cat-like ears perked up. We had woken it up and since we were downwind of it in fairly strong winds, it hadn't smelled or heard us. We'd camped within a half-mile of it.

It was the first mountain lion either of us had ever seen and I was ok if it was my last. It was big, it was fast, and thankfully scared enough to run away from us.

The rest of the day was focused on obtaining water. We'd both carried five liters from RB's home and the water was supposed to carry us almost twenty-nine miles. That was a bit of a stretch now that we entered the heat of the day with just a couple liters left. At one point in the day it was my turn to run to a water source with an empty pack, so I ran a half-mile down a dirt road to where I hoped to find a spring. I took the GPS and even found a herd of cows near the spring's waypoint, which I was sure indicated a flowing water source. After searching for ten minutes I found nothing but a wet spot alongside the dirt road; not even enough water accumulation for the cows to lick.

Disappointed and even a little embarrassed, I came back to Matt empty-handed and we continued on with very little water.

Sixteen miles into the afternoon we reached the water source that we had counted on, each of us with just a half liter left, and it was one of the worst water sources yet, a "tank" in our data book, which we learned meant, "a hole dug in the ground to accumulate water." The tank was so shallow that I would have had to walk in to dip my bottle, so brown that it resembled chocolate milk, and so stinky that we pinched our noses near it. Like Batton Pond, it was also surrounded by hoof marks and cow poop. There was no way I was drinking the water and I questioned how well our bleach would do against all those factors. From there we had another eleven miles to water, along with rolling terrain and at least a thousand foot climb, in the heat of the afternoon. We could do nothing but keep up our forward progress.

Just before an overlook at the top of the climb, we took a break to sip our water and I was so desperately thirsty that I sucked the sweat out of my shirt, just to see if I got any moisture out of it.

At the overlook point we walked on fresh tread, like it had been built yesterday, with fresh footprints, obviously boots of some sort, and we wondered where the tread came from, like it just popped up out of nowhere. We hadn't seen another person's footprints since leaving Raisins' and Joe's before Silver City.

Shortly after the fresh trail, we came across backpacks lying on the trail, along with water bottles. It took all my willpower to leave those bottles alone, which I was sure contained water. Minutes later we came across two people, trail workers putting up flags to mark where new tread should be laid. At that point the trail was back to connecting cairns over rocky, uneven footing, which made for slow progress as the trail rode the rolling Divide.

We talked with the trail crew for a few minutes before our thirst and desperation got the better of us.

"Do you have any water you could spare?" I asked, unashamed. I was reaching a danger zone of dehydration. We had walked thirty-three miles on five liters of water. We usually consumed a liter for every four to five miles in hot conditions and beyond that was downright painful.

The two trail crew didn't hesitate to walk back to their packs and let us drain their water supply of three liters. They were headed back to their base camp where they had gallons of water, so they assured us we could drink every last drop. The water went down quickly and we each left with a half-liter.

That evening we camped near Damian Springs, a water source a half-mile from the trail. This time it was Matt's turn to look for it, GPS in hand, only he came back empty-handed with another eerie story. While looking for the spring, he came upon an area with loads of animal bones strewn around on the ground. When he looked at his surroundings, he noticed he had entered a narrow passageway, surrounded by walls about ten feet high, with a dead end ahead of him. Red flags went off in his mind as he took in the trap-like surroundings and animal bones, and his thoughts went to that of a mountain lion, telling him to leave immediately. The fear of seeing another mountain lion, this time alone and most likely in its own den, scared him off and he hurried back to our camp just as the skies were darkening towards night, a bit shaken and still thirsty.

Our campsite that night felt creepy in general. We didn't get that feeling often but when we did, we both slept lightly and very aware of any sounds. It was low in elevation at 7,500', a full 1,600' drop from the high point just four miles before, it was choked among the trees, and it was near a forest road. We were happy for pre-dawn the next morning and started walking with headlamps before first light.

Six miles into the next morning, after an unexpectedly long, dry section of forty-seven miles, we reached Argon Well, a huge tank spilling over with fresh water. I nearly cried when we reached it and we each sat down and drank two liters with our emergency filter straws.

The goal that day was to put up some big miles. It was Friday morning and we were still forty miles away from the road to Quemado, which normally would be easy in one and a half days, but we couldn't afford a half day the next day, Saturday, because the post office was only open until 10:30am. On other trails like the PCT or AT, we could look at the elevation and have a fairly good sense of how fast we could move. Sure, both trails had moments of rocky, rooted terrain, but they always had reliable tread. The CDT did not give us that luxury. A day could look pancake flat and easy on paper, but if there wasn't an actual trail to follow, forget about moving fast if route-finding was involved or if signs had been knocked down. We simply couldn't plan on anything certain with the CDT; we could only put in our best effort and see where that took us.

While it bothered me, I knew from research ahead of time that this was simply the nature of the trail and so all I could do was accept it and move forward.

That day the terrain obliged with fairly easy walking, most of which was on dirt roads or jeep trails. Like all the days before, the sun was out in full strength in clear, blue skies. We even shared some tread with Raisins and Joe again, their footprints not as fresh on the trail but still visible, until they took a turn-off to Pietown, another route that nearly every hiker took. The route split from our current route and walked hikers directly into Pietown, a town with a dedicated trail angel and yes, lots of pie, while our route took us to a road that required a hitch into either Pie Town or Quemado. We had decided before the trail that since Quemado was larger than Pie Town, ironically so given just how tiny the towns were to begin with, we would hitch the eight miles to Quemado and see a town that was rarely visited by other thru-hikers.

We kept the pace steady all day despite the constant heat and even had a reprieve from the sun in the late afternoon at the Rincon Well, a swimming pool-sized well overflowing with clear water. We stripped down naked next to the well, washed our clothes and put them right back on so we could finish the warm evening miles in cold, wet clothing.

We walked until dark, leaving ourselves thirteen miles for the next day. At that point we were still hesitant to night hike because the tread was so unreliable. We easily got off-trail in the daytime so we didn't trust ourselves to navigate at night, and we knew we were approaching a long string of dirt roads. We could get stuck walking on dirt roads, near private property, and we felt uneasy camping anywhere near private property or even dirt roads, in the case that cars drove on them late at night. While it may seem crazy, we considered people to be just as dangerous as wild animals, especially given our remote location and vulnerability in a tent.

The next morning came around quickly and at 3:30am, we started walking again. The trail lead us past several herds of cows, all of us freaked out by each other's presence in the darkness, the cows mooing in response as we calmly talked back to them, their bright eyes the only things we could see in the light of our headlamps. Eventually we reached dirt roads by dawn.

As we suspected, we walked by a fair amount of private property, mostly large parcels of land with houses set back far from the road. I feared walking by the properties. To me, private property, especially property out in the middle of nowhere off a dirt road, meant dogs. Dogs that didn't like strangers, much less walkers with packs and hiking poles, and dogs that barked and usually weren't fenced in. People rarely knew a national scenic trail walked right by their home, especially given that so few hikers took this route, and they often let their dogs roam free in the daytime. In all honesty, I was more fearful of domesticated dogs than any bear or mountain lion and even after all these miles, the bark of a dog still raises the hair on my neck just as much as the rattle of a snake.

We finished our thirteen miles by 8:30am, with two hours to spare before the post office closed, and quickly stuck out our thumbs to get a ride to town on the paved road. About twenty cars passed us before we started jogging the road towards town in case we needed to run the entire distance. We didn't have to run long before an old Jeep Cherokee pulled over, with three weathered, somewhat crotchety, yet friendly men inside. They were on their way to a weekly Saturday morning breakfast in town, along with a stop at the post office for their weekly batch of mail.

The men were curious about our hike and quick to give advice.

"Are you packing heat?" one man asked. "And I don't mean for animals; I mean for vermin of the *human* kind," he added without a hint of humor in his voice.

"Uh, no," Matt answered. "We've never carried a weapon any more harmless than our hiking poles or nail clippers."

"Well, that's just stupid," the guy answered, the driver of the jeep.

Silence and awkwardness filled the car.

The guy in the back seat gave us a wink so I took that as a sign that I shouldn't take the driver too seriously, or at least not get too offended.

After pulling into the post office parking lot, the front passenger helped us get out of the back seat, holding my pack as I stepped out, and said to me, "By the end of this hike I reckon you'll either be in the best shape of your life or completely exhausted."

"Probably both," I answered with a smile, knowing he was absolutely right.

We thanked the men and stepped into the post office, only to face a critic of another kind, this time the Postmaster.

"Are you the Urbanskis?" he asked us.

We both felt kind of famous and answered, "Yes," simultaneously, with a smile.

"Well, you're in trouble," he answered gruffly as he hoisted our packages onto the counter.

6
Optimist

I immediately shifted from elation to concern. The Postmaster followed with, "Your mother has called a couple times, as well as your sister. They said that if they don't hear from you by today then they're going to call Search and Rescue."

He then lightened up a bit, as if he had planned all along to give us the scare, which seemed consistent with his fun-natured demeanor. He said he'd tried to help them out and had even called over to Pietown since that was where most of the hikers normally went for resupplying. He handed us our packages along with the little sticky note on which he'd noted all the calls he'd received about us.

We quickly went outside and managed to call home with Skype on our iPad. The signal was choppy but it was sufficient to let my parents know that we were doing fine, and that we were just a little behind schedule due to the difficulty of the terrain.

Our family had been tracking us on our blog, paying particular attention to the GPS map. Since our last cell signal had been eight days prior, our map was showing us in a stationary position not far out of Silver City, at the beginning of the Black Range. They reported having kept their cool early on but as the days began to pile up with no word from us and no sign of movement on our map, they thought the worst.

Even though we'd been on numerous long distance hikes, with our family supporting us the entire way, this trip was different. They knew we were in more remote locations, and they too were aware of all the unknowns surrounding the trail we were hiking. Consequently, my mother and sister felt a heightened need to look out for us from the outset. Emily, my sister, had contacted not only the Quemado Post Office, but also the area Forest Service Station, along with the local Search and Rescue. She talked with them about what to do and when to do it should we not surface soon.

We decided to come up with a plan for future situations so they knew how long to wait until making that call to Search and Rescue. We also tried to allay their fears a little by assuring them that though we were a little behind our original schedule, and in very remote locations, we were doing well and getting along fine. We also thanked them for their love and concern.

The call home was cut short though. Not only did we have a poor signal but we also had a steady flow of interruptions from all the locals as we sat out in front of the post office packing up our new supplies. It was Saturday morning and it seemed that everyone from the surrounding area was coming in to check their mail, and nearly everyone had something to say to us as we sat out front on the ground organizing our next few days' worth of supplies.

There were people interested in our adventure, there were people offering advice, and there were people sharing all kinds of scary stories relating to snakes, bears, wolves, and crazy people in these parts. But the one person who had the most lasting impact was Tom. He was interested in the trail and in what we were doing to the point of asking us our route and where we were heading. We pulled out our maps to show him our next section. He then continued about his business only to return fifteen minutes later with a proposal.

"I live right on the route you're planning on taking. You're welcome to stop by for the night, get some food and do laundry if you're interested," he said with a smile.

He then proceeded to give us specific details so we wouldn't miss his home off the dirt road we were planning on hiking out of town.

It was early in the day and we knew we would only get a few more miles in before getting to Tom's home, but the debate about whether to keep hiking or to take the afternoon off was a short one. We picked up our pace at the post office, hurried over to the general store for some additional supplies, and we were quickly on our way.

As we walked the dirt road toward Tom and April's home the contrast in landscape between our previous section through the Black

Range and our current surroundings was stark. The Black Range had a feeling of high prairie, often exposed with vast, wind-swept landscapes. It was wide open wilderness, and our elevation was high enough that it felt hot, more from being out in the sun all day, opposed to heat from higher temperatures. Rather than the clumpy prairie grasses, with the tough, lumpy footing of the Black Range, it was apparent that we were now back into more of a desert environment.

We could see the shift as we were making our way into Quemado earlier in the day, coming down from the mountains. As we came down, we couldn't see any substantial mountains that we would be heading toward. We proceeded up the trail with slight apprehension, not knowing what to expect from our upcoming section. We were also largely on our own as the Bear Creek route through this section again diverged from the route the majority of hikers took. Consequently, we were flying blind regarding water availability and footprints to follow.

The water situation looked somewhat bleak. From our last water supply before Quemado to our next available water, we had to cover sixty-eight miles. We did have the town stop to pick up liquids, but that still left us with over sixty miles to go before our next source. We were fairly confident it was going to be a challenging section.

At the moment though, as we walked the dirt road north of town, we were excited and not at all anxious for our visit with what already felt like new friends. Tom had a very relaxing and comforting personality such that we both felt at ease as we walked the long driveway to their home. We were greeted by their big friendly dogs, after which we met his wife April and were given their guest room for the night.

It was a spectacular home. They had built it themselves with a technique utilizing straw bales and adobe. There was no air conditioning and due to the ingenious design, it wasn't needed as the home provided for a refreshing reprieve from the heat of the desert. They had horses, a beautiful property, and they even had a green house with fresh produce they grew themselves. We were in heaven.

It had only been sixteen days on the trail so far and around 400 miles, but at this point we both felt like we'd been out there a long time. We had hiked every day since leaving Crazy Cook, we now had our hiking legs, and we'd adjusted well to the conditions of New

Mexico. It felt right to stop, and Tom and April were some of the best hosts we've ever encountered.

They were also both really interested in the trail, especially after learning that the CDT went right by their home. They were into the outdoors, having had many adventures themselves. They even had their own trail names, Wild Horse and Honey. We poured over maps together and talked trail for hours.

Tom then asked how we were going to deal with the long waterless stretch ahead of us. We told him our ideas, but our ideas were noticeably lacking. Tom was quick to offer assistance and said we could all get up early the next day in order to cache water for the next section. Problem solved!

We had a great dinner with fresh produce, more good conversation, followed by an early bedtime for all. We slept like rocks, and though getting up at 4:00am was a bit of a challenge, we were thankful for the chance to solve our biggest waterless stretch of the section.

We filled up seven gallons of water and headed out, placing two gallons twenty miles from their home, another two gallons twenty-one miles later, and then three more gallons another fifteen miles in. We saw the desert sunrise as well as some elk searching for breakfast as we drove around the desolate morning landscape.

It was then back to their home for breakfast before packing up and heading back to the trail.

The trail this morning consisted of forty-one miles of road walking, the first third on dirt roads, followed by paved road walking. It was 9:00am when we hit the dusty road, the sun already shining brightly and ready to roast any creature trying to do anything in its presence. But we had miles to make, we were refreshed from amazing trail magic, and we had twenty miles to get to our first water stash.

Though our packs were still heavily-laden with water, the road was flat and the footing fast. We talked a little here and there but we were both generally in our own heads as we put one foot in front of the other, making our way from the dirt road to the two lane highway. We followed private property nearly the entire way and shade was limited, so we just kept walking.

We reached our first water cache in the late afternoon. We tucked into the small shade provided by a lone tree and rested for a good twenty minutes, chugging water and thinking over the plan for the rest of the day. At this point we had twenty-one miles of paved road walking remaining before we were back to trail. We were headed for the intriguingly named section known as the Chain of Craters. As we rested from the afternoon sun, we both started getting the idea that we'd push on to finish the forty-one mile road walk before the day was finished.

The air cooled as the sun dipped below the horizon, but the pavement was still really warm. We had been able to feel the heat through the soles of our shoes all day and we were anxiously awaiting reprieve from the sun. As darkness settled around us, we walked on into the night on the desolate highway for half an hour without our headlamps before it simply felt too creepy to continue walking the road in the dark. Though the stars were spectacular on a perfectly clear, desert night, the thought of snakes warming on the road and who-knows-what else out there enjoying relief from the sun was enough to motivate us to turn on our lights.

When cars would come by, which was very infrequently, we'd step off the road and turn off our headlamps. We could see them coming for many miles ahead on the open road, their lights shining brightly. We didn't want to draw attention or freak anybody out. Around midnight, with only a few miles to go, a big truck actually noticed us and turned around. I said to Julie, "If there seems like any danger, we both drop our stuff and run." We were both a little uneasy in such a vast, remote place, but were relieved and comforted when the travelers asked us if we needed any help.

We pressed on and the last few miles were the most painful. My feet were aching and I could feel the formation of blisters on my foot pads as I limped my way in. The pounding of pavement and the sheer heat from the road had done some damage. Never on any of my previous hikes have I had blister issues, but I went to bed that night concerned.

When we got to our turnoff around 1:00am we went just a few hundred yards from the highway and onto sandy ground. The wind had picked up tremendously but we were focused and determined to stop walking and to get some sleep. Despite our tent flapping in the breeze for hours, we set up our little home and were asleep within moments.

We awoke the next morning around 6:00am to the heat of the sun and to the noise from the highway. We realized how exposed our crash landing from the previous night had left us and we quickly packed up. From what we could tell from our maps, we were hiking through a section of lava rocks to start the day, followed by some treeless desert walking. We mildly anticipated the lava but also dreaded how it might feel on our torn-up feet.

We found the lava rocks early. We gingerly and slowly made our way through, stopping frequently to look for the next rock cairn to guide us through the lava rock maze. We were both calm and quiet as we recovered from the previous day's push, and neither of us seemed too concerned with the slow pace.

We eventually picked up our rhythm after clearing the lava fields. We were now on wide open, parched land. We went from cairn hunting to post hunting as we attempted to traverse the vast landscape filled with small scrubby bushes, rocks, and sand. Pronghorn antelope, elk, and cattle dotted the horizon as we gathered momentum.

We reached our last water cache around lunchtime and we relaxed in the shade of some small bushes as we snacked. We were off the side of a rough dirt road when a Forest Service truck pulled up to post some new fire ban updates. The area was now under a total fire ban and no fires, including alcohol stoves, were permitted. Thankfully, they were willing to take the seven empty gallon jugs we'd been toting around, strapped to the outside of our packs.

As we enjoyed the quickly diminishing shade, we snacked on our standard dehydrated refried beans with tortilla chips. The fire ban didn't affect us at all because we'd chosen to go stoveless, relying solely on cold food. We never made a fire and we didn't cook food so the fire ban had no impact on us. We would simply put cold water into an empty peanut butter jar along with our dehydrated beans, and after twenty minutes, they were soft and ready to eat.

Had there been wood to burn, it would have burned quickly, given the heat and dryness. Plus, we'd hiked nearly 500 miles and not come across a single natural flowing water source. We'd had troughs of water pumped from springs out of the ground, but no creeks, streams, rivers, or lakes.

We pushed on through the Chain of Craters and into similar country named the Malpais or "Bad Country." This was another lava-filled section, but before setting off into it, we had the pleasure of stopping at the Malpais Ranger Station. We loaded up on water, had lunch at a picnic table in the shade, and then, from the advice of one of the rangers, we used their hose and took cowboy showers which consisted of drenching ourselves and our clothes with cold fresh water before heading back out into the hot desert afternoon.

We weaved our way through the lava rocks, peering down into caves and tunnels, all the while watching our feet for snakes. It was slow going but interesting. We'd learned that it was seen as a special place to natives where people would place offerings in the hidden rock formations. It also seemed like a place with plenty of places to hide out as it would be easy to get lost in the various rock formations and caverns.

As the day wore on, we began anticipating an early stop for the day. We were both feeling worn down. My feet were blistered and sore, and it felt like the string of early wakeups from the past couple weeks were taking their toll. However, early wakeups seemed like the best way to beat the heat. Our hope was to reach the highway, which lead to the town of Grants, in the early evening in order to go to bed as the sun was going down. From there we had a twenty-two mile road walk into town. We knew it'd be hot and we wanted to be sure to make the post office hours so we planned yet another early wakeup.

As the day was ending, we climbed in and out of some major rocky sections in the late afternoon sun, rocking out to Led Zeppelin before descending back toward the highway in the early evening. After camping out in the sand just off a deserted highway, we were up early the next morning and were on the road by 3:30am.

It was still surprisingly warm out. We tried to walk as quickly and efficiently as possible, only stopping for a few short breaks. Our phone worked for the last couple hours and we took turns calling friends and family as we neared I-40 and the town of Grants.

We got into town around lunchtime and we made our way to the post office. We were both a bit grumpy at this point, suffering from the hangries, an unpleasant combination of being slightly angry due to hunger. Thankfully, there was a park with a pavilion nearby that enabled us to spread out and relax with our new supply of food. We snacked and came up with a game plan as we packed up.

We decided to push on and get back to the trail. We stopped at a grocery store first though. We gorged on what was now our standard town food: canned fruit, canned vegetables, Pringles, and Gatorade. We then hit the road again in order to get back to the trail. It was mid-afternoon and hot, but we figured that with a few miles of road walking before getting back to the trail, we could push through, stop early for the night, and catch up on some much needed sleep.

We were slow as we walked the few miles of hot highway miles out of town, passing a Ranger Station and a large prison. We reached the trailhead worn out. We sat and chugged some Gatorade and then began the climb. We were heading toward mountains again and our goal for the day was now to simply get up in elevation, find some trees and a nice spot to camp, and call it a day. We needed rest and upon finding a flat spot under some small trees we quickly set up our home for the night and crawled into our tent. We hadn't seen bears for nearly a week, so with our new supply of food under our feet, we were quickly asleep.

7
Stopwatch

No matter how tempting a town stay, it was always nice to wake up on the trail after a town stop. We inevitably got more sleep on the trail, without electricity to keep us up, and we awoke earlier with the sunrise. Hiking in New Mexico still entailed beating the sun and getting in as many miles as possible before the heat of the day kicked in.

We knew by that morning, Thursday, June 13th, our twenty-first day on the trail, that we didn't have it in us to push to Cuba by the Saturday post office deadline of 11:30am. Cuba was still ninety-nine miles away so we decided to recharge our tired batteries and take four days to get there, with plans to get a hotel room Sunday night and to pick up our resupply boxes on Monday morning. Before the trail, I hadn't realized how dictated our schedule would be by the post office hours, as we'd never used them to this extent on other trails for our resupplies. It made absolute sense when I really thought about it; I'd just never experienced it first-hand. Now that I was on the trail, I was kicking myself for not doing a little more research into the selection of the grocery stores in each town, choosing to send boxes only to towns with little or no selection of food. However, I didn't lament that mistake for long because all the food was already purchased, packaged, and ready to be sent out in Matt's parents' basement.

There wasn't any water on the trail until ten miles into the morning, ten miles that went fairly fast because we talked nearly the entire time. All the phone conversations we had the day before on the walk into Grants finally gave us something to talk about. We often walked in silence for the simple fact that we ran out of stuff to talk about after spending so many long days together. The first water source of the day was a cache of bottled water, placed there by trail angels who lived in Grants and who drove the dirt road up to Mt. Taylor to keep water stocked. We were grateful for the water because at that point all springs were dry, tanks were disgustingly shallow and nearly dried up, and streams were small, stagnant pools of muddled liquid.

Our route took us around Mt. Taylor after the water cache, a common split-off point from Ley route hikers who went up and over Mt. Taylor. To our surprise, we had good tread nearly the entire afternoon over small, rolling elevation changes of a few hundred feet at a time, often deep under the cover of trees. As we took a break off the side of a dirt road, under a small, pavilion-like structure that offered soothing shade, we saw a runner pop out of the woods, running on the trail we'd just come from. He was rail-thin with sharp facial features and wore nothing more than short running shorts and a hydration pack on his thin, shirtless chest and back. He was an ultra runner from Albuquerque, training for the Hardrock 100 mile trail race, doing back-to-back long runs around Mt. Taylor. He'd been following our Brooks Cascadia shoeprints all morning, hoping we were runners that he could run with. We stood under the pavilion's shade and talked with him for forty-five minutes, mainly about trail running and racing. In real life, running is our true passion, so it was a good mental break from the hike to be able to talk with someone else about running. Both Matt and I dreamt about moving faster on the trails without a pack.

After we left the runner, we realized he was just the third person we'd seen on the trail. We had yet to meet any hikers.

That afternoon, we had another wildlife encounter. We were talking to each other when we heard the sound of claws scratching on tree bark. We both looked to our left, just in time to see a small black bear running away from us; it had just slid down the tree. We thought we were in the clear and almost started walking again, but then I had an instinctual feeling to look closer at the top of the tree that the bear had just come down from.

"It looks like there's something else up in that tree," I said to Matt. "All I can see is a big black shape."

After my eyes focused in on it, I recognized that it was a second cub; only one had come down from the tree. I immediately wondered where the mama bear was and I didn't have to question this for too long.

"Oh. There's the mama bear," Matt said, uneasily. "She's just ahead on the trail."

I didn't move an inch closer to the tree or farther up the trail. A huge brown bear was moving with confidence towards the trail, perpendicular to us, as if to say, "Don't go any farther or this could get ugly."

We talked in calm, audible voices as we backed up slowly, telling the bears we were moving away and asking them to do the same. Just after we were out of sight from the bears, we took a break and luckily sat upwind of them. Two minutes later, we heard the other cub slide down the tree and a few minutes later we walked back on the trail in our original direction, no bears in sight.

Whew! I had never run across a bear with her cubs and was pleased it was a fairly friendly encounter.

Our nerves were a bit shaken that afternoon and we were glad when the trail changed back to dirt roads, in wide open expanses with cows dotting the hillsides and barbed wire fences crisscrossing the land. As we walked the dirt road, I wondered if most Americans knew how much of this kind of land existed, far from any hint of concrete or electricity, or if they'd be surprised by how many miles of dirt roads and barbed wire fence actually cover the country.

Though we were more exposed to the elements on the dirt road, I could see my surroundings better, knowing what wildlife we were encountering well before we were right on top of it. The wind had picked up significantly and the skies filled with dark clouds, looking like rain as we walked the roads. It had been so dry throughout New Mexico that we never entertained the possibility of rain. Just as evening was arriving Matt suddenly had to poop, which meant he found the closest bush to hide behind off the side of the road. As he was cleaning up, I swore I heard a car.

"There's no way there's a car out here," I said to Matt as he hurried to wipe, afraid people would catch him pooping. He'd found a bush but it didn't do much to cover him. We felt about as far away from civilization as possible and the dirt road was full of sharp, tire-popping rocks and strut-ruining ruts. It would have to be a monster truck with indestructible tires to navigate the road.

Sure enough, we looked back on the road we'd just come from and cresting the hill was a big truck, moving slowly and carefully over the road. As the truck neared us, it stopped and the driver and passenger got out, two men in jeans, cowboy boots, and big belt buckles. They both had strong builds yet kind faces and the driver looked to be about twenty years older than the passenger. The driver, dressed in a black t-shirt in contrast to the passenger's striped button down, had a deep tan, weathered face, while the passenger's was both smoother and lighter in color.

"You guys ok?" the driver asked.

"Oh yeah, we're fine. Just taking a break," Matt answered.

"We could see your footprints in the road as we were driving and we wondered if we'd catch up to you," the driver said.

We explained our CDT hike, as we imagined they saw very few hikers out there. The driver quickly offered us a place to stay for the night in his cabin, just a couple miles up the road. We were a little skeptical because we were in the middle of nowhere, in the company of two strange men, obviously bigger and stronger than us, but we couldn't exactly discuss it between ourselves right in front of them. Nevertheless, we trusted them and agreed to meet them at the cabin, just a half-mile off-trail.

I was worried as we continued walking, fearing we'd made a bad decision. We tended to trust people fairly quickly on thru-hikes and it had always worked out for the best, but we wondered if we'd made too hasty of a decision. We contemplated hiking on and not stopping at the cabin, but seeing that our route was so exposed, it would be impossible to hide ourselves in case the cowboys came looking for us.

Holding our breath as we arrived at the cabin, hoping our fears were unfounded, we stepped inside the two room cabin and sat down at the square kitchen table. It was a small, simple cabin with a propane range, bunk beds, a central space for a small square table, and an outhouse. No running water, but there were huge jugs of fresh well water and they heated up water for us to clean our faces with. Within minutes of our conversation, our fears were assuaged and we were glad we had stopped. The men were two local ranchers, Mark and Cody, who raised cattle on the land around us and who were fixing a water tank that evening. We learned all about the cattle business as we sat and ate our granola and instant mashed potatoes, while they ate their meat and potatoes. It was surprisingly fascinating to learn about the cattle business, mainly because cows were the one animal we saw the most and which we slightly feared because of their size and erratic behavior. I'd even heard the CDT called the "Cattle Drive Trail," because of the amount of cows that crossed paths with the trail.

When we admitted to Mark and Cody that we were afraid of cows, they chuckled from the seemingly irrational fear until later, when we stood up from the table to go to bed. Mark said to Matt, "Damn you're skinny! How much do you weigh?"

"I'm guessing about 130," Matt answered.

"No wonder you're afraid of cows," Mark laughed. "I've got calves that weigh more than you two combined!"

It was nice to spend a night inside, especially because it sprinkled rain that night, but neither of us slept very well. Matt had a sore throat and was feeling the start of a head cold and we both heard the pitter-patter of mice more than once, but the gesture of the cowboys was too nice for us to pass up. It also made for a great story, meeting real cowboys who knew how to shoe horses and raise cattle, two things we knew so little about that it was almost awkward to utter those phrases. As an added bonus, we left the next morning with enough water to get to the next source, twenty-four miles away.

Just a few miles into the next morning, as we continued walking on dirt roads that went in and out of patches of trees, I suddenly stopped walking and Matt stopped abruptly as well, looking at me for an explanation.

"What? What is it?" he asked.

"Two cubs and a mama bear, just ahead," I said as I pointed them out. They had just started crossing the road about a hundred feet ahead of us.

"How in the world did you see them?" Matt asked.

"I think I look ahead a little more than you," I answered. It was true; Matt tended to walk with his head down while I looked up and around, contributing to my tendency to trip and fall more often.

We started talking louder to each other so the bears wouldn't be startled, but it had the opposite effect. Instead of continuing to cross the road, the mama bear hoisted the two tiny cubs into the tree and they both climbed up. Then the mother just stood at the bottom of the tree, watching us.

Disappointed that our tactic of making noise had backfired and led the cubs into the trees, we again walked backwards very slowly, then sat down out of eyesight but within earshot of the bears. Mostly, we were shocked this was our second encounter with a mama and her cubs within the last fifteen hours. The cowboys had been surprised to hear that we had seen so many bears already and we wished we could have told them about this encounter, not more than three miles from their cabin. About ten minutes later, we hadn't heard the cubs get down but we decided to keep walking and made lots of noise as we passed by the tree. There was no sign of the bears and we again walked on, both relieved and shaken.

By 9:00am we hadn't covered many miles and we were both dragging because of the lack of sleep from the night before. Matt said his signs of a head cold were getting worse so we set up the tent in a shady spot and took an hour nap. I had never felt so sleep deprived on a trail before and we weren't even in a hurry to get to Cuba.

Once we lost our shade to the rising sun and the tent started heating up inside, we knew it was time to walk. We still drug our feet for much of the rest of the day but since we weren't in a rush to get to town, we just accepted the slower pace and agreed to stop a little earlier that evening.

In the heat of the late afternoon, I was quickly pulled out of my half-stupor in a split second. I was leading and not only did I stop in my tracks, but I also backed up into Matt, unsure of what I was looking at on the side of the trail.

"What is it?" Matt asked.

"I don't know, but there's a big black figure lying two feet off the trail. I can't tell what it is yet," I said.

"I still don't see anything. Where are you looking?" Matt asked, confused and frustrated that there was a possible threat within fifteen feet of us, yet he couldn't see it.

We walked slowly towards the black mass to get a better look. It still didn't move.

"It looks like maybe a dog or something. Oh wait, it has hooves," I said as we moved closer.

"It's a dead calf," Matt said, once we got close enough.

We could still see blood trickling from its hide as it lay dead on its side. Whatever killed it must have killed it recently and was most likely close and even watching us. Our guess was a mountain lion so we calmly but quickly distanced ourselves from the calf. Unfortunately there was so much brush around the trail that we had to walk right next to it to get past it.

There was an eerie silence around us as we took a break a few miles later, sitting off the side of the trail with nothing but the wind making noise. For the first time on a trail, I actually felt unsafe because of the amount of wildlife surrounding us and because we were seeing the circle of life first-hand. We'd already had more wildlife encounters than the sum of all our other trails combined, and we weren't even out of New Mexico yet.

Later that afternoon, we reached the edge of a plateau and looked out into an open expanse of land, a few hills rising up from the flat valley bottom and several dirt roads cutting across it. It looked hot, dry, and waterless, and we had to cross it to get to Cuba. We had been above 8,000' since Mt. Taylor and our data book indicated that we were dropping into the low 6,000' range, which for us indicated hotter temperatures to come, especially since we could literally see the valley we had to cross. After losing 1,700' in less than four miles, we picked up our first water of the day at Ojo Frio Spring, a decent water source, though likely contaminated by the cow poop surrounding it.

Our wish for sleep unfortunately wasn't granted that night. Around midnight we both awoke to the sound of our tarp tent flapping in the wind. With a full moon to light the way, we got up to move the tent behind a tree. The new position still didn't help; the wind picked up even more and we slept even less.

We woke up sluggish once again; I nearly cried because I was so tired of not sleeping well, with the wind being the primary culprit. It made sense that the wind would be so strong because the areas we were walking through were so barren, with so few trees to block the wind. I was also worried about the upcoming terrain because it looked so hot and exposed the day before, but it ended up being one of my favorite sections in New Mexico. We walked through unique, colorful rock formations, worthy of a Flintstones cartoon. Some areas had large, smooth rocks, some had millions of pieces of loose rock, and all sections were different shades of reds, oranges and browns. Having such interesting scenery took my mind off the day's heat.

In the heat of the day, we came upon a pumped spring and quickly put our hot heads under the spigot, along with our dirty, dusty clothes and socks. The afternoon sky was clear and unrelentingly hot, even after putting on cold, wet clothes. The hiking actually got harder after that, or it was just fatigue setting in. We walked a slower pace over large slabs of rocks, tiny rock cairns guiding the way, gaining and losing elevation in quick, steep sections. While we had a goal of getting to the next water source that night, by 7:30pm we were so spent that we agreed to wait until morning to get more water. It was windy yet again that evening.

The next morning, as we came upon our last water source before the town of Cuba, we realized that it was a blessing that we hadn't reached the water the night before. As we approached the Jones Canyon Spring, a trough of fresh spring water, I noticed something furry on the ground. A closer look revealed a half-buried coyote in the ground, with its full head and half its spine visible. It made me sick to my stomach and we hurried to get water.

Looking at our surroundings at the spring, it made sense there would be a dead animal nearby. The spring was located at the end of a canyon, a dead end, with high, slick rock walls around it, and it was the only water source for miles. Again, we guessed a mountain lion was probably close.

The rest of the eighteen miles into town was uneventful after the dead coyote. All we saw on our walk over dirt roads and eventually paved roads were herds of cows. It was a hot afternoon and after five miles on hot blacktop into town, we were ready for a long break in Cuba. It was 2:00pm on a Sunday and we weren't leaving town until the next morning, so we booked a motel room and headed to Subway for lunch. It was our first real town meal on the trail, and real vegetables and bread tasted delicious.

As we sat in the Subway, we talked with an older couple sitting next to us. They warned us to be careful of wildfires with this kind of heat and wind. We heeded their advice, only in the sense that we listened. Other people's advice usually made us more aware of our surroundings, but rarely changed our actions. Even if fires were a threat there wasn't much we could do but keep walking until something stopped us.

The rest of the day was spent sitting in the motel room, using the iPad to communicate with the rest of the world. As I sat on the bed reading Facebook updates, I was surprised and saddened to read the news that one of the beloved trail angels, Sam Hughes, had died. He was the trail angel that had planned to pick us up at the airport in El Paso, but he never showed, most likely because he was having health problems that we didn't know of at the time. Sam had played a large part in the CDT thru-hiker community in New Mexico and every hiker that had an interaction with him had nothing but positive things to say about him. Though we never met him, we considered ourselves lucky to be in a circle of such good, caring people who gave up their own time and energy for the well-being of both the trail and its hikers.

8
Optimist

As we were heading into Cuba on Sunday, through the hot, colorful, and sandy terrain, we could see across the dry valley that was home to Cuba, a high wall of mountains to the north covered in green. We knew the desert was coming to an end and we knew it had to be coming soon because we were at our last town stop in the state of New Mexico. We were ready.

We were also ready for some rest. We'd been pushing due to post offices, we'd been pushing to stay on schedule to visit various friends in Colorado, and we were pushing because that was what we liked to do. However, there were times for resting, and Cuba was the quintessential trail town for the rest we wanted.

We arrived into town after a five mile hot road walk. We quickly picked our motel, the Del Prado, and found out after securing our room that we'd picked the classic thru-hiker pick without even checking with our guidebook. Mrs. Yang and her son ran the motel. They smiled, they took all the hikers' pictures for their scrapbook, and they charged forty-two dollars for a room. It wasn't the Hilton but compared to waterless hot desert, the Del Prado was an oasis.

We headed over to Subway for our first trail food other than canned veggies and grocery store fare. Fresh veggies and bread were so refreshing after twenty-four days of dehydrated trail food. By then our room was ready, we showered up, and we chilled out.

Admittedly, there wasn't much to the town of Cuba. It was primarily one road, a few restaurants and motels, a grocery store, and the post office – at least those were the important parts we remembered. We checked out the grocery store and this time, our world of possibilities was greatly expanded because we had a microwave. We also had Mrs. Yang, and she was grateful enough to provide us with bowls so we could cook meals in the microwave.

Food was a major attention getter for any thru-hiker and we were no exception. On this trail we had added the challenge of being vegan to the mix. We had both been vegetarian, eating no meat but still eating dairy and eggs, for well over a decade. We had been living the vegan life in which we didn't consume any animal products at all for just about a year. While largely motivated by health reasons, we also simply felt better not eating meat or animal products.

The challenge for this trip wasn't so much the trail food, which we easily found good meal choices for, but instead, the challenge came in towns. Quite frankly, there wasn't much hope for any vegan fare in the little mountain towns we knew we'd be going through. Burgers, pizza, milkshakes, and BBQ were what we found in most any place we stopped. We were mentally prepared for this challenge though and we were happily eating everything we could find in grocery stores to satisfy our cravings and our diet.

I think the terrain we'd been in for the first 600+ miles was evident in our food choices that day. We still did our obligatory four cans of vegetables, along with a big can of fruit, guacamole, salsa, chips, fresh bananas, a box of pasta, marinara sauce, a Thai noodle dish, a jar of pickles, orange juice, V8 Juice, and V8 Splash fruit juice. Lots of salt and lots of sugar. We paced ourselves all day and by the time we departed Cuba the following morning we had managed to eat everything but a small amount of salsa.

It was a great stop to say the least. We spoke with family, updated our blog, ate plenty, and simply let our legs rest. We also got caught up on sleep. It wasn't until the early afternoon on Monday that we finally hit the road heading out of town, toward what appeared to be greener mountains.

The trail went from paved road with houses and people, to dirt roads, to remote Forest Service roads, to a dead-end parking lot with a trailhead into the San Pedro Parks Wilderness. We were under trees and though we hadn't traveled far for the day, we stopped to rest as we were struggling a bit under the weight of our heavy packs. We were used to carrying plenty of water, never wanting to risk it too much because we never knew how reliable our maps and resources really were regarding water this late in the New Mexico hiking season.

But at mile 640 it finally happened. There was actual undergrowth, plenty of trees, and then we heard the old but familiar sound of running water. There was a stream winding its way down the mountain we had been steadily climbing. We ended up crossing the stream numerous times, but that first time we dropped everything and rejoiced. We photographed the water, we videotaped it, and the smiles on our faces were gigantic throughout. We were so happy to finally see flowing water. Never had we gone so long without it and never had we appreciated seeing a flowing stream more.

With brightened spirits and bellies full of cold water, we continued up the hill and were greeted with a lush mountain meadow. There were immediate signs of water pooled up throughout the meadow, the temperatures were significantly more comfortable, and we felt like we were finally out of the desert. That evening, we even saw and briefly spoke with another person out on the trail. He was out photographing the area for the weekend and to us it didn't matter if he was out for an hour or five months, it was simply nice to see someone else out there. It seemed as if the harsh New Mexico part of the hike was finally behind us.

It was around this time that we also instituted a new game between the two of us to deal with the ever challenging aspect of route-finding on the CDT. We hadn't had the major mishaps of the first week and a half but we were still going astray on nearly a daily basis. We decided to declare a "captain of the shift." Up to this point I carried the GPS and maps, and whenever we were in doubt, we'd pull the maps and GPS out and reason together the best decision; we were not batting a very high average with this approach. With the Captain approach, it was decided that one of us would be responsible for decision making and would carry the map and GPS for the shift. This way, someone was always paying attention to the route and taking accountability for staying on track.

It was a good thing we did because the next day we dropped down from the beautiful San Pedro Mountains and back down to desert as we headed toward the Chama River. It was back to dry, desert-like conditions and we were lulled into a false sense of water security. We were carrying too little water and were parched much of the day. Thankfully we found a cow trough that afternoon that hadn't been marked on our maps shortly before the river.

Once we got to the river we stopped and I rinsed off my body and clothes, and we cooled down. It was late in the day and the rushing water of the Chama River, the biggest river we'd seen yet on the trail, was very refreshing. It was especially so given that we had a couple thousand feet of hot, exposed terrain to climb to finish our day. It was often our motto to get the climbs in to finish the day, even though we'd often be sweatier when getting into camp. We generally preferred sleeping up higher and away from water. Temperatures were cooler and we felt we were often less likely to have animal encounters.

The next day was the most challenging day to be "Captain" that we had had yet. We were walking on a dirt road until we saw a sign marked CDT taking us to the left and off the road. We had discernible trail for a few minutes and then it slowly faded away. There was the occasional pink ribbon tied to a branch which we assumed was meant to guide us through the dry, though difficult-to-maneuver forest. But the ribbons would come and go and we never could make much sense of them. We tried the GPS only to realize we were now off course. We tried to aim ourselves in the right direction but could never seem to get back on track. Finally, getting frustrated, we decided to just hike straight toward the nearest GPS waypoint, regardless of the terrain. This lead to some steep, hands-grasping-the-dirt climbing as we made our way back to the same road we were taken off of an hour earlier.

The day continued on and unbeknownst to us, we were heading right for another no-trail CDT nightmare as we entered Martinez Canyon. The trail was fine at first, as usually was the case, and then it was gone. We were following pink ribbons back into trees which got more and more dense the farther in we got. We didn't know if we were occasionally on deer paths or if we happened onto remnants of an old trail. Somehow we magically found water. This was amazing because we rarely came across unmarked water. We chugged some with our straws and pressed on.

At one point the overgrowth got so bad we jumped down into the little creek and walked in the water. We did this until reeds sprouted up all around the creek, completely covering any path we could conceivably take. We were trapped, and our GPS was telling us we were right on course! It took so much force to push through the reeds as they clung to our packs, attempting to keep us stuck in the creek bed.

We eventually found daylight and found our way back to hikeable trail, but not without scrapes, scratches, and quite a lot of emotional energy. The worst part was that when we were expecting water near the end of the crazy trail-less section, the creek had dried up. There was no way we were going back into that mess, but we weren't sure when we'd get water again.

So we kept walking and the heat of the afternoon weighed on us. I got ahead as we climbed a steady dirt road. I heard the buzz of a machine come up from behind and a man on an ATV told me to slow up and wait for my wife, and that she promised to share with me. Julie was back up within a couple minutes and in her hand was a can of Minute Maid Orange Juice and a little baggie of ice from the ATV driver. Apparently, he was out looking for his cattle, had asked Julie if she'd seen them, and then she asked him if he had any water since we hadn't had any for a few hours. My wife was becoming quite the trail yogi.

However, one twelve ounce can of orange juice wasn't going to solve all our hydration issues and as the day turned to late afternoon we still hadn't found water. We thought we were finished with this game of searching for water but were quickly jerked out of lush mountains and back into the desert, reminding us that we were still in New Mexico.

Our biggest hope, a spring that was reportedly still running, was our last chance for water for the day. I was the captain at this point and the GPS said we were literally standing on the spring, but there was no sign of water anywhere. There was green grass around but no water. We dropped our packs and searched all around but still nothing.

I pushed us forward and a few minutes later we saw what looked like a tent. We had seen literally one tent on the trail in twenty-seven days thus far. The thought also crossed our mind that if there was someone camping, there was a good chance there may be water around too. We hurried over toward the tent and sure enough, there was another hiker.

As we approached the woman I held my arms out with a big smile and said, "I need a hug! You're the first hiker we've seen in nearly a month and that deserves a hug." She obliged and we sat down to talk trail. Her name was Late Start and she was out doing her second big section of the CDT, this time from Grants to Steamboat Springs, CO. We chugged water, we bleached more, and we snacked as we chatted it up with Late Start. Julie and I both seemed to think we were going to keep hiking that day, but as we ate and drank more, it became more and more apparent that we weren't going anywhere.

We eventually gave in and found a spot a little away from Late Start. She was really friendly even though we probably seemed a bit crazy to her after not seeing people for so long. She explained that she was an introvert and often traveled alone. She wasn't that introverted though because she gladly gave us hugs and we enjoyed our evening together.

That night, she told us about fire concerns up in the San Juan Mountains in Colorado. There were rumored to be fires just north of Chama, and they were rumored to be big, serious, and potentially covering the trail. We listened to all the info she had to share but we did so with a bit of an air that said, "It won't affect us, we always find a way through whatever challenges the trail may throw at us."

The next morning we took off early. We were yet again in the midst of a town push and this time we were hoping to get to Chama before the Saturday morning post office deadline. We had two and a half days and over seventy miles to hike, but we were energized and the terrain seemed to be changing for the better, and hopefully this time for good.

Much of the morning was dirt roads up in the mountains. There may have been one or two pickup trucks the entire morning though so to us it felt like glorious trail. We walked side by side and we didn't have to worry much about getting lost. At one point we came across a camper on the side of the road and then heard a bunch of big dogs barking. Thankfully, a guy was quick to quiet them. We then met our first shepherd.

We'd seen sheep on the trail the previous summer on the Colorado Trail and we'd had encounters with sheep dogs before as one had bitten Julie's pack as we tried to hike through a flock. We had camped with cowboys already on this trip and had learned about the livestock life, but Ron was our first shepherd. He was finishing his breakfast and seemed just as happy to have someone to talk with as we did. He told us about what it was like to be a shepherd and about the terrain we were heading into. Our assumption from the evening before, that we were out of the desert, was confirmed as Ron said we were in the foothills of the San Juan Mountain range and that we would only be going up from here.

We left ecstatic and we cruised up the mountain roads. We covered over thirty miles that day which was made easier by not having to carry nearly as much water as we'd become accustomed to. We were still carrying a couple liters each, but that would eventually drop to sometimes not even carrying any as we got more comfortable with the trail farther north.

That night we found a spot off a dirt road that was not visible from the road. People were often the scariest animal on the trail and we didn't want any late night confrontations or surprises, especially given all the littered beer cans sadly lining much of the National Forest Service roads that we hiked.

We set up camp and were sitting down to eat when we both noticed an abnormally large number of squishy, green, caterpillars. Upon further inspection, they were everywhere. They were crawling up our shoes, on our clothes, on our mats; they had literally covered our tent. We flung as many of them off as we could find, quickly finished our food, and crawled into the tent, hoping they couldn't eat through our tent walls.

We woke early and were moving. We had plans for a big day and the trail obliged. However, it didn't take long for us to see our first sign of trouble. As we crested a ridge and looked out to the north we got our first glimpse of what appeared to be a huge smoke plume. Though it was thick and white, like a big fluffy cloud, it was not shaped like a normal cloud, and it was massive. The optimist in me was quick to say that it was likely some strange winds or funky Colorado clouds, but it was around this time that Julie began to really wonder what was going on, especially since we were heading straight for it.

Later that morning as we crossed through a large open meadow, our heads pondering the potential fire, we came across the mother lode of elk. We were walking through a swath of treeless, grassy terrain about a hundred yards wide with two thick clumps of trees to both sides. We had seen plenty of elk by this point in our hike including males and females, small and large, but nothing like what we saw on this day. All told, there were at least one hundred elk that continuously ran out from the trees to our right, across the meadow and over to the trees on the left. They appeared to be all females and their fawns. The fawns were the smallest I'd ever seen, Bambi-sized, and they ran for their lives. While adult elk ran with what appeared to be a bit of snobbery, with their noses high in the air as they pranced away, the little ones awkwardly ran all out to keep up with the adults and to avoid being prey.

Midway through this amazing nature show, one particular subgroup of the herd, which had let us get just a bit too close before deciding to bolt from one side of the meadow to the other, took off running. The adults easily cleared us but one of the babies failed to do so. Whether it was defeat or defense, the fawn simply dropped to the ground a little ways from us and buried its head in the grass. I didn't know if it was giving up, playing dead, or thinking that if it couldn't see us, maybe we couldn't see it, but either way, it seemed like we could have gone right over and picked up that little fawn.

As the day went on and our apprehension quietly grew regarding the huge and strange clouds to our north, we encountered a herd of another type, this time in the form of livestock. We'd seen plenty of cows and while the elk tended to run perpendicular to us when we came upon them, cows inevitably ran parallel. On this afternoon we were driving cattle for a good mile before the trail narrowed between a fence and a drop off down to a creek. We approached in our normal way, talking to the cows and singing a bit, letting them know we meant them no harm.

However, this herd was different. We noticed as they all huddled up together next to the fence that on the other side of the fence was a large bull. With the bull's presence the cows were emboldened. They turned and faced us; it was a standoff.

At this point we became a bit fearful. They probably wouldn't do anything to us but if they wanted to, or realized what they could do with their huge 1,000+ pound bodies, we would be destroyed by these large vegetarians. So we shuffled down the hill and hiked around the herd, carefully eyeing each other the entire way. Once past them we climbed back up the hill and carried on with our day.

After a couple near misses with getting displaced on the trail that afternoon, we found a spot high in the mountains, tucked in between some coniferous trees and out of the wind for the evening. The smoke plume was still a dominant part of our landscape and we were continuing to get closer to it. We were also getting closer to Chama, our last trail town before being out of New Mexico for good. It had been nearly a month in the state and almost 770 miles, and while we had a treasure trove of unique experiences, we were also ready to be moving on.

We now had twelve more miles and an 11:00am post office deadline. We made good time that morning and without so much as a sign we found ourselves in Colorado a few miles before the road to Chama. We stopped and gave each other big hugs. It felt like a major accomplishment. Plus, not only were we excited to be out of New Mexico, but we were really happy to be in Colorado. We'd hiked in Colorado the previous summer, and we had particularly special memories of the San Juan Mountains, so it felt like we were entering familiar and more comforting terrain.

We got to the road by 10:00am and immediately set about trying to get a ride to town to beat the post office closing time. There was a surprisingly high amount of traffic that morning given that we'd read it wasn't a very highly traveled road and that it was reportedly a tough hitch. Thankfully, a mountain biker in a Subaru was quick to pick us up and take us into town. On the way he told us about the fires and how, on his drive to Durango for a mountain biking trip, he'd had to reroute due to some road closures due to the fires. He didn't know the full extent of the fires other than that the road we were hitching on was really busy because the other main road through the mountains was currently on fire.

We went about getting our food from the post office first and then we got into problem-solving mode. On our way out of the post office we ran into a volunteer firefighter. We were quick with the questions. While he wasn't too sure about the extent of the damage, his words let us know there was a real problem at hand. What hit us hardest was his parting line, "It's not likely you'll be hiking out of Chama anytime soon."

PART 2

1
Stopwatch

"We need to eat something," Matt said.

While it wasn't the response I was expecting after hearing from the firefighter that our thru-hike was essentially in jeopardy because of fires, I knew exactly where he was going with his desire for food. We never made good decisions on empty stomachs and we had already planned on eating a meal before leaving, so we might as well eat while we sorted out all the details of the fires.

At the west end of town was a Subway, the one restaurant that we could still frequent as vegans. Once inside, we stood in a long line of customers with the primary conversation being about fires, as most of them were passing through Chama because of evacuations. The big-screen TV inside was showing news reports and footage of fires raging all over Colorado, yet we still couldn't tell if the fires directly affected us.

We consulted the iPad to see if there was news on the CDT Facebook page, but we didn't have a signal. People all around us were on their phones but we couldn't manage to get a signal; it was maddening to be in a town but still feel so disconnected. We asked several patrons in Subway if they knew anything about the actual location of the fires in relation to where we were headed. One particular man was extremely knowledgeable of the area, especially the trail, but he didn't have good news.

"The fire is at zero containment right now. They're just trying to save the towns at this point," he said.

I didn't know much about forest fires but zero containment didn't sound good to me and if the concern was over saving a town, forget the insignificance of our thru-hike in the grand scheme of things.

We walked back to town in search of a wifi signal, our heads hung low. The winds had picked up and were blowing from the west, heading in the same direction we were walking. The fine particles of dirt off the side of the road stung our calves as we walked back to town and eyed the huge smoke plume up in the sky, directly ahead of us.

A local bookstore and coffee shop let us use their wifi as we sat at a table in front of the shop, drank coffee, and finally connected with people online. Another hiker, Peru, had tagged us in a Facebook post, telling us to check with the Forest Service before leaving Chama because of the ever-changing threat of fires. Other than that, we couldn't find any definitive information on trail closures.

At that point, around 2:00pm, we didn't feel safe leaving town because of the fires but we also didn't have clear information on what we should do. Both our minds went into problem-solving mode and we started throwing out ideas: do we skip ahead and go north of the fires, do we flip-flop up to Canada and hike south, or do we wait it out in Chama until the fires are contained?

Meanwhile, we needed a place to stay if we were going to wait to make a decision. The trouble was, with so many nearby towns evacuated, there was absolutely no vacancy in a town already so small and so limited in lodging. I posted a desperate call for help on the CDT Facebook page, asking for advice on trail angels, and other hikers were quick to respond. Apparently the woman at the local ice cream shop sometimes let hikers stay in the empty apartment above the shop.

We headed to the ice cream shop, which happened to be across the street, where we asked for Patsy. Inside it was packed with people and we felt cumbersome. Patsy saw us and immediately knew we were hikers and knew we were looking for lodging, but she was so busy that she asked us to come back later. We completely understood that the business had to come first. All that mattered was that she knew we were in town, so we headed back to the coffee shop for more problem solving.

While waiting for the ice cream shop to calm down, we talked with locals, especially Robin, the kind owner of the bookstore and coffee shop, we sent messages to other hikers like Joe and Raisins, who were just ahead of us, and we called the Forest Service to hear their take on it. The bottom line was that we most likely would not be able to take the normal route heading out of Cumbres Pass, but since there was nothing officially decreed by the Forest Service, and since we really didn't like any of our other options, we decided to not decide just yet. We were still in the information gathering phase, as more information was trickling in on Facebook by the hour.

Eventually the ice cream shop patrons dwindled in number and we headed across the street once again, hoping that Patsy would let us stay there. We had no other options and were both on the brink of tears because of our current situation. We literally had no idea what to do next or how to make forward progress on the trail. It was a predicament we'd never had before because we'd always been able to push through tough moments and strange scenarios, but never had nature literally barred us from continuing on the trail.

Patsy and her husband Gino looked exhausted but they must have sensed our heavy hearts. Patsy was quick to offer up the empty apartment, apologizing for the lack of furniture, which was almost funny to us because anything indoors was more luxurious than our little tarp tent in the woods. We both showered in scalding hot water, just the way I liked it after several days on the trail, and Patsy and Gino were so kind that they brought over fresh towels, dishes, pots and pans to use on the stove, and lawn chairs. Gino even drove us to the grocery store, a mile down the road, to help us load up on fresh food for the evening.

Though we were in low spirits because of our present situation, we were in good hands with Patsy and Gino and we went to bed knowing something would work out, even if we had no idea what that something would be quite yet.

It was a pinch-me moment to wake up on the floor of an empty apartment, on a quiet Sunday morning in a small town in New Mexico, without an inkling of a plan for leaving that town and continuing up the trail. The morning also represented the start of our first zero, ever, in a trail town. We never took a day off on the PCT, we took a week off on the AT in Myrtle Beach, far from the trail, we never took a day off on the Colorado Trail, and now here was our first real trail town zero on the CDT, thousands of miles later.

Over the course of the day, we weighed all our options and talked to several people, including locals in town and hikers up the trail. Matt woke up with the mindset that we should just try and go through the burn section. I vetoed that option with staunch conviction and let it be known that I wasn't even considering that option. Online, we asked for advice from both the Forest Service and Jerry Brown, the Bear Creek route mapmaker. He suggested we head west to Durango, where we could pick up the Colorado Trail and then meet back up with the CDT. That option was also quickly deemed impossible when yet another wildfire popped up on that section of trail. We looked at maps of Colorado to see if there were any trails or forest roads we could piece together from Chama. That option presented about 200 miles of paved road walking to swing far enough west of the fires, and since we didn't know anything about water sources or safety on the route, it also didn't seem viable.

Later that day we spoke to several hikers over the phone about our options. First was Joe, who had just barely made it through the fires and was currently in Lake City, CO, just north of the fires. He said he was so scared that he literally got down on his knees to pray for safety and was nearly running the miles. He also warned us that fires on the trail weren't as big of a threat as the heavy smoke that sat like a thick cloud over the trail, which got heavier as the day progressed because of the afternoon winds. Our friends that lived in nearby Creede, CO, emailed us several times over the course of the day with updates. We had planned on staying with them as we passed through, but they headed to Durango because the smoke and ash were too strong for them, making it difficult to breathe. Finally, the Forest Service issued a notice that the trail was officially closed from around Cumbres Pass to nearly Monarch Pass, around 280 trail miles. If anyone was found on the trail, it meant a fine of thousands of dollars or imprisonment.

Clearly, going through the burn section was not going to work.

We then thought about waiting out the fires. It seemed like in the past we heard about fires popping up all the time, only to be contained several days later, allowing for trails to be open again. But, each passing hour seemed to bring more and more stories of the worsening fires and rumors online said that the trail wouldn't be open again until the following spring, after a snowfall. Since we stayed at the ice cream shop on the main street, where most cars and

people passed as they evacuated nearby towns to head west, we saw a lot of people come into the shop for ice cream, and each one of them had a story about the fire. Exaggerated or not, we knew waiting out the fires wouldn't work either.

Next we talked to our friend Alex, who had just started going southbound from Montana less than a week prior. He was in East Glacier at the time and we eagerly asked him about the snow levels up in Montana, worrying that our inexperience in snow would hinder our progress if we were to flip up north and head south. Our fears were confirmed when Alex said that not only was there still plenty of snow, but also that the route we wanted to take wasn't even open until mid-July, and we still had over a week of June left. Another door closed when we learned the idea of flipping up to Canada would not work.

In between the moments of problem solving, we continually found our way back into the ice cream shop or the bookstore across the street, just to talk to Patsy and Robin. Both of them had such warm, welcoming personalities that we felt surrounded by good people who cared about our well-being. Upon Patsy's suggestion, we even tried hominy, one of her favorite foods, and added that into our vegan rotation with chips, guacamole and salsa. They were the human connection we'd been craving so badly for the past month on the trail.

As we explored each of our options, only to find a dead end in our path, it was as if we were going through the different stages of death, the death of our pure thru-hike. This would not be a one-way trip from Mexico to Canada. We would have some sort of asterisk to overcome and it was difficult to swallow that reality. At first, when we were walking into Chama, seeing the plumes of smoke in the sky, we were both in denial, not accepting that those plumes might affect us. There had always been threats in the past to our thru-hikes, but nothing that actually affected us personally, so we denied that the fires were that bad.

Then, upon entering Chama and hearing the stories about the thousands of acres burning, the zero containment of the fire, and the near-loss of a town, we realized we would be greatly affected and we were angry. We felt like we had obtained a good rhythm and we were finally finished with New Mexico miles, ecstatic to enter Colorado. We entered Colorado only to be faced with fires and snapped back into New Mexico, our forward progress threatened.

That first full day off from hiking, the day spent working on logistics to save the hike, was the bargaining stage. We were trying to think of any option we could to keep going, whether it was walking right through it, walking around it, flipping up to Canada, or skipping ahead.

After several of our options ended in dead ends, we were depressed. I felt like we had come so far and had already overcome so many obstacles, from no ride at the start, to heat stroke, to getting lost on a daily basis, to bear and mountain lion encounters, to sleep deprivation and complete isolation. And yet, there we were in Chama, unable to move on the traditional way because of factors completely out of our control. I was not only depressed about our situation, I was anxious. We were already behind our schedule and each dead-end option presented an even greater challenge of finishing before our deadline. I would say that I even began to lose hope.

But then we talked to Peru.

Peru was a fellow thru-hiker that was also affected by the fires. She and Radar had been in Chama just days before the fires, so that by the time the winds picked up and the fires spread, they were deep into the woods. Luckily they came across a dirt road, where a vehicle picked them up and evacuated them to Del Norte. In Del Norte they met a woman from South Fork who heard their story and wanted to help, so she drove them up to Salida, CO, (the town near Monarch Pass) well north of the fires.

It was from Salida, CO, that we heard from Peru over the phone. She relayed her and Radar's story to us, which gave us the hope that we needed to lift us out of the depression of the death of our thru-hike. She told us that the woman who gave them a ride to Salida, Karla, was headed through Chama the following day and had offered to take us up to Salida. It was our best option yet, so we jumped on it. Karla was our ticket out of Chama, a town so small a car was necessary to get in or out of it, and most importantly, she was our way to continue up the trail. Before we went to sleep that evening, plans were already in place for Karla to pick us up the next afternoon. If all went well, we'd be on the trail by the next evening. Things were already starting to feel normal again. It was as if we had finally accepted the death of a pure thru-hike and were moving on the best way possible, given the unique circumstances.

The next morning, we both woke up at peace with our decision to skip the upcoming section, promising ourselves we'd come back and finish it after reaching Canada. While I was happy we had a plan in place, I was also anxious. I ran the numbers in my head, calculating at what time we might get back on the trail that evening, and therefore how many miles we might get in. From there I calculated when we'd reach the next few towns, noting that we'd have trouble with the weekend post office hours in Breckenridge and the upcoming Fourth of July holiday in Grand Lake. I was completely accepting of our plan, but now that we needed to pick up the pace not only to get back on schedule, but also to allow enough time after Canada to come back to Colorado, I felt overwhelmed. I didn't know how it would be possible to fit it all in and my anxiety started building inside me.

As much as I didn't want the anxiety of the numbers, I simply work that way. I'm always running numbers in my head, even if it's not in thru-hiking. As a kid, when I sat in the car and looked out the window, I did math in my head with the mailbox numbers, trying to add them, multiply them, make each set of numbers relate in a pattern. Now as an adult I do the same with running, always calculating paces in my head for races or workouts, and that propensity to constantly calculate followed me on the trail. I couldn't help but run the numbers. It was the anxiety part that I could normally control but with this new wrench in our plans, I had a hard time containing it.

At 1:00pm, Matt and I sat in front of the ice cream shop, looking for a woman that seemed like she was looking for us. At 1:30pm, we started to worry a little. At 2:00pm, I sent her a text, "Hi Karla, hope you're ok and that we see you soon." She was doing us a huge favor so I didn't want to seem pushy, but we were genuinely concerned about her and about our chances of getting back on the trail. At 2:30pm, I could barely sit still I was so flustered with the feeling that we were being stood up. Then, a woman not more than five feet tall, wearing jeans, cowgirl boots, a floral button down and turquoise jewelry, rounded the corner of the ice cream shop and looked right at us with a nervous smile. She had shoulder-length blonde hair and a warm smile that spilled over into her eyes. I felt a flicker of hope in getting back on the trail as I thought, "Please let this be Karla!"

After introductions, Karla said in a uniquely blended Oklahoma/Texas accent, "So I have a proposition. My son's car broke down in Pagosa Springs, so I can either take you with me while we solve the problem, or leave you here and come back and get you."

My heart sank. My visions of snuggling in the tent that night with Matt floated off into the sky like the surrounding black smoke. Still, Karla was our one hope of getting back on the trail and I wasn't going to let her go. We had no idea what we were getting ourselves into, but the unknown sounded better than letting our anxiety build while we sat still. Matt and I simply looked at each other to confirm we were both thinking the same thing, "Stick to Karla like glue."

From Chama we headed to Pagosa Springs with Karla and her husband, Mark. Though they were complete strangers, we hit it off well with them and the fifty miles between towns flew by. While Karla was quite a bit more talkative than Mark as she drove quickly over the rolling highway, Mark's witty responses in his southern accent were downright charming, and Matt and I were immediately won over by their warm, energetic personalities. We met their son and the broken car, a fifteen-year-old, faded-red Jeep Cherokee named Rosie. Because her son and husband were working against a deadline to get to Texas, they immediately left with the good car we'd just been riding in. At that point, we were stuck at the repair shop. After a verdict from the repair shop that the car was drivable, yet not dependable at high speeds on curves, such as mountain passes and most Colorado roads, Karla decided to take a chance and drive us to our destination. It was 5:00pm when we left the shop and we had a 220 mile drive. We would be arriving at the trail in the dark.

Karla knew the roads well. As we talked to her during the drive, swapping stories of camping and hiking in Colorado, she took each bend in the road like she could drive with her eyes closed. But, because she knew the roads well, she also knew the drive up to Monarch Pass would stress Rosie beyond her limits, so she called a friend in Del Norte, asking to borrow their car in order to drive us the rest of the way. It was almost 8:00pm and nearly dark when we arrived at her friends' home, a farm that grew hundreds of acres of barley. We stopped inside to stretch our legs, use the bathroom, and muster up the energy to continue. It had already been a long, fairly stressful day, and we still had another two hours of driving to the trail, all in the dark.

As we walked towards the car in the dark, our feet crunching on the gravel amidst the silence of the wide open expanse of farmland, Matt and I both looked at each other and knew this was asking too much of Karla. We all looked exhausted, there was space at Karla's friends' home for all of us to sleep, and the moment we suggested waiting until morning to hit the trail, Karla sighed relief and said, "Oh thank goodness. I really don't want to drive there and back in the dark tonight and I would really love some sleep."

The tentacles of anxiety grew longer and wrapped more tightly around my chest when I admitted to myself that it was simply asking too much of Karla to drive through the night, and therefore we'd wait another day to start hiking again. But, there was nothing I could do. The situation was out of my control and likely would be for the rest of the trail. I had only deceived myself on previous trails by thinking I was in complete control; it was just that the factors out of my control were much more subtle and much less effective in knocking me off-balance. The CDT had proven itself as the wild, uncontrollable, unpredictable beast that people had made it out to be.

My sadness was set aside that evening when all of us gathered around the living room and drank wine and swapped stories. We learned about the fascinating and grueling lifestyle of a farmer, their business hours anything but normal and determined by humidity in the air. They sold barley and raised two girls who competed in horseback riding and goat-raising. The vast differences in American lifestyles continually surprised us with every new person we met on the hike.

By midnight, my eyes were drooping from the combination of a long day and red wine, and I had to call it quits. As we went to sleep I knew my anxiety was still there but I also knew the next day was again a fresh start. I was just happy we'd come this far with Karla and grateful for the unexpected friendships we were forming.

2
Optimist

We woke to cool morning air and a sense of loose plans. We knew we were headed up to Monarch Pass that morning to pick up our resupply box and to get back on the trail again, nearly 290 miles north of where we had gotten off the trail at Cumbres Pass near Chama, but we didn't know when we were leaving because there wasn't much of a plan. We learned quickly that our new friend Karla wasn't much into planning, but it was obvious that she got results, so we rolled with it.

We had coffee and breakfast, we chatted some more with all the good people on the farm, and we eased into our day. We eventually loaded up the truck, said our goodbyes, and were on the road again. As was often the case, it was bittersweet leaving. I would have enjoyed staying around with everyone, helping bale hay and learning a little about their lives on the farm, but the trail was the mission and it was our life, and it was time to get back to it.

After a pit stop for vegan breakfast treats, since Karla knew all the good spots in the area, we finally arrived at Monarch Pass. We could practically taste the trail again as we were above 10,000' and enjoying the fresh high mountain air yet again. There was a little store atop the pass alongside the highway and the store had opened its doors to thru-hikers by allowing us to send ourselves boxes of food. We excitedly got our package, eager to show Karla all the details of what we carried and what sustained us while living out in the woods.

Before saying our goodbyes, we debated our shoe situation. We'd packed new shoes in our Monarch Pass box, meant to be switched out after our first 1,000 miles on the trail. However, we'd just skipped nearly 300 miles so our current shoes didn't feel completely used up just yet. Karla offered to take them, saying she'd clean them and hold them as ransom so that we'd be sure to come back to finish our last section of Colorado once the fires were out. She became one of our biggest cheerleaders and we really were set on seeing her again as we set off north that afternoon.

As we crossed the highway and headed up the trail, it was literally within minutes of being back on trail that all the stress and concern over the past few days about changing the hike disappeared for me. I was on the trail and all was good. The moment felt natural as we eagerly climbed up from the pass, our poles digging into the ground as we propelled ourselves up. We were back in our element and life was seemingly back to normal.

While our hiking life was back to normal, we were now in totally different terrain. That afternoon we were battered by winds on exposed sections above tree line. We saw snow for the first time during the trip, and we were up high, getting well over 11,000' that first day out. We also were treated to amazing views of the surrounding mountains with all the snow, the major peaks, and the vast mountains. We could see smoke to the south, reminding us of what we'd just been through, pushing us forward with the knowledge that fires could strike up anywhere in Colorado at any time during this part of the year.

We also saw people. That first afternoon we saw people working on ski runs that the trail skirted around, we saw other hikers, and we even saw ATVers and mountain bikers. We saw more people on our first day in Colorado than we saw the entire state of New Mexico. We were also excited by our jump up the trail because we knew we were now around other thru-hikers. While there were more than 100 people on the trail attempting a CDT thru-hike, we hadn't been around any of them yet. We had started nearly a month behind the main pack of hikers and though we had been gaining on them with our faster pace, we were now right in the thick of the pack with our 290 mile move.

Two hikers we were especially on the lookout for were Peru and Radar. They had hooked us up with Karla and they'd been really kind and helpful to us while we were stuck in Chama trying to solve the fire problem. They were also both active on the CDT Facebook page so we felt as if we knew them a little already.

While life was good and seemingly back to normal, there was inevitably some pressure. There was both immediate pressure due to post office hour deadlines and there was the larger looming pressure of our finishing deadline of September 18th, when we needed to be back in Seattle for my nursing school. Julie and I dealt with these pressures differently.

My trail name is Optimist and while my optimism serves me well most of the time, I sometimes tend to think I can take on more than I probably should. So with our immediate pressure of getting to Breckenridge before the weekend, and Grand Lake after that before the Fourth of July, I knew we needed to push, and that when it came down to it, I felt like I could push and get it done, even if that meant crazy plans involving hiking straight through the night.

Thinking big picture, it was now June and I couldn't conceivably feel much pressure for our September deadline. While many, including Julie, would say that we were hiking with a deadline, I didn't really feel that way and I had a general sense of calm regarding something so seemingly far away. I knew what our daily average needed to be in order to make it happen and I was checking with that average daily, but doing so as a game and a way of monitoring what sort of effort it would take to get it all done.

Julie on the other hand is Stopwatch. She thinks about all the details and calculates and sees all the potential roadblocks to accomplishing our goals. Together, we tend to balance each other out. She keeps my visions realistic and I keep us pushing forward with the optimism that we can often do more than she thinks we can. At this point in the trail, she was not only focused on the short term post office pushes, but she was for the first time on the trail, seeming to focus much more intensely on the September finish date.

Though we often balance each other out, it was evident at this point in the hike that we were not balancing well. Julie was noticeably more agitated and worried as we pressed forward on our way to our next resupply point at Twin Lakes General Store. It was a familiar state that took me back to times on the AT when she wanted to quit the trail. Despite the warning signs, we just kept walking.

The next morning began with a climb to a pass with our first ever snow cornice. As we headed toward the ten-foot high wall of snow that blocked the pass, we learned what a cornice actually meant. We then set about figuring out how to maneuver past the huge wall of snow. The challenge was intensified because it was early morning. The sun was not quite hot enough yet to melt the snow, which would make it slushy enough for us to kick little steps into the big snow wall. Instead, it was hard and slick. We managed to slowly and precariously climb our way up and over it to safety and to the other side which revealed more beautiful mountain terrain.

Once we made it over and were heading down the other side we talked about how narrow the window in Colorado was and how we had been so close to nailing it. Part of the reason we'd started later than everyone else was that we didn't want to get stuck in the snow in Colorado. We'd seen pictures of hikers ahead of us, and while they looked like they were having an adventure, we knew we weren't all that comfortable with snow travel. So we had tried to avoid the snow by swapping snow for desert heat. However, we hadn't counted on the fire season stopping us. All told, we had just over a week from the time snow levels dropped to the time the fires started up to get through, and we'd narrowly missed the window.

One feature of thru-hiking we'd not had to deal with in New Mexico but which made its presence known immediately in Colorado was mosquitoes. We hadn't had to deal with them at all thus far, only some really persistent flies. They were here now though and as we camped our second night in Colorado we began worrying about our tattered tent.

Our tent was a gift from another hiker we'd met near the end of our AT hike in 2011. It was a well built, classic tarp tent, but with all the sand of New Mexico the zippers were shot and we could no longer close the door. So our tent was good for keeping us dry, but not so reliable for keeping the bugs out. Thankfully, nights were cold in Colorado so we could get all bundled up under our sleeping quilts. If mosquitoes were getting into the tent, we weren't noticing them.

The next morning, as we were making our way toward some familiar Colorado territory, we finally met Peru and Radar. They'd camped a few miles north of us and we caught them as they were getting ready for their day. We were so excited to meet them.

As is often the case with long distance hikers, they were quick to open up and to share how they were feeling about their CDT adventure. They were struggling. They told us they had recently decided on a plan to get off the trail at the next town, saying that the elevation was really getting to them and that there weren't enough distractions on the trail. They told us how they loved the AT with the vast community and all the different festivals along the way, and how, instead of pushing through parts of the CDT they weren't enjoying, they had decided to do more hiking on the AT.

While quitting rarely feels good, they seemed to genuinely love the Appalachian Trail, and having hiked the AT ourselves, we could clearly understand the parts of the AT that were drawing them back, as well as the aspects of the CDT that were pushing them away. Nonetheless, we knew it was likely a tough decision for them and we attempted to be as supportive as we could, regardless of which decision they made. We were simply happy to have met them and that they were so instrumental in helping us stay on the trail.

As we moved through the miles of the day, we knew we were quickly approaching the Leadville 100 course which was a race I had run in August of 2012. The Leadville 100 mile run is a race that starts and ends in the small mountain town of Leadville, Colorado. With a thirty hour time limit, hundreds of runners race off into the mountains, attempting to complete the 100 mile course. I had managed to complete the race in 2012 and knew that much of our hiking for this particular day would be on the same trail I raced the previous year.

Our route had us first going through the historic town of Winfield, a deserted old mining town with restored cabins lining the dirt road, and then up and over Hope Pass before heading down to Twin Lakes, where we had a resupply box waiting for us. I had tried not to talk about this upcoming section too much because I didn't want to annoy Julie by reveling in my own memories, when she herself had heard these stories so many times already. To my delight, she was actually eager to see the course I'd run. She crewed for my race, driving to all the aid stations and helping me out with food, drinks, first aid, and all the moral support I needed to get me through the race. We talked memories as we walked through the remains of the old town to the base of the climb. I remembered it all vividly as we relived the moments together.

Then we turned left at a trail junction to climb to the pass. It was a

2,300' climb in two and a half miles, and it was relentless. I remembered having to stop and rest during the race. For me, it was normal to walk in mountain races, but this climb in particular was the only one that ever made me feel the need to actually stop walking and rest. I smiled as Julie repeatedly talked about how tough the climb was and how amazed she was that people ran this on a 100 mile race course.

The pass rewarded us with great views in all directions. I took a video from the cairn atop the pass which had a small Leadville 100 course marker blowing in the wind. It was cold and windy at 12,500' though, so after two minutes of picture taking and yelling into the wind we hurried down from the pass. We were also hurrying because we weren't sure what time the Twin Lakes General Store would close and we still had over ten miles remaining to get there.

We picked up our pace and as the late afternoon dragged on Julie became more stressed. She was downright upset by the time we hit the junction with the Twin Lakes cutoff. The cutoff was exactly that, a short cut to the little town of Twin Lakes that cut off nearly eight miles from the official route, which walked the entire perimeter of the lakes. We'd hiked around the lakes last year on the Colorado Trail and it'd been our plan to hike around them again this year. We'd stuck to the official route from the beginning and I had no intention of changing at this point.

She begrudgingly followed me and we walked the flat, fast miles around the lake. It was hot in the exposed sun as we came out of the trees to follow the northern side of the lake. Thankfully, around 6:30pm, we got a cell signal and I was able to call the General Store. The new owner said she'd be open until at least 8:00pm and that she would be around if we were later in order to get our package.

We hiked a little more relieved after that but Julie was still not happy. I thought it likely had to do not just with hiking around Twin Lakes but with the entirety of the situation. It was Thursday evening and we still had over seventy miles remaining to Breckenridge for our next resupply, which had Saturday hours closing at 1:00pm. We were also planning on meeting our friend Eric in Breckenridge on Saturday afternoon. On top of that, we were behind schedule to make Canada, and we had also told ourselves we'd come back to hike Colorado.

I wasn't sure what to do though. We'd made plans already so we felt obliged to push on and to keep them. Despite the general pain and discomfort associated with crazy binge hiking, I tended to enjoy the occasional push so I didn't mind trying to stay on the schedule we'd made. But I could sense Julie was unhappy and there wasn't anything I could do to change that. I knew that she would not want to slow down but I also knew that the pressure she associated with the challenge ahead of us was weighing tremendously on her. I also knew I couldn't simply tell her to be optimistic and to not worry. That wasn't the way she looked at things and since she was already down, telling her to not be down wasn't helpful at all.

Our answer was to push even harder. I picked up our food at the general store and we set up camp close to Twin Lakes. We were hot, tired, and a little grumpy as we planned our push to Breckenridge, ultra marathon style. We'd get up early and hike all day, taking small breaks along the way. Then, we'd push through the night. If we kept a steady pace, we'd make it to Breckenridge in time for the post office and to see our friend. Our thought was that if we could get through Breckenridge and then through Grand Lake's Fourth of July post office deadline, we would be back on schedule and then able to slow it down a little. It was a big challenge, but not out of our league. However, given Julie's pessimistic mood of late, I had my doubts about the plan.

3
Stopwatch

We woke up early to start the push to Breckenridge, only this time the push felt different. In New Mexico, when we pushed to town, the unknown factor that often slowed us down was the ever-changing terrain and the complete lack of tread. In Colorado, it was simply hard hiking. There was no telling what kind of pace we could manage over thousands of feet of climbing and descending. Plus, there were more people on the trails, people to talk to and spend precious time with. Because of the desolation in New Mexico, I liked talking to people. I felt that if I didn't have enough time to stop and say hello to people, then I was missing out on a valuable part of thru-hiking. Matt loved people. He was like a black lab that lit up and wagged its tail when he saw new people coming down the trail.

Yet I felt conflicted that day. As much as I wanted to stop and talk to people, I felt so much pressure in making miles that each conversation was bittersweet, melting away the minutes needed to hike at the same time of adding to the quality of our experience.

The section out of Twin Lakes was special to us and I wanted to savor the memories from it, which made it all the harder to go so fast through the miles. We had hiked it going the other way the year prior and Matt had run much of it during the Leadville 100 mile race a year ago. Aspen trees lined much of the trail, their leaves blowing in the wind and mimicking the sound of running water. The trail took us through Mount Massive Wilderness and Holy Cross Wilderness, all the time above 10,000' and over fairly smooth tread. We even took breaks in the same spots as the year before, just so we could sit there and rehash the memories. While I enjoyed reliving so many memories, I still couldn't shake the underlying pressure of getting to Breckenridge.

I started the game of running numbers in my head throughout the day, losing hope at times, yet gaining it back at others. This mentally exhausting process went on all day and by the time we reached Tennessee Pass, thirty-four miles into the day, I was torn over the decision to night hike. I'm not a fan of night hiking but at that time, it was absolutely necessary if we were going to reach Breckenridge. Matt and I were debating how long to night hike when we came upon a cooler just before the pass.

The cooler of snacks and sodas had been left there by trail angels, a fairly rare occurrence on the CDT compared to the large amount of trail magic on both the PCT and AT. As we bent down to check the cooler's contents, we saw a hiker lying on the ground about fifteen feet away, covered in his sleeping bag even though it was fairly warm outside. He was surrounded by at least six empty cans of pop and bags of chips all scattered on the ground around his head. It was as if he had overdosed on junk food and we were sincerely concerned.

Matt walked over to the lump of a hiker on the ground and whispered, "Hey, are you ok?" at least three times before the hiker's head popped up in surprise.

"What? Oh, oh yeah, I'm ok."

"I'm Optimist and that's Stopwatch," Matt said as he pointed to me, still standing by the cooler. I was afraid to get too close to the hiker just yet.

"I'm The Michigan Wolverine," he said. "There weren't any rooms at the hostel in Leadville so I'm just staying here tonight while I nurse my blisters."

It was then that I noticed the bin of first aid supplies sitting next to him. I also remembered the swarm of mosquitoes that had attacked us in the late afternoon and realized why he'd covered himself in his sleeping bag.

We sat and chatted with him while I downed a Dr. Pepper and as we discussed our plans of hiking through the night. We still had around thirty-seven miles to go to Breckenridge. Based on our pace over the course of the day, I doubted our chances of making it on time, given that we'd be hiking in the dark for half that time and that we had two more climbs and descents of almost 3,000' each. I started feeling hopeless.

Still, we continued walking and left Wolverine to the rest of the cooler as we started off with headlamps to guide the way. As we walked through the evening, I started to mentally unravel and it didn't take long for me to reach the point where I was questioning my desire to be on the trail. Looking back, I can see it all taking shape: the pressure to get to Breckenridge, the tough terrain of Colorado, and the disconnect between time on our feet and miles completed. Colorado was like the John Muir Trail on the PCT and the White Mountains on the AT. It was slow, technical, challenging, and unforgiving. Most importantly to us at that moment, Colorado took time and effort, but didn't always give back miles, and as we hiked through the night, the uneven give and take relationship between me and Colorado finally cracked me. I started thinking about how much more of Colorado I still had left and how far behind schedule we were, and I began the process of convincing myself that I didn't want to be out there.

I voiced these concerns to Matt, but I knew he didn't want to hear them. He'd heard them all too often on other trails and was dealing with his own acceptance of the harder, slower miles. He listened to me in silence as I talked aloud about my motives for being on the trail, including the big question, "Why am I doing this?"

Matt was the original reason I was exposed to thru-hiking and he's a big part of why I keep going back to it. He loves the trail life and while I don't always love it, I love him and therefore want to spend time with him, living out both of our dreams, the CDT being a big dream of his. That night, I questioned if supporting his CDT dream was enough motivation for me to keep pushing through such hard days. I also questioned how much I actually enjoyed hiking. Was I really that much into hiking after all or had I been fooling myself all along? If it wasn't truly my dream and if I was having such a hard time getting through the CDT from a mental standpoint, should I consider supporting him in another context? Should I have been on the sidelines instead, rooting for him at home while he did these adventures with other hikers, hikers that were more passionate about the trail than me?

When I brought up the idea that maybe I should be supporting him from the sidelines rather than literally being at his side, where my cloud of negativity historically tended to move in over his sunny skies, he admitted something that I always knew was true but never wanted to fully believe.

"I think my favorite trail," he started cautiously, "when I was most happy and had the most fun, was the first time on the Appalachian Trail, back in 2000."

It was the only trail I hadn't been a part of. It was the trail he hiked with two friends, Animal and Rocketcop. I winced when I heard his admission, only because I knew he was being completely honest. I could tell my negativity was starting to gnaw at him as we passed the miles in the dark and I worried that if I continued on a downward spiral for very long, my unhappiness would ruin the trip and drag him down. I didn't want to be a "Turd of Misery" for the rest of the trail, a term a friend had used to describe my demeanor at times on past trails. It was in those dark miles that I considered quitting the trail so that I could cut off my negativity before it permeated Matt's hike. It was the first time I had uttered the word, "quit," on the CDT.

After walking nine miles in the dark, we reached the base of a 2,500' climb and set up the tent. It was 1:30am and we were exhausted, both of us doubting our climbing ability in the dark, given the possibility of lingering snow near the top of the passes. We looked ahead and decided to target Copper Mountain, a manageable sixteen miles away, as our stopping point rather than Breckenridge. We knew there was a free shuttle from there to Breckenridge. We set the alarm for 4:30am just before we both fell into a deep sleep.

The climb up to Kokomo Pass, starting just before 5:00am, was an easy way to wake up after so little sleep. We couldn't ignore 2,500' of elevation gain and since it was a chilly morning, we welcomed the uphill to warm up. As soon as we reached the pass, a flood of Colorado Trail memories came back and I suddenly remembered the rest of the day's miles to come. All I needed was that one view at the top and I could piece together the rest.

After reaching Searle Pass a few miles later, we ate breakfast on a cold rock as the morning sun gained strength. I felt like a dark cloud of sadness had moved in over my head and I couldn't shake it. Matt recognized my mood but didn't make much of an effort to help the clouds move out. He'd seen me unhappy so many times before and I couldn't blame him for finally tiring of my moods. We ate our granola in silence, the water still very cold from the night before, never truly tasting like milk with the powdered soy milk mixed in with it.

The rest of the morning was nearly all downhill and we had clear skies and cool temperatures. We met at least fifteen people in the span of just a few miles, including mountain bikers, a family of hikers, and trail maintenance crews. We were incredibly close to civilization and since we knew we were stopping early at Copper Mountain, we took the time to talk to each of them.

At 11:00am we arrived at Copper Mountain, feeling triumphant in allowing ourselves two hours to get to Breckenridge. There were people milling about, the skies were blue, the grass was green, and I was starting to feel better.

We reached the bus stop, only to find that we missed the most recent bus by a few minutes. Not only did we need to wait a half hour for the next bus, but it also stopped at a transfer station in Frisco before transferring to another bus to Breckenridge, and that ride took at least a half hour. It looked like we were going to miss the post office hours if we relied on the bus system.

Our friend, Eric, was on his way to Breckenridge to visit with us for the day, so we quickly called him with a new plan. He first stopped in Copper Mountain to get us and then took us to Breckenridge. By the time this plan was executed, we made it to the post office with just five minutes to spare, our closest call yet.

Eric had just graduated from Grad School with Matt's brother and had moved out to Steamboat Springs, so we were some of his first visitors in his new home state. Since it was the weekend, he was happy to spend his free time with us and we were happy to see a familiar face. He was also an ultra runner, having run several races with us before the CDT.

In Breckenridge we hit every possible restaurant with vegan food, including a hot dog joint, a sandwich shop, a café with cookies and cupcakes, and finally a coffee shop. It was in the coffee shop that the subject turned to my unhappiness on the trail and it quickly turned into a therapy session for me. Eric and Matt listened patiently as I explained my unhappiness on the trail and I have to say, I had a convincing argument for considering quitting. I felt that I wasn't supporting Matt's dream of the triple crown by simply being by his side on the trail. Even if I was with him, being anxious and negative was not helping his hike and was even possibly hindering it. I also felt it was time to admit to myself that I simply wasn't that into thru-hiking and that I had to be ok with that. I wondered if I could be a better support person if it was in a different capacity, from the sidelines. As Eric left the table to pay the bill, it was just Matt and me and the general feeling was that this might be the end for me. Matt looked at me with sad eyes and said in a heartbreaking tone, "Does this mean you're leaving me?"

I started crying because I knew the decision to quit meant that not only was I getting off, but that Matt was staying on, alone.

Before making a final decision, we booked a hotel room to talk it over for the night. Eric was headed back to his home in Steamboat Springs, a trail town up the way, but he offered to come back and pick me up the next morning so I could stay in his home while Matt continued hiking to Steamboat.

That night we talked it over. I had so much anxiety over finishing on time and I knew it would only get worse, pushing me farther down the deep hole of negativity. Once I entered a downward spiral, it was very hard for me to climb out; it's a personal fault that I've dealt with in normal life, not just in hiking. At one point, I thought about continuing on, but I looked ahead at the data book and I let the numbers get the better of me. The upcoming climbs and terrain scared me, thinking we'd slow down even more and be even more indebted to the miles, and we still had 280 miles of Colorado left to finish after Canada.

One thing that was different from past times when I talked about quitting was that Matt didn't fight me this time. He listened to my reasoning, let it be known that he preferred that I stay on the trail, but he didn't try to sell me on staying on. He simply said it was my decision to make and admittedly, it hurt that he didn't put up a fight to try and keep me on the trail. I wondered just how much my presence really mattered.

The saddest moment of the night was when Matt looked at me with a surprised look on his face and said, "I've never camped alone!" and started crying. In all his trails, he'd always hiked with another person, camped with a friend or with me, or had stayed in a shelter with other people. He'd never hiked or camped alone.

Looking back, that should have turned things around for me. I wish I would have stepped back from the situation and gotten my head on straight. I wish I would have given more weight to the fact that I was about to start my period the next day and was therefore emotional and slightly out of sorts. I wish so many things had been different.

The next morning, I made the phone call to Eric, asking him to come get me. When Matt called his parents to tell them the news, Matt's mom said what I was thinking.

"It's going to be so hard for Julie to watch you walk away," she said to Matt.

I packed Matt's pack while he lay on the bed, most likely in shock that I was moving forward with this decision. In the past I tended to drag out my thoughts of quitting, debating the decision for days or even weeks, greatly affecting his normally positive mood, but I was simply done with that. I didn't want my CDT story to say that I pushed through the rest of the trail in a dark cloud of negativity, just to say I completed the CDT. Completing it wasn't enough for me; I wanted to enjoy it, all the good and the bad, and I wanted Matt to enjoy it just as much, if not more. The way I felt then, I doubted I would pull out of my unhappiness and I decided to make a clean break from the trail. Though it seemed like a quick decision, it felt well-thought out and I was ready to support him in a different role.

The guilt started to creep in as I gave him all the shared gear I'd been carrying, including our first aid kit, the chargers, the maps, and the camera. He was already carrying our two-person tent but that seemed excessive now that his tiny frame would be the only thing occupying it. My head and my heart were so confused at that point and in all honesty, it could have simply been an impending menstrual cycle behind all of it.

But at the time, I didn't see it that way. I saw myself going to dark mental places that I had been tired of visiting and I only wanted to be a bright spot for Matt, so I felt he was better on his own. I knew we were in the thick of thru-hikers so I felt confident he would make friends very quickly.

Eric picked us up in the late morning and drove us back to the spot at Copper Mountain where we'd left off from the day before. Matt picked up his pack, this time much heavier, and kissed me goodbye. Even though I still felt good about my decision, it ripped my heart out to watch him walk away. My decision came crashing down on me and I couldn't stop the flow of tears as I saw Matt look back at me one last time. He had his head up but I knew he was feeling low. He'd heard me talk about quitting so many times and yet saw me continue each time, so it had to be shocking to him that I finally got off the trail.

I held back my tears for the drive back to Steamboat with Eric; I'd already made it miserable enough for Matt and I didn't want to drag Eric down too. Inside I was crumbling and couldn't stop my mind from repeating the picture of Matt walking away at Copper Mountain. As we drove to Steamboat, the skies unleashed lightning and pea-sized hail. The guilt I felt in leaving Matt to traverse those challenges alone was overwhelming.

4
Optimist

None of this seemed truly real until I started walking by myself from the Copper Mountain Resort and back to the trail. Up until now, Julie had merely talked about getting off the trail, convincing herself she wasn't into hiking at all, and that it was best for her to get off the trail. But she had done this on every trail and she had finished every other trail we'd hiked. We'd hiked over 6,000 miles together, sometimes with her kicking and screaming, but she always kept walking.

But this time was different. From the beginning, I was different. I treated her unhappiness differently. In the past, I would often be the salesman, continually selling the trail to her, pushing and convincing her to keep going, encouraging her to be positive and to make the most of the experience. This time around, I didn't take this approach. I listened to everything she said, but I tried to avoid telling her what to do or convincing her one way or the other. I certainly wanted to keep hiking with her, but I wanted it to be her decision.

So as we made our way through the trail, be it little whining sessions in New Mexico, or serious struggles in Colorado, I listened and talked with her but it was her show and her responsibility to make decisions. As we'd talked over the situation while in Breckenridge, she continued to worry about the idea of failure and quitting. The only thing I said was that she was the author of her story and that she could tell the story of her life however she wanted, and positive or negative, it was up to her. Would leaving the CDT be a failure for her or a victory? It depended on how she wanted to see it. She then built her story which centered on the idea that she never really liked hiking to begin with and that she would do better by supporting me without actually hiking herself. Now, here I was walking back into the woods alone.

Thinking back, I didn't get very emotional as she was agonizing over her decision. It all went so fast and before I realized it, a strong current had built and swept Julie off the trail.

It was in this state of semi-shock that I began my 145 mile journey from Copper Mountain to Grand Lake alone on the afternoon of day thirty-eight. I got going in the middle of the afternoon, and I just walked. Then I actually cried. I don't cry much, I actually have underactive tear ducts, but it all hit me then. While Julie and I often didn't talk much while hiking, we always knew we could, even if it was small and insignificant. Now, it was just me. So I walked. I walked nonstop almost the rest of the day.

About thirty minutes into my hike the skies opened up. I'd just passed the Copper Mountain Ski Resort and Golf Course and was headed up the Ten Mile Ridge to Breckenridge when I began getting pelted by hail. It was the type of hail that was big and hurt as it hit my neck and head. It then turned to rain. I don't think I even changed my stride as I walked on up the mountain.

Thankfully, the skies cleared as I neared the top of the climb for the few miles of exposed ridge walking above the tree line. I remembered this section very well from our hike the previous year and each memory drove home the fact that Julie was there before and not here now to talk about it and to share in it. I passed an old campsite where we'd camped. Then I passed a spot where we'd been photographed by some day hikers, and then painfully, I passed a section where we'd taken a break and Julie mimicked the pikas. She loved making their squeaky noises and was quite good at imitating them.

I steadily walked down the other side of the ridge toward the road to Breckenridge. By the time I got there it was early evening with maybe an hour of daylight remaining. I saw two huge rainbows which lingered for all of three minutes before storm clouds blew in. The skies opened up and it poured again, this time bringing lightning. I made a wrong turn after the road crossing and as I was trying to use the GPS in the rain to find my way out of a resort neighborhood and back to the trail, a flash of lightning came down so close that I could actually hear the sizzle of electricity as it touched down. I waited a moment and then cautiously continued on. As I was tracking the next waypoint, I was stopped by a gushing creek.

"What the hell is going on?" I thought as I stared in disbelief at this now gushing, swollen creek. I had been on my own for merely five hours. I'd been pelted by hail, stormed on, nearly struck by lightning, and now, here I was facing a precarious water crossing. I managed to slowly and cautiously balance myself on a downed tree, steadying myself with my poles as I crossed. I then found the trail and started the climb out of town and back into the woods.

The rains began to let up and now it was a race with the sun to find a spot to camp for the night. At first I was only looking for a flat spot. Then I got the idea to find the spot we'd camped at the year before. I knew it was somewhat close to the road crossing so I kept hiking, passing up good camp spots in the name of nostalgia. But then it got dark and I started getting anxious about night hiking alone. I eventually found a flat spot and set about trying to set up our two-person tent by myself.

I had been somewhat concerned about the process of getting the tent standing by myself because it required staking ropes to the ground and balancing the front of the tent support with a hiking pole. With two people, this was no problem at all, as one person held the hiking pole while the other staked in the support lines. I was now attempting this alone and in the dark. Thankfully, it went smoothly and I crawled into the tent.

I was still wet from head to toe and so was my pack. I got my sleeping mat out, took off my shoes, got out my sleeping quilt, and curled up for sleep. I didn't take out my contacts because I didn't want to be blind while in the woods alone. If there was ever a threat, whatever was threatening me wasn't going to wait while I put in my contacts. I didn't even brush my teeth that night. I did check the iPad to see if I could call Julie to tell her about the crazy storms but I didn't have a signal. So I turned it off, turned off my light, and thought about going to sleep.

Within moments of turning off my light the coyotes howled. It seemed as if they were surrounding my tent. I thought, "Really, my first night alone and the coyotes are spooking me!" I lay there for awhile, awake, cold, and wet, and I realized that this was one of my first intentional nights camping alone ever on any of my trails. I'd walked nearly 10,000 miles and spent nearly a year of my life living in the backcountry of the United States and I had never camped alone. It was a heavy thought to fall asleep to.

I woke up the next morning with thoughts just as heavy. In fact, I was an emotional wreck. I had moved in silence the entire time since leaving Julie the day before and as I went through each action of the trail life, it felt as if part of me was missing. As I cried and lamented the situation, I began to realize that I was essentially mourning the loss of my hiking partner. Stopwatch was gone. Her life had been so intertwined with mine that without her there, a huge void was now present, and I could feel the immensity of that void with each trail life action I undertook.

I tried to call her that morning, but again, there was no signal. I ran into a couple hikers later that morning and when I started talking with them, saying "we" instead of "me", I started getting choked up, so I just kept hiking.

I thought briefly about ending my hike. How much did I really care about completing the hike? Why should I have us both unhappy because of something I wanted to do so badly, but that she disliked so much?

Around lunchtime I'd gotten to Georgia Pass, the point where the Colorado Trail and CDT diverged, with the CDT turning left and heading up to a higher route above tree line. It was at this time that I met another thru-hiker, Green Flash. He was a few years younger than me and he seemed eager to have someone to hike with. I warned him that I was carrying some heavy emotional baggage, but from that moment on, we carried on a positive and uplifting conversation that carried us through one of the tougher sections of trail I'd hiked thus far.

We were above tree line, above 12,000', and there was often no trail whatsoever. Sometimes there were cairns to guide us, and sometimes it was just known that we needed to follow the ridgeline through uneven, rocky terrain, regardless of whether there was a path or not. We talked for hours about travel, trails, and adventuring and it eased my mind tremendously.

We stared in amazement at a herd of shaggy mountain goats high on the ridge as clouds cleared, with Green Flash stating that that moment in and of itself, made his entire hike worth it. We walked towards them, eventually watching them dip off the side of the ridge into seeming oblivion, their agile and nimble legs perfectly adapted to such treacherous terrain.

We luckily dodged a storm that afternoon as thunderstorm clouds rolled over us but didn't unleash their fury. We sat on the hillside in our rain gear, looking at a mountain face with a steep pitch and an orange-red hue, both feeling as if we were on our way to Mordor together.

By early evening, the route I was trying to follow diverged from his route and I headed off to find my way down the ridge. I managed to get pretty off track, but with the GPS I was eventually able to route myself back on track through some heavy bushes and down a steep ravine. I managed to get set up just before dark, happy and exhausted after a thirty plus mile day. But the only thing I could think about as I went to sleep alone again was how tremendously much I missed Julie.

The next morning I woke up early with the sun. I crossed the rushing, cold Peru Creek and then headed up toward the highest point on the entire trail, Grays Peak. The weather was crisp, clear, and cold that morning. However, I had over 4,000' to climb and I wanted to get up and over the peak before the afternoon storms.

The first part of the climb was steady and there was nice trail. Once I got to Argentine Pass however, the trail turned off to the left and I followed the cairns up the rocky terrain. I sighted my way, staying along the ridgeline and made my way to Mount Edwards. At over 13,800' it was the second highest point on the trail. From there, I had to follow a spine of rocks connecting over to Grays Peak before beginning the big climb.

This spiny section was probably one of the scariest portions of trail I've ever hiked. There was no trail, there were no cairns, and there were precipitous drop-offs on either side. Yet, there was nowhere else to go in order to feel safe or to get down other than following the spine and heading toward Grays. While I missed Julie tremendously, I knew she would be hating and cursing this section. I smiled a little and carefully made my way alone along the spine and climbed Grays.

At the top, at over 14,000' I came across many other people

enjoying the beautiful day. The route I was taking down was the route most everyone else had come up and it led back to I-70 with an easy access point. I had someone snap some pictures of me up on that amazing peak and then I ran. I ran down that mountain jumping down steps and racing past the day hikers. I felt so strong and I pushed myself. I thought, "There is no way I am going to quit this trail," as I felt my will and my drive surge strength through me.

I got to the bottom and had a quick bite to eat before heading down a forest road to a bike path that followed along I-70 for a few miles. Finally, the iPad worked and I was able to Skype with Julie.

The emotions came flooding back and it was difficult for either of us to talk without crying. She updated me on everything she'd accomplished and she told me about her plans. I told her that I thought I could get to Grand Lake a day sooner than we'd originally planned in order to be in town for the Fourth of July. We picked a time and agreed to meet at the trailhead in Grand Lake a couple days later.

I packed up, and then I listened to music on my mp3 player for the first time since hiking alone. I had energy in my steps. I sang aloud and began my climb after crossing under the highway. I pushed all day, barely stopping. Taking breaks alongside the trail was an entirely different experience when hiking solo. There wasn't anyone to talk with, and for me, sitting there idly by myself felt weird so I just kept walking.

I was above tree line again and though it was getting dark, I didn't want to stop to camp so high up if I could avoid it. I was energetic and kept hiking well into the night. By around 10:00pm the trail had barely dipped into some scrub brush in the alpine zone and I found a spot to tuck in behind some bushes. I quickly set up camp and was immediately asleep.

I was building strength but I was also feeling lonely. I would classify myself as a hugs kind of guy, requiring multiple hugs per day. However, not only were there no hugs, but there were rarely even people to talk with. I had a new respect and appreciation for our hiker friends that went it alone. I had always known they'd had a different experience than we did, but it felt like an entirely new one to me now that I was actually hiking solo.

The day after Grays Peak was challenging as well. I had three huge climbs, and three times I was over 13,000'. I chugged along though, hardly stopping, and sometimes walking for hours on end.

I hadn't been eating much. When I was packing up prior to leaving Copper, I'd packed all the foods I liked and left behind stuff I was tired of eating. So I had the best food but I wasn't hungry. As a result, I was carrying too much. But I didn't seem to notice the weight on my back much. I walked all day, deep in thought or sometimes simply numb.

As I made my way up James Peak during the afternoon, chancing storms, I met a couple, Mike and Carrie. They section-hiked one month every year and by doing this year in and year out, they have tackled thousands of miles of trail. We stuck together for the afternoon and thankfully so because the ridge walk after James Peak was one of the most brutal I'd ever hiked. We were battered by gusty winds and pelted with rain. It was cold and miserable and there was no trail. We'd walk through thick, wet, scruffy grass, followed by patches of slick rock fields. At one point I had to stay clear from the edge of the ridge for fear that the wind may actually blow me off the mountain.

We eventually descended back into the trees shortly after dark and found a camp spot. I was really happy to camp with them. We swapped details on gear and food strategies and talked about our future miles left to hike.

The next morning left me with thirty miles to Grand Lake and I was to meet Julie by 5:00pm. I knew I had a downhill to start the day and relatively flat terrain for most of the day. The previous three days were probably the most challenging miles I'd ever hiked and I'd managed to hike over thirty miles each day. I felt like the thirty into Grand Lake should be easy.

The miles clicked by as I walked around some pretty lakes and met families out celebrating the Fourth. I walked dirt roads and even had a guy give me some Gatorade as I walked by his cabin. All was rolling along nicely until I hit a section called Knight's Ridge.

I generally didn't read much about the trail or know much about what was coming as I entered each new section of the trail. I had my maps and data points but other than that, I had quickly developed the routine of waking with the sun without an alarm and pretty much hiking all day until the sun went down. This was working well for me and I was developing my own rhythm on the trail. However, the Knight's Ridge was a section of trail that had been decimated by bark beetles, and as a result, the entire ridge was littered with dead, fallen trees. The trail was covered and was nowhere to be found. All I could see in any direction was downed trees piled up like matchsticks.

I had my GPS out and ready. I had grown in confidence over the past few days with my GPS skills. I proceeded slowly from waypoint to waypoint, continually hoping to find more trail, but I was losing time. I crawled under trees and over them. I snagged myself on branches and I climbed up and over hilly terrain as I tried to stay on course. I stayed calm briefly but my patience eventually gave way as I yelled out into an empty forest in anger, "Where the hell is the trail?!"

I could also see the afternoon clouds building up and knew that storms were on the way. I eventually cleared the section of blow downs and found the trail again. I was now totally off schedule though. As I saw signs indicating I was entering Rocky Mountain National Park, I also encountered signs stating that the section I'd just passed through had been unmaintained and was dangerous due to all the downed trees. Not that it would have changed my course had I seen that sign on the other end, but maybe I would have been better mentally prepared.

I was now thankfully at a lower elevation and following along a large lake as the thunderstorm hit. I was happy to no longer be up high on the ridge but lightning was scary nonetheless. With clear trails again, along with sections of flat and downhill trail, I began running. I shuffled my feet quickly whenever possible, trying to make up time. I knew I was getting close to the meeting place with Julie but I also knew there was no way I was making it on time.

I was sopping wet and eventually gave up on avoiding puddles as water built up on the trail. As I came around a bend I noticed something big off to the side of the trail. It was my first moose encounter of the journey. It was a huge bull and it didn't seem too concerned with my presence. It looked at me, and I at it. I dug my camera out of my dry sack, snapped a couple pictures, and was quickly on my way.

Not more than a mile later I saw another bull just off the side of the trail. I again took pictures and just as I was walking away another bull stood up. It had been lying down close to the other bull but out of sight. Here in front of me were two huge moose. I'd heard they could be aggressive, and if so, they could absolutely crush me, so I got my pictures and hurried along.

At 5:40pm I popped out of the woods and into the trailhead parking lot where I saw Julie eagerly awaiting me. I was so happy to see her again. She raced to me, embracing me in all my wet, trail grossness.

I took off my heavy, wet trail running shoes and got in the car. She'd prepared a feast for me. I gorged myself as she drove us to Steamboat Springs where we were celebrating the holiday together. It felt so good to be with her again.

5
Stopwatch

The first phone call I made as I tried to make sense of things at Eric's apartment was to Matt's brother, Jeff. He'd hiked half the Appalachian Trail in 2004 and was one of the few people that would understand the emotional roller coaster I'd gone through on the trail thus far.

"Jeff," I started calmly, which quickly changed to sobbing and unrecognizable words, "I quit the trail."

"What?" he asked. I knew he wasn't asking out of surprise, but because he literally hadn't been able to understand what I said.

I took a deep breath and repeated, clearly this time, "I quit the trail. Matt continued on and I'm at Eric's while I wait for him to get here to Steamboat Springs."

"Oh my gosh...well, I don't blame you; that trail sounds awful," he said, which helped lift my spirits a little. Talking to Jeff was refreshing because he knew Matt well and confirmed that Matt would be just fine on his own, that he'd make friends and push himself to finish the trail alone. Still, I couldn't believe I was sitting indoors, talking to Jeff, having quit the trail. Jeff had been the first to ask me before the trail started, "Why do you keep doing these trails? You don't like thru-hiking."

I had to finally admit he was right. While there were some aspects I liked about thru-hiking, such as spending time with Matt and challenging myself both physically and mentally, other factors like extreme discomfort over so many continuous days had overwhelmed my desire to continue.

I didn't sleep much that first night on Eric's couch as I watched thunderstorms roll past the windows, bringing heavy rain and wind. I knew Matt was out in that storm, alone in our two-person tent, without glasses to see, and with nearly 2,000 miles left to walk. The darkness surrounded me with sadness rather than sleep and I couldn't wait for daylight.

I woke up before sunrise. It was a quiet, calm morning. I pictured Matt going through his morning routine of getting dressed, going to the bathroom, taking down the tent, packing up, and finally starting his day with an energy bar in one hand and the GPS in the other. I thought about the silence that surrounded him in the early morning, a silence that was unique to walking alone in the mountains. He had the sounds of nature surrounding him but hiking alone was a different kind of silence, where the only possibility of a voice was his own. I felt incredibly lonely as I thought about him walking alone.

To take my mind off the mental video of him walking away, I made a to-do list. It included buying two important things for Matt: a one-person tent and bear spray. The list also included booking a one-way flight home to Seattle. Once in Seattle, I planned on finding a new apartment and a job, two tasks I looked forward to because they would take my mind off missing Matt.

All within a few hours I had already ordered a tent, booked a flight home, and booked a rental car to see Matt in Grand Lake in just a few days. The new tent weighed a scant twenty-six ounces, stakes included, a fifteen ounce improvement from our current tent. My flight would leave a week later, after I'd seen Matt come through Steamboat, and the rental car allowed me to see Matt at different points along his way to Steamboat. I was almost too efficient in my to-do list because by early afternoon I was left to face my own thoughts once again, and they were sad thoughts.

I missed Matt tremendously. I still didn't want to be hiking, but I wasn't dealing well with being so physically disconnected from him. When I started to feel down, I consoled myself with a walk around town, holding back tears in public as waves of sadness ebbed and flowed. I also visited the local natural foods store very often. A big consolation of being back in the real world was that I was able to eat fresh fruits and vegetables once again, so I cooked and baked several different dishes to pass the time and take my mind off Matt. After dinner on my first full day off in Steamboat, Eric and I watched one of several documentaries that Eric loved, all about people overcoming obstacles and pursuing their dreams. It didn't have quite the effect on me that I imagined Eric was hoping it would. Instead of lifting my spirits, the movies made me feel lame for quitting a challenge that I had taken on and I felt that much worse about myself and my decision. I wasn't questioning my decision to get off the trail but the documentaries showed me the grit and toughness that other people possessed, which I felt I had lost.

I went to sleep yet again amid thunderstorms outside the window, feeling like a massive disappointment to myself, my family and friends, and most of all, to Matt.

I heard from Matt the next day around lunch time. He'd kept the iPad so he could make phone calls on Skype. He was around I-70 and I could tell by his voice that he sounded pretty roughed-up.

As I talked to family members over the course of those days, they all said I had the harder job of having to start up a new life in Seattle by finding a new apartment and a job. They were wrong. I knew Matt had the harder job of hiking the trail alone. I had creature comforts to make life so much easier. He not only had no creature comforts, but he also didn't have me. He didn't have his best friend by his side to support him, to help navigate the tricky trail, to join him in walking through thunderstorms over lightning-rod ridges, or to lie in the tent at night and listen to strange sounds amid the darkness.

We talked for almost an hour and he was surprised to hear I'd already bought a plane ticket. I had bought one so that I wouldn't be tempted to get back on the trail but he'd hoped I hadn't bought one in case I thought about getting back on.

"Oh, it's been so hard, Julie," he said. "I thought about quitting too; it's just not the same without you. But it's getting better and I think I'll be ok on my own," he said, his voice cracking into tears. "I was thinking, maybe if the trail got easier, you could get back on," he added with hope as the tears continued to flow.

"I can't," I said. "It's done, I quit and I can't go back," I said through gushing tears. It saddened me that he was considering quitting because I wasn't there; it felt like my plan was backfiring if the end result was him quitting as well.

It was hard to say goodbye. Neither of us wanted to continue going on alone but he still had two days to go to Grand Lake, and that was our beacon of hope to look forward to. The guilt was overwhelming afterwards as I pictured him putting away the iPad and slinging his pack on his back, continuing alone up the trail.

Later that afternoon I called my sister. I had dreaded telling her firsthand that I had quit the trail. This was the first trail she'd become really involved in, sending us mail to every stop along the way and even going so far as to bake vegan cookies for us. I knew she was rooting for me and I felt like I'd let her down. If she was disappointed she didn't show it on the phone, but I knew there had to be some piece of disappointment in her feelings. She had done so much for me and it felt like I betrayed a part of that support by quitting.

There are so many clichés in life, one being that we shouldn't worry about what other people think. I think that cliché is bull. If I really look at myself, I discover that I act each day according to what others might think about me, in my dress, my diet, my habits, etc. In quitting the trail, I thought a lot about what others might think. I knew so many would be sad, disappointed, angry at me, supportive of me, worried about Matt…I cared about what they thought because my actions still affected others, outside of both Matt and me. I thought a lot about what my sister thought because it was one of the first times in my life that she was on my side, cheering for me like we were on the same team. I feared what quitting might do to our already fragile relationship since the trail was a building block that was helping to build a better foundation for us. I hoped she would understand my feelings and actions, but it hurt to know that she saw me fail at the CDT.

After watching another documentary with Eric, I went to bed excited to make a new to-do list the next day in order to prepare to see Matt the following day. Matt's arrival into Grand Lake carried some logistical difficulties since he was getting to town on the Fourth of July. There wasn't vacancy at any hotels within a thirty-mile radius of Grand Lake so Eric and I both agreed that I would drive Matt back to Steamboat that evening, ninety-four miles each way. All I had was time on my side, so it didn't matter to me how much time I spent in the car.

It was Wednesday and I was starting to feel slightly better. I still had tears in my eyes when I pictured him walking away at Copper Mountain, but I was getting better focusing on other things, and that day I focused on menu planning for Matt's visit. I knew he'd want fresh vegetables, fruit, and some kind of baked dessert.

Just like I had done the past few days, I talked to my mom that afternoon and let her know of my plans to see Matt the following day and all the food preparation I had done in anticipation of taking care of him for the evening. I had read one of his recent blog posts and it sounded like tough terrain he was going through, including days and nights of powerful thunderstorms. I also couldn't help but repeat myself in telling her how much I missed him.

"Wow," she started, "I guess I didn't realize how much you guys loved each other," she said. I didn't quite understand what she meant and she seemed to sense that.

"I mean," she paused, "I'm just so proud that you have someone that you love that much and I'm happy for you that you've found that kind of love," she explained.

"Well, thank you," I said, unsure of what to say. Both my parents had been divorced twice. It saddened me to think that I had left the one person I shared such strong love with, but it also made me grateful for my relationship with Matt.

That night was the worst night of thunderstorms yet, with hours of lightning, strong winds, and heavy rain. The guilt I felt seemed to have rooted itself in me. The only comfort was that I would see Matt the next day.

Matt and I planned on meeting at 5:00pm that day but I was so excited to meet him that I reached town at 3:00pm and parked at the trailhead, my eyes fixed on the trail. As I sat there, a cooler in the backseat full of sandwich fixings, vegan pesto, homemade lentil burgers, and salad, two moose crossed the parking lot just ten feet from my car. It was the first time I'd ever seen moose so close and in such clear daylight, and yet so ironic that I was just sitting in a car rather than out on the trail. They sauntered through the parking lot and slowly made their way through trees and bushes at the edge of the parking lot, eating as they walked. I wondered how many moose encounters Matt had had so far.

As I waited for Matt, a group of four older day-hikers parked next to me. They went for a short hike and returned to find me still waiting, this time standing outside of the car because I felt antsy sitting down. We struck up a conversation and I told them how I was waiting for Matt to arrive and how I had just quit the trail. Maybe they could hear a hint of regret in my voice, because one of them asked me, "Well, can't you get back on?"

"Nah, I can't," I answered. "If I did, then I wouldn't have a full thru-hike and that's the whole point, to go from point A to point B."

The moment I said it, I realized the absolute fault in that reasoning. I had just spent the last few days telling people that the reason I ever thru-hiked in the first place was because it was Matt's dream and that I was there to support him. The whole point wasn't just to go from A to B, something I learned on my very first trail, the PCT, but obviously something I had forgotten in all my anxiety of completing the hike before our September 18th deadline.

It occurred to me that I was making my own rules on what I could and couldn't do, and I could easily get back on if I wanted. Not that I had really considered getting back on, but I missed Matt so much that I was starting to regret my decision and to think of other options. If I got back on, that meant I would have skipped a section, which indeed meant an incomplete thru-hike, but there was no rule saying once I was off, I couldn't get back on. If getting back on meant that I was once again with Matt, and that I could still help him complete his dream of triple crowning, wasn't that a win-win situation? That moment, I started tossing around the idea of getting back on the trail when Matt went through Steamboat Springs. There was no one keeping me on or off the trail other than myself.

As I drove Matt back to Steamboat that evening, happily watching him eat and listening to his stories from the last few days, I kept quiet about my latest idea. I didn't want to give him hope, only to take it away if I changed my mind, so I kept the focus on him. I was playing the role of a support person, so that's exactly what I did at Eric's home. Once in Steamboat, I took care of Matt like I always wanted others to do when I was in town. I did his laundry, cleaned out his pack, repacked his new food, gave him fresh towels and clothes, and fed him vegetables, pasta, and vegan brownies and coconut ice cream. He was exhausted from the previous big mileage days in tough terrain, not to mention the emotional drainage that he'd gone through in missing me. Before we went to bed, Matt pulled up his latest pictures on Eric's computer.

As he showed the pictures, it occurred to me that I was missing out. I didn't know the places in the pictures and I loathed the fact that he needed a stranger to take his photo atop Grays Peak, the highest point on the trail. In seeing such unfamiliar scenery, I was hit with the realization that I was missing a huge, important piece of his life that I'd never understand. I wouldn't be able to share in those memories because I wasn't there to take part in the original scenes.

The seed of getting back on the trail had been planted in my mind and that moment had watered the seed and given it sunlight. Still, I didn't mention many details to Matt. I simply built my mental case in order to talk it over with Matt and other family members before making any final decisions.

Matt fell asleep immediately as we lay next to each other on Eric's couch. We'd been so used to sharing a small tent space that sharing a couch was still roomier and more luxurious than any night outside. As he slept, his breathing heavy in such a deep sleep, I lay wide awake, my mind racing with thoughts of getting back on the trail, debating so many conflicting feelings that had grown over the last few days of being apart.

6
Optimist

The stopover in Steamboat Springs was an ideal trail stop. I was treated like a king and though I was ecstatic about seeing Julie again, I was also seriously in need of a town stop. Julie knew all about what I needed and she quickly fed me, cleaned out my pack, and started getting the next section of food ready for me. I was able to shave and shower and I was even given some of Eric's clothes to wear for the evening to escape my hiker wardrobe.

It was the Fourth of July and Eric's company had a party down by the Yampa River with a great view for the fireworks. They also had a catered dinner. We crashed the party and had a great evening of socializing. I reveled in the small spotlight as people eagerly asked questions about the craziness of a CDT thru-hike.

By the time we got back to Eric's after the party I was spent and I was quickly asleep on the couch. I knew Julie had been thinking about options other than going back to Seattle so we talked briefly about them but saved the rest for the drive back the next day.

The original plan was for her to fly home to Seattle in a few days time and then begin the task of setting up life for us there, finding an apartment and looking for a job. She'd also thought about flying home just to pickup our car so she could then drive along and support me as I made my way north, seeing me at towns and road crossings along the way. She'd also thought about getting back on the trail.

My response was that I simply wanted her to be happy and for the choice to be her own. I told her I definitely loved hiking with her and that I would be overjoyed if she returned, but that I'd also be happy if she were crewing for me. I would also be happy if she was back in Seattle if that was what she wanted to do, even though I knew I'd miss her tremendously.

By this point I had begun to find my own rhythm on the trail. I had given up using the alarm on my watch to wake up in the morning. I found that I was actually getting up earlier, beginning my hiking day as the sun was coming up. I took fewer breaks and I would hike for hours on end. I also began hiking until dark and sometimes into the night. I felt good pushing myself, and my growing confidence in my ability to do the trail on my own was fueling me forward. However, I also knew that I was lonely and that having my wife back on the trail with me would be wonderful.

I got back on the trail in Grand Lake in the early afternoon, once again in time for the afternoon storms. I again entered Rocky Mountain National Park where I faced a potential dilemma. A portion of trail in the park had burned earlier in the summer and had been closed. It was a longer, higher route, but it was supposed to be beautiful. I'd planned on hiking it knowing that it was part of the official route I'd stuck to thus far. However, it was not meant to be this time around because the signs clearly indicated that the section was still closed and that it was illegal to hike that section. With circumstances like this, I was wholly flexible and ready to adapt my plans, and thankfully, my maps guided me through the park and around the burnt section.

As I moved up the trail, within the first ten minutes the rains began. They kept up for the rest of the day, stopping briefly, only to restart again. I made my way out of the park in the early evening and into the interestingly named, Never Summer Wilderness. The name proved to be very fitting as my surroundings were dark and damp as I climbed for more than an hour that evening, eventually finding a flat spot by a creek next to an open meadow just before dark. I'd pushed about as long as I was willing to push and when I looked out into the meadow and spotted a female moose and her calf, I quickly debated whether to pack up and move on, or to take my chances.

I hoped we could all get along and I set up my tent amidst the tall, wet grass. I was in a small opening surrounded by trees. For me, the spot was not ideal, but I'd been climbing for over an hour and I knew I had more climbing ahead. I didn't want to hit the pass after dark and my camping options had been limited. I usually avoided camping near water due to wildlife, especially if the wildlife was standing right there when I set up camp.

Nonetheless, I called it a day, and around midnight the skies unleashed. It was a huge lightning storm with strong winds and lots of rain. I was awake for much of the storm and was actively checking my tent to ensure that everything stayed as dry as possible. At one point I spotted a place where some water had pooled up in my tent. I quickly adjusted my things, dried the floor with a bandana, and hoped for the best. The storm eventually calmed and I managed to fall asleep again.

I was awoken again shortly before dawn to the sound of heavy footsteps and crunching sounds. I figured right away that it was the two moose. They were eating right outside my tent and my hope was that they wouldn't trample me as I lay there in my tent. I opted for silence and stillness so as to not startle them. Eventually they moved on.

I was up early, ready to get out of there. However, since I hadn't slept much, it was a bit more challenging than normal to get myself moving faster than a sluggish plod to start the day. I had told Julie I'd meet her in two and a half days, meaning I had two thirty-plus mile days ahead of me in order to reach our meet up point at Rabbit Ears Pass outside of Steamboat Springs.

After leaving the Never Summer Wilderness, I found myself atop the Divide for many of my miles, often on exposed terrain following along the ridgeline. Sometimes there would be trail and sometimes I was simply walking across open land with no path. Antelope and elk kept me alert as I would spot them from a distance dotting the landscape. Thankfully, there were no storms on my first full day out of Grand Lake and I was rewarded with a day filled with panoramic views of the Rocky Mountains. Alone in the wilderness I belted out rock ballads from Guns 'N Roses. I sang along with Dave Matthews and I picked up my pace as I rocked out to Led Zeppelin, all the while soaking in the expansive wilderness around me.

While the section between Copper and Grand Lake had been dominated by long, continuous ascents and descents, this section was more deceptively challenging. The maps and data sheet didn't indicate many huge climbs but instead seemed a bit steadier. However, following the Divide proved challenging as I was constantly going up and down, usually in steep bursts. This roller coaster section took its toll on me and I called it quits shortly before dark. I was up high again but the weather was clear and I had a few trees to tuck into. I was still thirty-seven miles out from my meet up point with Julie.

The next morning I was still sluggish. The miles were still tough and the terrain wasn't letting up. The Divide was unrelenting and I began to doubt whether or not I'd make it in time. To compound my concerns, I managed to lose the trail that morning, eventually going waypoint to waypoint up a steep hill, stepping over downed trees and getting my feet soaked in tall grass, still wet with morning dew.

By 8:45am I finally made my way back to trail and then to a Forest Service road. I now had thirty miles of road and just over eight hours to do it in. However, I was exhausted. I sat down by the side of the dirt road, alone and high up in the mountains, and I gorged. I attacked my food bag like I had yet to do ever since heading out on my own. The hunger hit suddenly and it was as if the lower calorie intake of the past week had finally caught up with me. My desire to fuel myself kicked in again and I ate. I ate chocolate, I ate dried fruit, and I ate energy bars. I ate salty snacks and soy jerky and I wasn't even getting full.

Finally, after forty minutes of non-stop eating, I felt like I was ready to move again. Energy pulsed through me and I came up with a plan to run the trail. I missed running quite a bit on my thru-hikes, especially with so many beautiful sections of trail to run, and I figured that with a long section of dirt roads and downhill, I could make up a bunch of time.

I needed to average close to four miles per hour to make it on time. I knew I had to keep breaks to a minimum and I had to be efficient with my time and energy. I was recharged though and suddenly felt adrenaline pulsing through me. The challenge was on.

I spent the rest of the day checking my watch and GPS to see how fast I was going. The first ten miles were mainly downhill on dirt roads. They then led to rolling hills past cattle farms and eventually to a paved highway for the final twelve miles. As I ran down the hill and toward a large herd of cattle, I realized they probably weren't used to seeing crazed-looking hikers running down these mountain roads. They freaked out and all started running, eventually congregating in one spot. They made a huge circle with all the calves in the middle. The large mothers would then take turns coming to the front of the circle facing me while belting out an aggressive and loud moaning noise.

As I passed the herd, a little frightened by their behavior, one of the cows stepped forward out of the group and began walking towards me with a moo I'd never heard before. It was as if she was screaming at me, barking orders, telling me to get away. Her head was down low and she followed me down the road for thirty yards. I continued to check over my shoulder to make sure I wasn't going to be charged and as I distanced myself from the herd, I continued to hear them well after they were out of sight.

I was making good time and the 5:00pm meet up seemed doable again. I even surprised myself by walking nineteen miles straight without stopping. I took a quick break for some snacks and realized my water was low and that I still had over ten miles remaining. It was hot and sunny now, and I was on a highway, surrounded by private property.

I pushed on, looking for water. There was ditch water but it was behind fences and inaccessible. Eventually I found a spot where the water from a drainage area off the side of the highway had swollen such that it had pooled up outside the fence, allowing me to dip my bottle in. I put an extra drop of bleach in the water and chugged it as soon as it was ready.

As I made my way up the final stretch of highway I began to get concerned regarding our planned meeting spot. We'd agreed to meet along the highway. We hadn't looked at my trail map too closely, but we had discussed some mile markers on the highway to aim for.

As I followed my route, moving at a focused and fast clip, my route took me off the highway for what I thought was a brief mile or two of trail. I was paralleling the highway for a mile but then it began to get quieter. I was getting farther from the highway and eventually found myself at a trailhead taking me farther into the woods. I nervously got out my map and realized I was not heading back to the highway.

I panicked a bit and hurried to call Julie. I had a signal but she didn't answer. I knew I had to get back to the highway. I was on a dirt road and knew the highway was to my west so I hurried up the road, quickly scoring a hitch back to Route 40.

As I sat on the corner of the highway, hoping Julie would find me, a couple in a Subaru pulled over and asked if I needed help. I explained my situation and they were quick to offer assistance. It was now 5:30pm as they went on down the highway looking for where they expected Julie to be waiting. I stayed put in case Julie was driving up and down the highway looking for me.

They came back empty-handed. I jumped in their car, now really feeling the effects of my hard effort from the day's hike. We made one last attempt together to find Julie, knowing that I'd head back to town with them if we couldn't find her. Thankfully, we spotted her a few minutes later and the run-around was over.

Julie had a huge smile on her face along with cold drinks and food for the ride home. We thanked our new friends for helping us out and we headed back to Steamboat. I quickly found out that Julie had gotten a lot accomplished in the two and a half days I'd been out on the trail. It was also obvious that she was feeling much better about her plans going forward.

7
Stopwatch

Before I drove Matt back to Grand Lake, I let him sleep as long as possible while I prepared breakfast and finished organizing his pack. He'd hiked some tough miles in the previous section, probably the hardest ones on the trail so far, and I'd somehow managed to quit just before those miles.

While Matt was showering, I hinted to Eric that I was considering getting back on. First a look of surprise swept across his face, but then he lowered his head, looked at me through serious eyes and said in a deep voice, "Julie, what's the definition of insanity?"

"Doing the same thing over and over again and expecting different results?" I asked, knowing exactly where he was going with his question. Part of me felt silly and embarrassed, but another part didn't care. The bottom line was that I'd seen the other side, the side where the grass looked greener, and I didn't like it if it didn't have Matt in it. Eric didn't offer any other advice; I had a feeling I had run out of his free therapy sessions over the course of the week.

As Matt and I drove back to Grand Lake, it began to sprinkle outside. Not only had Matt had hard terrain, he'd also experienced a lot of rain in the last few days and it didn't look like it was letting up. Part of me was glad I hadn't been in all that rain; being wet and cold made for difficult hiking and rain gear never seemed to be fully functional in continuous rain. As we neared the end of the drive, the sadness I felt in missing him started to creep back in. At that point he knew I was contemplating getting back on the trail, but that I hadn't come to a conclusion yet. I assured him I'd make a decision by the time he got back to Steamboat, which was about eighty miles away for him.

As I stood in the parking lot, watching him walk away yet again, I felt the pull to get back on and to be with him again. I had thought about driving the rest of the way up the trail, supporting him along the way, but it was too heartbreaking to see him walk off alone each time. It was also just as tortuous to think of being back in Seattle while he continued facing these challenges alone. I had set out from New Mexico with a promise to be by his side and here I was violating that promise and creating a big, hot mess of things.

Upon arriving back in Steamboat, the first person I called to talk about my idea of getting back on was my mom. She wasn't a hiker but she'd listened to me talk throughout the week and she knew how much I was missing Matt. She was quick to support the idea and even said she was surprised when I bought a plane ticket home, thinking I might change my mind and get back on. I guess she knew me better than I realized.

In thinking of getting back on, I was embarrassed. I'd written a blog post explaining why I was quitting and here I was mentally forming the content of my next blog post, saying why I was getting back on. I was afraid people would be angry with my indecision and tire of my inability to simply hike a trail without the drama. But, those people that might be angry were not the ones hiking, were not the ones getting heat stroke, running out of water, or getting stuck in lightning storms. They wouldn't understand what went through my mind and therefore shouldn't be the ones making the decision for me. I had to step back and not rely solely on what others might think in order to make as objective of a decision as possible.

Before making a final decision, I called one more person, my friend Jessica, Rocketcop's wife. Rocketcop and Matt met in 2000 on the Appalachian Trail and have been friends ever since. Rocketcop also started the Pacific Crest Trail with us in 2007 and finished just two weeks after us. Jessica and Rocketcop were dating in 2007 when he hiked the PCT, so Jessica had the unique perspective of being a thru-hiker's significant other. She stayed at home while he hiked and from what we gathered, she wasn't thrilled about it. I had no idea what that felt like until now and I wanted to talk to someone who had the experience of being at home the entire time that her (now) spouse was on the trail.

When I first mentioned to Jessica that I was thinking of getting back on, I felt stupid. Matt's mom had just sent all of our resupply boxes to Rocketcop and Jessica's house in Seattle so that I could repackage them once I got home to Seattle. If I got back on the trail, they'd now have the duty of sending out our resupplies, a fairly daunting task considering the logistical implications of getting the timing right with our arrival in each town.

Once I got over feeling stupid, I voiced my concern to Jessica that I felt like I was missing out on a huge part of Matt's life by leaving him to hike the rest of the trail alone. I wanted to know if she also felt that way about Rocketcop's hikes. She was quick to agree, saying that thru-hikes were a part of Rocketcop's life that she would never fully understand or grasp because she'd never been through one with him.

That conversation sealed the deal. I wanted back on. I didn't want to miss any more of Matt's life than I already had and I no longer cared about an official thru-hike. I just wanted to be with Matt in the simple act of hiking, not putting any more emphasize on titles like, "Triple Crown," because that really wasn't what it was about. Even Matt had said that before, that his dream was that of experiencing the CDT, not just gaining more titles to put behind his name. I was tired of putting importance on the accomplishment rather than the actual journey and once I switched my mindset to see it that way, I saw how it was possible to still be physically present with Matt. That meant I needed to be hiking.

The next day, Saturday, was spent untangling the mess I'd created over the previous week. I was not going to use the upcoming one-way plane ticket to Seattle, so there was $170 down the drain. I'd also done my job to support the US Postal Service, because I'd paid for postage two times on the same boxes, once for Matt's mom to send them to Seattle, and then again for Rocketcop and Jessica to mail them out to us. I typed up a list of the remaining post offices and UPS locations for Jessica to reference in order to send out each box. I also set up a ride with a friend of a friend in Steamboat to take Matt and I back to the trailhead at Rabbit Ears Pass on Monday morning. Eric was going out of town and I didn't want to rely on a hitch to drive us over twenty miles to the pass.

One thing I didn't do was tell people I was getting back on. I was tired of stirring up so much drama, I was also partially embarrassed, and all I truly wanted was to be out in the woods again with Matt. I wrote a blog story explaining my reasoning for getting back on, but I didn't post anything on Facebook or Twitter, and assumed people would learn about my return much more slowly. The title of my blog post was a tribute to Eric, "I Never Claimed to be Sane."

That night, before going to bed, I wrote Matt an email that I hoped he would see on the iPad sometime before Steamboat, with the subject line, "I'm Back."

I said to him in my email, "Count me in to be by your side until the end. I love you too much to not experience this with you. I love you and can't wait to see you again and to walk off into the woods with you."

So sappy but damn, did I miss him. He was my best friend. And still is.

Along with cooking up good vegan food once again for Matt, I completed what I called my Starbucks Training. I had just read a book about habits and one of the most interesting sections in the book was about a guy who worked for Starbucks as a barista. He had a fly-off-the-handle kind of personality and part of his training at Starbucks was to go through exercises simulating how he would react to difficult customers. He anticipated both external and internal problems before they happened and was ready with a response for each one, so when those things happened, it wasn't the first time he'd thought of how to deal with them.

I did the same for the external and internal challenges of the trail. I made a list of all the negative things that could happen to me both externally and internally and came up with a plan for how I'd deal with them, such as a rainy day or a lack of motivation to walk. It certainly wasn't a fool-proof plan, but they were things I needed to think about before they happened, before I was in the throes of a mental downward spiral, as I'd been a week prior. Had I had better habits in dealing with negative experiences, maybe I would have been able to deal with my emotions rather than quit the trail. It was a waste of energy to think of what might have been, but I felt positive about my approach to negative external and internal situations going forward.

That evening I picked up an exhausted, thirsty Matt at Rabbit Ears

Pass. He hadn't looked very carefully at the water sources for the day and ended up walking a nineteen-mile dry stretch with hardly any water. He'd also hiked thirty-seven miles by 5:00pm, a feat fairly unbelievable even to me, who'd been with him on other epic hiking days.

Just like I'd done a few days earlier, I washed his clothes and cleaned out his pack while he showered and relaxed, and fed him plenty of vegetables, pasta, bread, and brownies. This time the atmosphere between us was happy once again since I'd decided that I was leaving Steamboat with him. He fell asleep before I'd even brushed my teeth for the night and I lay awake on Eric's couch as he slept, my mind racing with excitement for getting back on the trail.

This time the excitement felt different than anxiety. I really was excited to simply be with Matt again, to be his best friend by his side. I felt free from the mileage pressure of the trail because I was going to be out there as support and no longer had to worry about the title of a true thru-hike. I'd already messed it up so much that the official triple crown aspect didn't matter anymore. All that mattered was that I was getting my wish of being with Matt and helping support his dream.

PART 3

1
Stopwatch

The trail knew just how to welcome me back. The moment we started walking away from Rabbit Ears Pass, towards our next town of Rawlins, Wyoming, a somewhat intimidating 165.2 miles away, I heard thunder. It was 1:30pm, prime time for thunderstorms in Colorado, and soon I felt the wind kick up and even noticed a sprinkle of rain.

Our friend Keith, a friend of Jen, our ride back to Rabbit Ears Pass, found out that it had started raining right after Jen dropped us off at the trailhead, and we later received an email from him that read, "I hope you are well on the resumption of your CDT journey. From what Jen told me a major hailstorm happened ten minutes after she dropped you off. Clearly you are being F'd with by the trail gods. You must perform a penance/sacrifice. Maybe burn some of that granola."

I had a feeling Keith was right; there was a little vengeance in that hail as it welcomed me back to the trail. I was paying back my dues for leaving Matt just before some of the hardest, most weather-volatile miles of the trail. The rain and hail barely lasted long enough for us to put on our rain gear and once the rain stopped, we were welcomed by swarms of mosquitoes, forcing us to sweat it out in our "full armor" as we called it, including our wind jacket, wind pants, and mosquito head nets. We reserved our tiny bottles of DEET only for the most extreme mosquito conditions.

Considering my historic emotions in rainy, mosquito-like climates,

I couldn't have been happier. I was walking with Matt once again, he seemed tickled to have me back, and I felt like a completely new hiker, with a fresh, positive attitude and a different perspective. While I still felt regret and sadness for having left Matt for a week, I felt grateful for the new insights I gained, something I wouldn't have been able to do had I kept trying to trudge through the miles with my negativity. Each time I felt that sadness well up inside me, each time I pictured Matt walking away at Copper Mountain, I stopped hiking and hugged and kissed him, simply because I could. He had that sparkle back in his eyes and I felt so lucky to have another chance to spend the rest of the trail with him.

The miles were surprisingly easy that day despite heavy packs full of five and a half days of food. I was worried I'd gotten out of shape over the last week while Matt got stronger over such tough terrain, but I was able to pick up where I left off. The freshness in my legs countered the fatigue in Matt's, so we quickly found a good rhythm for both of us.

We walked past dusk, leaving us about fifteen minutes of daylight to set up the tent. Over the course of the last week, Matt had created a new routine of rising without an alarm and walking until almost dark. He took fewer breaks and was able to get in high mileage with the approach of long, steady days, and he'd been happy with the results, so I wanted to adopt his new ways. From then on, we vowed to not set an alarm unless we absolutely had to get up at a certain time. Freeing myself from the alarm felt like I'd cut another cord that was binding me in my unhappiness on the trail.

That night we set up our new tent for the first time. I'd bought Matt a one-person tent, thinking he'd use it alone for the rest of the trail, but when we received it, I kept it for the two of us because we both fit in it. Sure, there wasn't much wiggle room and only one person could really move around at a time, but we could both lie down in it, shoulder to shoulder, and have plenty of room to sleep, along with room at our heads and our feet for our gear. We welcomed the cozy, warm space that night in the chilly Colorado air at 11,000'.

As I went to sleep, I was overwhelmed with gratitude for being with Matt once again.

At 6:15am the next morning we both popped up, ready to begin another day, partially because it felt like a whole new trail again, but mainly because we were cold. There had been a cold breeze blowing all night that didn't let up and we still had more climbing to start the morning.

Nine miles into the morning, just as we reached the crest of Lost Ranger Peak, we saw another hiker coming towards us, a woman dressed in a yellow wind jacket and a long purple hiking skirt.

"Fancy meeting you here at the top!" Matt said to her as he opened his arms in a welcoming gesture, as if we'd all planned this morning meeting at a remote mountain peak.

The hiker's name was Crow and she was hiking a large section from Rawlins, WY to Pie Town, NM. We guessed she was sort of a trail legend by the context of some of her stories, after we'd heard what trails she'd done and who she'd hiked with, including Billy Goat, an older hiker who's said to have hiked over 40,000 miles.

As we stood and talked with Crow, I felt like an imposter because I had spent the last week off the trail. I felt wrong introducing myself as a CDT hiker now that I wouldn't have a true thru-hike, but it felt like I'd make it all the more awkward and painful if I went about telling my sob story to everyone. I didn't want to take any credit for being a thru-hiker anymore, which was sad since I was so accustomed to that label. But, I was out there with my Matt, which was what I wanted in the first place.

The rest of the morning and early afternoon truly was all downhill. We descended from 11,800' at the peak to 8,000' at the Elk River. If I had been Crow, I would have felt very triumphant for having just climbed almost 4,000'.

At one point in the late afternoon, Matt was listening to music on his mp3 player to help pass the miles. We had been walking a long, gradual uphill combination of trail and dirt roads and the mosquitoes were out in full swarm. We were in our full armor once again. It was a typical moment on the trail where normal conversation had ended and we were left to our own thoughts as we passed over the inevitable miles. It was a fairly unsexy moment on the trail because it was a typical scene not seen in Hollywood versions of the trail life, but which actually made up most of the trail's miles.

As Matt listened to his music on random, a special song came on, the live version of "Crush" by Dave Matthews Band. It was one of our favorite songs because we loved to play it on long car drives, turning the volume up so high that we could sing along and not hear how bad we sounded. Matt started singing the song aloud as he hiked and I joined in. I knew every word, every note and even every voice inflection of Dave's in that song; I could nearly hear it without any music. We sang loudly without a care for who heard our poor pitch.

There we were, walking through a remote section of Northern Colorado, belting out the song in unison, with no inhibitions and only each other there to share that moment with, and I started crying. I was crying out of sheer joy for being with Matt, for being present in that moment, in a moment that otherwise wouldn't have been had I not gotten back on the trail. Those were the kinds of moments I knew I'd miss if I wasn't on the trail with him, the moments that made all the crappy ones worth it. It was one of the happiest moments on the entire trail. It was a moment that I was truly present in, when I wasn't regretting the past or looking towards the future, but rather completely lost in the moment at hand and fully living it, one precious second at a time. I turned around to hug him as I cried, so happy that I had returned to the trail.

The next day was fairly momentous. We crossed the border of Colorado and Wyoming and I breathed a sigh of relief. I had felt like my re-entry to the trail was a fresh start and now it really felt that way by starting a new state. Colorado was behind me, a state that ended up being my downfall, which was ironic because I was so excited to enter it and because I felt like I knew it fairly well from previous hiking trips. But, that was the way nature worked. It never acted the same from year to year, it was fairly unpredictable, and it was rarely forgiving of weaknesses in mind or body. I had lots of unfinished miles in Colorado but I put that thought behind me as we entered Wyoming.

Wyoming was the mystery state for Matt and me. We hadn't done much research on it before the trail started but we knew there were two important sections in the state: the Great Divide Basin and the Wind River Range. Both sections were important because of the lack of water in the former and the beauty and ruggedness of the latter. We were fairly ashamed to admit that we had no idea where either of those sections were located within the state, so we entered Wyoming with a slight fear of the unknown and a promise to each other to simply give our best each day over an ever-changing route.

As we walked through much of the latter half of the day, we saw several glimpses through the trees of barren, open land. It was as if we were on a platform above a valley and the trail was keeping us in the mountains for as long as possible. It also seemed like we would inevitably run out of mountains and have to descend into that open, dry, barren land. Part of me was actually excited to see it because it felt familiar to New Mexico and I'd been fairly successful at hiking New Mexico. Apparently I wasn't a mountain goat after all, but rather a desert lizard who loved hot, dry landscapes.

The next day, our fourth day out from Steamboat, the mountains ended.

Throughout much of the first half of the day, we walked the edge of the mountains, shifting between two types of terrain as we rode the roller coaster Divide, constantly gaining and losing elevation over exposed ridges and then dropping down into dense patches of forest. Much of the open, exposed ridge was a matter of hopping from one cairn to the next. There was little to no tread to guide the way and plenty of sagebrush to maneuver around. At the bottom of each dip in the roller coaster, we entered dense forests with good tread, only to encounter blow downs blocking the entire path, giving further evidence to the need for more love, attention, and money for the CDT. I couldn't guess when the last trail maintenance had been done in that section, yet I could see that the area had little appeal, at the edge of the desert in a very remote section. It was easy to see throughout the state of Colorado why so many trails were so well-maintained. Because of the amazing views from nearly any point along the way, along with the proximity to so many trail users, the trails were often well-kept. We were already seeing that the same wasn't exactly so in Wyoming, at least thus far.

In the early afternoon, we literally walked down the side of a hill and out of the mountains, soon meeting up with a dirt road. We turned around to see where we had come from and saw the mountains growing in elevation in the distance. We definitely weren't in Colorado anymore. I was happy to have such a stark contrast between the states and to have Colorado behind me and Wyoming ahead of me. I felt positive and excited about what was to come.

For the rest of the day we walked a mixture of rolling dirt roads, jeep roads, and cross-country sections of trail. It was hot, dry, and windy. Most of all, that barren feeling of New Mexico crept back in and it felt like it could once again be days until we saw another soul on the trail. I kept imagining Matt hiking this section alone and kept fighting the feelings of guilt and sadness with those of gratitude. My mind ran over the same scenarios over and over again, the guilt of leaving him alone versus the possibility of becoming more negative over the hard terrain had I not quit. I questioned whether that short week off the trail was actually better for both of us in the long-term since I gave myself the chance to be happy for the remainder of the trail. This fight between guilt and gratitude was an undercurrent in my mind during those first few days back and still surfaces every once in a while, even now, well after my last steps on the trail.

Though the dirt roads that we walked were barren, there were plenty of signs describing the different types of lands, including private property and BLM lands. We worried we wouldn't know the difference in the land we camped on so we were a little concerned about where we'd camp for the evening, as it didn't look like the dirt roads were ending any time soon.

As dusk approached, we crested a small hill and looked down at our next road intersection, about a quarter mile away, and saw hundreds of cows scattered about. There was a fairly sizable patch of trees about a quarter mile west of the intersection, so once we reached the cows and the intersection, we left the road and headed for the trees, hoping to find coverage in them. We were able to tuck into the edge of the woods and set up camp. From our tent we could barely see the road so we felt safe in case anyone happened to drive the road that night. Of course, we were surrounded by cow poop and every so often the breeze would carry the nauseating smell right into our tent.

As we looked at the data book that night, we saw that we had almost fifty miles remaining until Rawlins. Our first instinct was to hike thirty to thirty-five miles the next day, then have a short fifteen to twenty miles into town the next day. Unfortunately it was Thursday, so that meant we'd arrive into town late on a Saturday and have to wait for our resupply boxes until Monday. In looking at the maps, we also noticed that nearly all of those fifty miles were on roads.

In Matt's week alone, he'd started running on the dirt road sections as long as they were flat or downhill. He was able to make great time in doing so and it actually helped relieve his legs of the usual soreness of walking. It also gave him something new and exciting to work towards, as running took a bit more concentration and it was downright more fun than walking, at least for us.

As we both looked at the black lines on the maps into Rawlins, all indicating roads, we both knew what the other was thinking.

"Think we can make it to Rawlins tomorrow?" I asked.

"It's certainly worth trying," Matt answered.

From there the plan was hatched. We agreed to start early the next day, run the flat and downhill sections, and let the chips fall where they may. If that meant we got to town, great, and if not, maybe we'd get close enough to make the Saturday post office hours. The idea of a hotel with a hot shower and real food was plenty of motivation for me to feel good about the new plan to push to Rawlins as we went to sleep that night.

Both of us easily woke up before dawn without an alarm. The cows were already up, crowding the dirt road ahead of us, and we ate much of our food as we walked, taking care not to waste too much time in breaks. We made sure to drink several liters of water that morning, as the water sources looked sparse in the upcoming miles.

From the get-go, we ran the downhills and the flats, which was especially easy and even enjoyable because we had such light packs, each weighing around ten pounds. The dirt roads were well-graded, with very few rocks or ditches, so we were able to scoot along over the tops of the roads, lifting our legs just enough to shuffle along.

As the day progressed the roads started to roll a little more, offering bigger ups and downs, but we welcomed the uphills as a change from running the downhills. Though running felt liberating, it didn't feel completely free since we were still trying to run with some pack weight, so we created a comfortable rhythm of walking the ups and running the downs. It actually felt like our very own ultra marathon, the way we worked the miles and took turns pushing each other to keep running the easy parts as the day's mileage wore on.

Fifteen miles into the day, it was hot on the exposed dirt roads and any lingering coolness from the morning air was gone. We took a snack break under clear blue skies, only to start up again and see dark, ominous clouds heading our way from behind us. As we continued walking, it felt like an old horror movie in which the blob chased people down the street, moving deceivingly fast for its size. After forty-five minutes of trying to outrun the storm, it was right over top of us. Matt wanted to continue walking but I didn't feel safe being the tallest beings on such an exposed road. A little annoyed at each other, I at him for not taking lightning seriously and him at me for being overly cautious, we agreed to huddle in a ditch off the side of the road. We sat with our tarp tent over top of us while the storms passed overhead, waiting a full twenty-five minutes before we felt safe enough to start walking. As we walked, we watched the storm move on ahead of us, lightning still striking in the distance.

We were able to keep a steady rhythm after the storms, but the next challenge was the lack of water. While there were still several water sources, such as clear, innocent-looking pond water, every ensuing water source tasted like a combination of bitter and salty. It was shockingly disgusting for how normal it looked. I couldn't place exactly what was wrong with it, but each time I tried taking a sip, trying to ignore the taste, I gagged and couldn't drink it. That was in the early afternoon.

As the day progressed, every scarce water source we tried tasted like the last and my thirst started driving me crazy. I tried putting flavored drink mixes in it, doubling the normal amount, but that didn't help. I tried making mashed potatoes, but that was even worse. Each time that I couldn't finish the water, Matt was able to magically drink it without even making a face. I couldn't fathom drinking even a half cup of it, yet he was downing liters at a time. It baffled me.

Thirty-three miles into the day in the late afternoon, we left the road and walked a difficult cross-country section. It was partially difficult because there was no tread and all the signs were missing or had been knocked over, but it was mostly difficult because most hikers skipped that section. There was an alternate route to stay on the road and cut about fifteen miles. While I was a little envious of the shorter route, I knew Matt wanted to hike each official step and if I truly was out there as support, then it didn't matter what I wanted to do. At that point I was over the alternate routes and just along for the ride with Matt, so if he wanted to stick to the official route, so be it.

After the cross-country section, we neared a water source that I hoped was good. It was nearly 5:00pm and I'd only had about a half-liter of water since late morning. Our hopes plummeted when we could smell the lake before we saw it.

The lake was at a lower level than normal and the banks were covered in a black film that stunk of dead fish. It smelled and looked so bad that we could only get within ten feet of the water before we started gagging. My thirst continued.

We made up some ground by running pieces of the remaining miles and we started gaining hope that we'd reach town. At that point we needed to reach Rawlins just to get water, something we hadn't planned on happening until we found ourselves very thirsty from going nearly fifty miles on just a few liters.

With just a few miles to go to town, so close we could hear a train's horn blaring as it chugged past Rawlins, we walked past piles of garbage that we guessed locals hauled up there. I saw a Pepsi can on the ground that looked unopened. My heart jumped at the thought of liquid so I picked it up, only to find it barely open and almost full. I was so thirsty that I contemplated drinking it, but thought better of it, given the surroundings.

Our last mile took us through neighborhoods before we reached a main intersection on the east side of town. It was 9:00pm, just getting dark, and as we stood on the sidewalk, fairly in awe at what we'd just accomplished, Matt and I hugged each other in relief. As I was hugging him, there on the corner of US 287 and Cedar Street, I saw that we were standing on the edge of a wine store's parking lot. I didn't care if all they had was wine; I was going inside to get liquids while we figured out a hotel situation.

As soon as I walked inside, four sets of eyes turned to me, three store employees and a customer, as they all asked in near unison, "Are you ok?"

I must have looked downright haggard and half-crazed. We'd just walked/run nearly fifty miles on barely any water, my skin was the color of rust, a mix of my existing tan and a fresh burn from the long day of sun exposure, my calves were covered in dust, and I stunk of thru-hiker funk.

"I just need something to drink," I said, really no pun intended because I was too tired to be witty. "Do you have any water or Gatorade?" I asked, clarifying what kind of drink I wanted.

They directed me to the case with Gatorade, Coke and juices, and I bought two Gatorades, one for Matt, a Coke, and a lemonade-blueberry wine slushy to go. I wanted to cover every type of beverage.

The store employees were intrigued to hear about our hike and one was quick to offer Matt and me a ride to a hotel down the street. Within the next half hour, I was showering in scolding-hot water with my wine slushy in one hand and a bar of soap in the other.

After showering we dined on Subway and grocery store vegan food like canned chili, chips, and almond ice cream, as we watched TV and lay on hotel beds. Every ten minutes or so, one of us would look at the other and say, "I can't believe we made it!"

Before going to bed, I peeked at the CDT Facebook page and read a post from another hiker, saying the water heading into Rawlins was alkaline, undrinkable, and would certainly cause diarrhea if consumed. Whoops! That explained why it tasted so gross and given that Matt drank at least three liters of it, I was concerned for his well-being, but he never reported even so much as a grumble in the gut from drinking the bad water.

2
Optimist

The push to Rawlins was awesome. It was so good to have Julie back and to be playing our roles in the trail life once again. It was fun too as her attitude had changed dramatically. She was out there for the experience and she was no longer focused on miles. We of course paid attention to what was ahead and we planned our days in order to make towns and to not run out of food, but otherwise, we woke with the sun, hiked all day, and were enjoying the trail life.

We were exhausted upon arriving in Rawlins late on Friday night. Julie was bonking after such a challenging effort with minimal water and food. She was able to hold it together long enough to get us refreshments and a ride to a hotel.

While Julie made it to town with her body on empty, I had been able to stomach the weird tasting water and I was feeling relatively good. My feet and legs were tired from the effort, but once we checked into our hotel at 9:45pm, I was quickly in food mode. I headed over to Subway, which was next to our hotel. I got our subs minutes before they closed and then headed to the supermarket for vegan treats for the evening. It was a late night but it was so good to be back with my best friend, enjoying ourselves after a hard day's work.

The next day we made our way to the post office to pick up our resupply. Rawlins was one of the many stops along the trail that we'd designated as a "Feed a Vegan" stop on our website. Prior to setting out from New Mexico, we knew that finding food to fit our diet would likely be difficult in many of the trail towns. So we posted a list of a dozen trail towns on our website with expected arrival dates. Our friends and family enjoyed being part of the journey in this way and we received numerous letters, cards, and vegan goodies.

In Rawlins, not only did we receive some uplifting cards and snacks, but we also got a memorable card from our cousin's son. Andrew had made a homemade card with a colorful bear he had drawn with the caption, "Please don't be eaten by a bear!" At this point in Wyoming, it didn't seem likely we'd be seeing bears anytime soon, but we knew we would be entering grizzly country in the not-too-distant future so we both smiled as we read the advice from our young cousin.

While in town we met five other hikers that had just gotten into town. They were doing the traditional hiker activity of gorging on food first, and then figuring out town plans second when we met them. We joined them for lunch and though we were tempted to stay with them for the night, we were also eager to keep moving.

We had covered big miles since Julie had gotten back on the trail and we were having fun doing it. We hit thirty or more miles per day almost every day, capping it all off with our biggest day ever on our day into Rawlins. I was keeping track of the total miles remaining including the Colorado fire miles we'd missed, and we were finally ahead. We needed to average twenty-six miles per day in order to complete all the fire miles we'd missed, so long as the trail reopened in time. This was a manageable distance for us and while Julie wasn't paying attention to the total numbers, I still kept them in mind as we headed out of Rawlins.

The terrain had changed markedly over the past couple days. We were no longer in huge mountains and the trees were now gone. The elevation wasn't very different, as we were still in the 6,000' to 7,000' range, but the landscape was entirely different. The expansiveness of the landscape brought with it strong winds and few places to hide. Afternoon storms were still a concern and though we weren't on mountaintops anymore, we were often still the tallest things out there. Consequently, lightning continued to instill fear in us.

We road-walked out of town on the highway for a couple miles and then headed off-road. For the remainder of the day we were sometimes on trail, sometimes on dirt roads, and sometimes hiking cross-country, dodging sagebrush.

As the day went on we noticed fresh footprints on the path and eventually on a hill Julie spotted another hiker. Seemingly noticing our presence, the hiker turned around while atop the hill, spotted us, and then sat down to wait for us to catch him.

Upon meeting Softwalker, we were surprised to have not heard of him. After learning that he wasn't much into technology and therefore not very active on the CDT Facebook page, we understood why we'd never heard of him. He also tended to travel solo up the trail, only occasionally sticking with groups as he made his way north. However, we did find out that we had seen signs of him before Rawlins, only we didn't know it was him we were following.

Softwalker had his name because he was a minimalist shoe wearer, and at times, he wore no shoes at all. We had been surprised a couple days back when we'd found ourselves suddenly following bare feet footprints in the sandy ground. They weren't always there but would occasionally pop up and then disappear. Softwalker explained that sometimes it felt better to walk with the sand between his toes rather than being confined in shoes, even if his shoes were thin soled, no heel, minimalist shoes.

We quickly discovered that we had much in common and the talking that started that evening would carry on for the next four days as we made our way to South Pass City, 118 miles north of Rawlins.

That first evening out of town, as the three of us were walking cross-country amidst the desert bushes and sage brush, Julie leading the way, we all stopped suddenly in our tracks upon hearing the eerily familiar sound of a rattlesnake. Julie quickly spotted the large, dusty green colored rattler coiled up in strike position a few feet off our intended path. We backed up a bit and the snake stopped rattling. We got out our cameras whereupon Softwalker noticed something peculiar about the snake. Its mouth seemed stuck in an open position and upon closer inspection the snake's mouth was stuffed with a fresh mouse. The snake couldn't bite us if it wanted to because we caught him in the middle of dinner. Furthermore, as we got even closer to take pictures, we realized that the snake was having a difficult time eating the mouse because the mouse's tail was stuck to a cactus, and therefore the snake couldn't swallow it.

We'd never seen anything like it and we continued getting

dangerously close to the snake, feeling immune from its bite due to its full mouth. The snake seemed to know the precarious situation it was in as it moved with purpose to get the mouse down. Finally the tail ripped free and down the mouse went into the snake. At that time we all knew it was time to move on.

While Softwalker wasn't big into technology, he did know a good amount about the trail. It was almost comical how little Julie and I actually knew about the land we were in compared to most hikers.

"What exactly is the Basin and where is it?" I asked as we walked along that second morning.

"We're in it right now!" Softwalker laughingly responded.

We learned that the Great Divide Basin was a unique stretch of land where the Continental Divide actually splits. Whereas normally, the Continental Divide is a line of mountains running north to south down the continent, delineating whether water flows east to the Atlantic or west to the Pacific, the Great Divide Basin is a place where there are actually two sections of the Continental Divide. The Basin is the circular bit of land in between this stretch of dual divides and the area in between is dry and desolate since the water flows from either side of the dual divide in opposite directions.

Along with being educated about birds, plants, and mountains, we also shared our stories. We had all done a good deal of adventuring and each story we shared seemingly fed right into the next. Softwalker was an ideal hiking companion as we crossed the vast Great Divide Basin, his character evident in all his actions.

While the weather in the Basin was hot and exposed, it was also very bearable. After being stormed on our first evening out from Rawlins, the stormy winds seemed to blow in some relatively cooler air. The temperatures were reasonable, being in the mid-eighties, and though we were constantly exposed to the sun, the three of us had fun together making our way across this unique section without much strain or discomfort. With the terrain being much flatter with no major climbs to speak of, we were able to steadily average thirty-plus mile days together.

Water was scarcer in the Basin but it wasn't nearly as bad as some of the stretches of New Mexico that we'd encountered. Generally, in the Basin we had water every ten to fifteen miles and most were reasonably good sources. We always bleached our water but some sources needed it more noticeably than others. One water source in particular had an oily film on top of it. We swished the top layer of the pool a little, dipped our bottles, and were able to get water. It tasted odd but we couldn't be too picky at that point. With our bleach method, we had continued to avoid stomach sickness and thankfully, the trend continued as we crossed the dry Basin.

On the middle of day three we came across our biggest water source, a man-made reservoir built by an oil company and stocked with fish for local anglers. It was a popular area and as we walked along the dusty road leading to the water we saw nearly a dozen men fishing and grilling out food. They were somewhat surprised to see us walk down to the lake and dip our water bottles in to drink. They eventually asked us what we were doing, as we were likely a strange sight for them, and after learning our story, they were quick to share food and drinks with us.

The wildlife in this section shifted from mountain mammals such as bears and deer, to more prairie animals with antelope dotting the horizon. We also saw wild horses. We came across a pack of ten on our third afternoon with Softwalker on a sunny day in the Basin. The horses playfully ran around and seemed to be having a good time. There was however an obvious social rank within the group as there were two ponies that would continually attempt to move to the front of the line of horses, only to be attacked and forced to the back of the pack. At one point there was even a standoff between the horses with two of them rising up on their hind legs and hitting each other with their front hooves.

Later that day, we came across a large flock of sheep. We were on the lookout for sheep dogs, and we were quickly relieved to see the dogs rounding up the sheep and leaving us alone. Shortly after distancing ourselves from the flock, we came across a young man on horseback. He was heading out to check on the flock. He told us all about the lonely, simple life of being a shepherd. He was a young guy, maybe twenty years old, and he was ready to get back to society. He told us he was working for an older guy and that we would come across him soon, as they were camped alongside the trail. He also told us they'd been helping hikers and sharing water.

We walked with some pep in our step at the prospect of fresh water that we wouldn't need to purify. We found the shepherds' trailers a mile later and sat down with the old timer. He seemed happy as could be to have company and to share stories of life in the wilderness. He told us about his elk hunting trips and his time spent in the mountains with his sheep. He was also quick to offer water. We guzzled some there on the spot and we took some for the next stretch as well. Julie and Softwalker even scored a couple cans of Mountain Dew.

We hiked until the sun dipped below the horizon that day, stopping with maybe ten minutes left of real daylight. Softwalker tended to cowboy camp so he could sleep anywhere, and with all the flat, dry ground, we had our choice of camp spots.

On our last night in the Basin, we all realized we had thirty-three miles to our next resupply in South Pass City. We decided that night that we'd push for town together the next day. The store was said to be open until 6:00pm each day and with the roads and flat terrain, it seemed doable, especially if we ran the downhills as Julie and I had done heading into Rawlins.

Softwalker seemed genuinely excited about the idea and the next morning he was the first to start running as soon as the terrain was suitable. During the sections that we weren't running, we were singing. We played the "lunch song" game which entailed thinking of as many songs as possible that had the word "love' in it, only we would substitute the word "lunch" in its place. We got on a Led Zeppelin kick with a favorite being "Whole Lotta Lunch."

The Zeppelin theme was still in mind as we began a long downhill run toward a herd of cattle. As Julie and I had seen in the past, cows got freaked out when we ran, and Softwalker and I had a blast as we barreled down the hill, riling up the herd.

I began singing the guitar intro to Zeppelin's "Immigrant Song", "da dun da da dun-na, da dun dad a dun-na." Softwalker jumped right in with the vocals: "ahhhhaa ahhhh ahh!" "We come from the land of the ice and snow…"

We were smiling and singing and enjoying the hell out of the trail as we ran those cows crazy.

Later in the afternoon as it was getting closer to store closing time, I fell behind Julie and Softwalker. I had to dig a cat hole and after falling behind by a couple minutes, I had to pull out the GPS. While I could still see them ahead of me on the open landscape, we had entered a nine mile section of cross-country hiking. I was tracking waypoints on the GPS, trying to stay on route, but I noticed that we were moving in different directions.

This was one of those annoying parts of the trail where the official route was not a trail at all, but instead, just a walk through bushes and unpleasant terrain, while a dirt road perfectly suitable for walking, and rarely used by any vehicles, paralleled the trail a half-mile to the west. However, I was sticking to the route, and nine miles later I caught back up to Julie where the trail crossed the road that she and Softwalker had walked.

We were now only a few miles from South Pass City with seemingly plenty of time to make the 6:00pm store closing. As we cruised on in and saw Softwalker sitting cross legged on the steps of the store, he said to us with a grin, "You are really lucky."

3
Stopwatch

As we approached the general store in South Pass City, savoring the fact that we'd hiked thirty-three miles and still had almost an hour to spare before the store closed, Softwalker shared shocking news.

"The store actually closes at five, not six," he said.

He was sitting cross-legged on the store's front porch, sifting through his resupply boxes. I was relieved to see our resupply boxes sitting right behind him, along with two Mountain Dews. Softwalker had gone ahead of us and arrived at the store with just five minutes to spare, picking up not only our boxes, but also some drinks for us in case the store closed before our arrival. As we stood there, the woman running the general store stepped out onto the porch and said to us, "Yeah, the tour goes until six but the store closes an hour earlier. I kept the store open in case you wanted a cold drink."

South Pass City wasn't so much a city, but rather an historical site with old, refurbished buildings that people could tour and walk around. Along with holding packages for hikers, the general store sold souvenirs, pop, and ice cream bars. Most exciting to me, there were bathrooms with flushing toilets. It made my day to sit on a porcelain bowl, flushing my waste away into oblivion and washing my hands afterwards with soap and warm water. We contemplated camping near the store just so we could have access to the flushing toilets the next morning.

Just before the store closed, I bought a Pepsi and a Snickers Ice Cream Bar. Ever since getting off the trail for a week in Steamboat

Springs, I had gone back to being a vegetarian. I wanted more opportunities to load up on calories in town and while I didn't plan on consuming large cheese pizzas or half-gallons of ice cream at a time, as I'd done on past thru-hikes, I gave myself the freedom to include dairy once again in my diet. Matt was still a staunch vegan and I was just fine with that, just as I was fine with his strictly official route.

For the next two hours we rested our legs on the porch, lacking any motivation to move. When we all agreed it was time to start walking, we felt refreshed and excited that we'd soon be in the Winds. Just two miles later we spotted the perfect campsite off the side of the trail, tucked inside a large patch of pine trees. All of us eagerly anticipated the next few days of hiking and fell asleep quickly.

We were finally knocking on the door of the Winds, an area we had heard so much about, including the beautiful, challenging terrain.

It took nearly all of the next day to feel like we were in the Winds. All of us had the same feeling that we were certainly out of the Basin, but not quite in the Winds. The terrain was a mix of trail, cow paths, and route-finding and we climbed gradually for most of the day, eventually heading into thick woods, surrounded by trees and flowing water. Every so often we got a stunning view of a lake and there was a tangible buzz of excitement among all of us for such a stark contrast in scenery as compared to the dusty Basin bowl.

At the end of the day, we came upon a rushing creek that offered no chance of fording without wet feet. Softwalker walked right through it without breaking stride but we didn't want to start the next morning with wet feet. He went ahead to pick a campsite while we took the time to take off our shoes for the crossing.

Within minutes after the crossing, there was a split in the trail. Someone had handwritten a sign that said, "CDT," with an arrow pointing to the right. The official trail, confirmed by our data book, actually turned left and the alternate, the Cirque de Towers route that Softwalker and nearly every other thru-hiker would hike, turned right. Suddenly we were in trouble. We needed to go left but we were sure Softwalker went right.

Matt dropped his pack and started running up the trail towards Softwalker, returning within minutes. Luckily Softwalker was just up the trail and he and Matt decided we'd all camp there together and say goodbyes the next morning.

As darkness fell, we set up camp on soft, pine-needle covered ground. There was a bittersweet feeling in the air as we quietly ate dinner, knowing it was our last night with Softwalker. Yet, it was time to part ways. All of us had been the companions we needed to get through the desolate miles in the Basin, but now that we were in the Winds, we were all ready to hike our own hike and get back into our own mileage rhythm. As I did with so many of the hikers we met along the way, I doubted we'd ever see him again on the trail and wondered if our paths would ever cross off-trail.

Our day started at dawn and Softwalker was still nestled in his sleeping bag when we exchanged goodbye hugs. We wished each other luck in getting through the rest of the trail and walked away, leaving him sitting alone on the ground. Even though I knew it was only temporary hiking with him, it still made me sad to say goodbye.

We felt good from the start, my pack feeling almost too light for a 172 mile carry to the next town. About two miles into the morning, Matt turned on the GPS and stopped mid-stride.

"We're not on-trail," he said dejectedly.

We pulled out the maps and saw that we'd missed a right turn over a mile back and were on a completely different trail, heading in a parallel direction with the CDT. We contemplated walking straight towards the next waypoint but could see that it involved crossing a meadow. At that point the normal trail was wet, squishy and muddy, so we could only assume that the meadow was more like a bog. We had no choice but to backtrack. Adding to our frustration, the mosquitoes were out in heavy swarms and the comfortably cool morning temperatures were increasing quickly.

We turned around, downtrodden but not broken, and went back to the missed turn. We walked around the area, looking for a turn, for at least three minutes. There was nothing there, no trail, no cairn, no indication of a turn. After a few minutes of blindly following the GPS and bushwhacking, we popped out onto an open field and saw a cairn, which led us to another cairn across the field. Still no trail, but at least there were cairns.

Ten minutes later, the cairns disappeared. At that point it was 9:00am and we'd covered less than three miles. We had learned that when we were going slow or getting lost a lot, we needed to sit down and eat because it probably meant we were tired or hungry. Just off the side of the trail, we sat under the shade of a tree and ate granola and energy bars as we tried to regroup before going any farther.

From that point on for the next ten miles, it was mostly cross-country through thick brush and over blow downs. We knew the alternate was popular but didn't realize that nearly no one took the official route and therefore no one maintained the official route or even seemed to have built it. We were shocked at such a difficult section. The section also kept us low in elevation and tucked into the trees, offering little to no views, while the alternate route, the Cirque de Towers, was known for 360 degree views. So far, the Winds were a letdown.

The trail eventually re-connected with the alternate and we climbed for four miles, all over well-established tread. At the top of the climb, we entered another world and the legitimacy of the beauty of the Winds was finally confirmed. We looked down a long meadow dotted with pristinely blue lakes, lush green grass, and craggy mountains towering on each side. Even the mosquitoes couldn't bring us down as we drank in the beauty around us. It was almost impossible to believe that just days prior, we were in a shadeless bowl of dusty, desolate jeep roads, with hardly any water and no trees.

For the rest of the day we were in awe at our surroundings and we gladly traded the harder hiking for such beauty. We were so excited about our new surroundings that we couldn't wait to contact family again just to tell them how beautiful the Winds were. I was also reminded of how grateful I was to be sharing experiences in such beautiful country with Matt.

Around dusk we called it a day and licked our wounds from the damage that had ensued that day. We'd barely hiked over twenty-four miles but it felt like the effort of a thirty-four mile day and the upcoming terrain didn't look much easier. Yep, we were in the Winds.

Just like so many other days prior, our energy was renewed the next morning. We were ready to keep tackling the Winds in order to see what else they had to offer. Part of what drove our excitement that day was that we'd had good trail ever since we reunited with the alternate route the prior afternoon. It seemed like we were in a fairly well-used section, so much that even signs of wildlife, like tracks and scat, were no longer present.

The morning started with a few hundred feet of climbing to once again crack the 10,000' mark and still we were surrounded by water and therefore mosquitoes. The water was both a blessing and a curse, the former because we carried very little water weight and the latter because the mosquitoes were horrendous and relentless in their pursuit to find any chink in our armor.

The terrain we walked that day was challenging with lots of changes in elevation. Luckily we had sunny, clear skies throughout the entire section, without a hint of bad weather. By around 5:00pm, we'd hiked twenty-four miles and decided to put in a late-afternoon push. Lester Pass was within six miles so we made it our goal to reach the pass. We put on our power music to get our legs moving fast and strong, and pushed it to the pass. Dusk was settling in as we neared the base of the pass. Though I started to feel weak with hunger, I tapped into all my available reserves and we pushed up the final climb to the pass as dusk turned over to darkness. We reached the top just in time to see the silhouette of the mountains on the other side of the pass, their cragginess the most noticeable attribute.

The moon was nearly full as we set up our tent, tucked out of the cold wind as much as possible, given we were at 11,120' among short, scraggly bushes.

Both of us were tired, cold, and achy as we started moving the next morning. I was also so dirty that I had trouble pulling up my shorts over my salty, sticky butt. I laughed out loud as I thought about renaming myself "Sticky Buns." It was fitting, given my often poor hygiene on trails, and downright fun. Matt was in complete agreement that I should be named Stopwatch Sticky Buns Urbanski.

Our late evening climb was rewarded with a beautiful sunrise to start the day and we saw craggy, gray mountains in the distance as we headed downhill from the pass. We pinched ourselves at that moment, along with many more moments in the Winds, amazed at the vast differences in scenery thus far in Wyoming, grateful for such a pleasant section that we doubted many other people had ever seen or even known about.

As much as we took in the beauty around us, the terrain was hard and our food supply was dwindling fast. The Winds were made up of lots of smaller increments of elevation changes sandwiched between larger climbs up and over the passes. It made for a constant, steady effort with very few easy, recovery miles. We had also under-packed on food and would be in fairly serious trouble if the terrain kept up at such intensity until the next resupply. Our resupply boxes had been different because I had re-packed them while in Steamboat Springs, when I had decided to get back on the trail. I didn't realize it until we were in the thick of the Winds that I had forgotten several essential snacks. We hadn't noticed it while we were sitting on the porch at South Pass City, but we certainly noticed it now that we were so hungry.

The elevation was above 10,000' for much of the day until Green River Pass. After that pass it was all downhill, literally. We dropped elevation quickly as we made our way down a series of switchbacks, following a long canyon with a fast-moving creek. We didn't know it at the time, but we were already heading out of the Winds with that huge drop in elevation.

Eventually the trail leveled out and we walked a long, flat, and fast corridor of trail that followed alongside a glacial-fed river. The terrain was so easy and soft underfoot that we found ourselves longing to run again. Despite our walking pace, we still put up some fast miles.

We reached the Green River Lakes Campground thirty miles into the day but there was still plenty of daylight and we both felt like we had gas left in our tanks. As we stood near the campground, we looked back and saw that the Winds were behind us and already a memory. For how much buildup there was to the section, it seemed so short and went so fast. Even though it was harder, we wished it was longer, as we were once again faced with cow pastures ahead of us. We walked two more miles to distance ourselves from the campground and nearby cows and camped off the side of the trail, in a patch of dense trees that barely afforded a space for our tent. We were so tired and elated with our progress that we didn't care what the campsite looked like or how lumpy the grass was underneath; we set up the tent and fell asleep immediately, the full moon overhead.

Though we were out of the Winds, we still had work to do the next day, which started with a 1,400' climb up to Gunsight Pass. We took a break at the top, knowing that it was too early in the day to feel that tired after just one climb. Our arms, legs, and lungs were already burning with the effort. I estimated that we were short by at least 1,000 calories per day and we could both feel the effects in our hiking. Yet, we were within fifty miles of our next resupply. We knew we'd make it but it would hurt a little more than we had intended.

We headed down to a creek over soft, pine-needle covered trail in a dense forest and I was still sleepy, not paying attention to my surroundings, when a large ball of fur rounded the bend in front of me and nearly ran into me.

"Uhhhaaahhh!"

I screamed, which came out more like a guttural bellow, and it echoed in the woods as the animal yelped loudly at the same time. The animal, which I assumed to a be fairly large coyote, veered to the right at the last second, just before reaching me, and all I saw was a brown, bushy tail disappear into the bushes. Matt was stunned behind me for a brief second before getting out his bear spray. My near collision with a coyote left me speechless and weak-kneed for several moments.

Later in the day, after several miles of cross-country navigation through high grass and rolling hills, with plenty of cairns to guide the way, the trail unexpectedly disappeared. Our waypoints pointed us into dense forest, which then lead to a drop-off on the side of a hill, and we were suddenly very confused. There were no markers, no cairns, and definitely no tread; just waypoints to follow in thick woods without a logical path to take.

As we stood there checking our GPS, an older hiker walked up to us, coming from the other direction. He was snippy and in a sour mood, as he'd just come from the section we were about to walk through. When we asked him how long the tough navigation lasted, he estimated around twenty miles. Gulp. We took his advice on the upcoming route and starting covering ground as best we could.

About a mile later, as we tried to make sense of our maps, three hikers caught us from behind.

"I hope you're not following us, because we have no idea where we're going," I said to them just as they reached us.

Their names were Aquaman, Adam, and Huck, and Aquaman seemed excited to catch us. We'd unknowingly passed him somewhere in Colorado. It was immediately apparent as we started hiking that they were hiking fast, and even though they were making quick decisions about the route, they were seemingly on route.

"Time to put on the big-girl boots," I thought to myself as I felt the shock of a faster pace through non-existent terrain.

For the rest of the day, it was a matter of trying to stay with them as they maneuvered through that trail-less section. It was quite possibly the most difficult section to navigate because the terrain didn't lend itself to a logical path and because the section was so long. At one point our waypoints led us alongside a creek, then they took us up on the Divide, only to go back downhill towards the creek.

I was glad for the company. Matt and I were undoubtedly the weakest link in the route-finding, while Adam seemed to have an internal compass, so we made sure to stick to them like glue. Huck parted ways when he stopped for water, but I wasn't going to let such good navigators go.

I made a resolute decision to stick with them no matter how thirsty or tired I was and Matt seemed to have done the same. They didn't stop for water or food and I wondered how they didn't burn out at that kind of a pace without breaks for the essentials, but I knew our time with them would be short-term, so I just buckled up and hung on for the ride.

While it was a fast pace, we still made a fun time out of it. I listened to Matt and Aquaman carry on a conversation while Adam did most of the navigating ahead, stopping every so often to check with us and agree on a route. We made our way over the Divide, trying to make sense of multiple snowmobile paths, at one point trying to walk through a creek to stay on route. Aquaman was sure that walking through the creek was the best way, his name implying a connection to water, until he stepped in a deep pocket and fell on his butt, soaking the bottom of his pack. We stayed out of the creeks after that.

We walked until dark because it took that long to finally get on route again. Before bed Aquaman and Adam looked at the upcoming maps and decided to take an alternate route the next morning. It was comforting to know that we'd return to our slower pace the next day, though I was grateful they'd pulled us through the worst of the trail-less section.

Both of us felt hungry and abnormally fatigued as we went to sleep.

Twenty-two miles stood between us and the Brooks Lake Lodge the next morning, and it was a fairly daunting twenty-two miles because we didn't know how much of it was still part of the treadless, sign-less section. We awoke early, only to see that Aquaman and Adam were already ready, and we packed up quickly in the cool morning. Much of the first ten miles were slow-going, but the amount of signs increased as we walked and we found that the worst of the route-finding was over. Soon we popped out onto dirt roads and were able to make up time.

We surprised ourselves by making it to the lodge by 3:00pm, good timing considering the morning miles had been through water-logged meadows and brush-heavy terrain. Despite our hunger for town food, there was nothing to purchase at the lodge, a five-star resort that was well above our price range and frankly, out of our league. We felt out of place at the lodge, knowing our last shower had been on day fifty in Rawlins, and today was day sixty. We stunk and we knew we stunk, so we didn't linger inside after picking up our box of food.

We sat on one of the benches outside while we packed up our new food, nibbling on some of it because we were so hungry. Both of us wanted to gorge ourselves on the new food, particularly the dark chocolate, but we couldn't pig out because we needed all our food to get to Yellowstone. Just as we were packing up to leave, an employee walked by and quietly told us to wait in case there was extra food in the kitchen. Five minutes later she came back and slipped us a white paper bag full of leftover food, including cookies, trail mix, and fresh bread. I was overjoyed. Matt showed an act of godly willpower by refraining from eating any of it because he assumed none of it was vegan. I wasn't messing around with being hungry anymore but since I felt bad stuffing my face with cookies and bread later that day, I gave him some of my vegan food.

That evening we hung our food and slept with our can of bear spray nearby because we were finally in confirmed grizzly country, a whole new twist to the hike. Our next stop was Old Faithful Village in Yellowstone, the edge of Wyoming and Montana, and we were excited to reach it.

4
Optimist

There was new energy and excitement as we left Brooks Lake Lodge. Trail magic was flowing, we were in a beautiful setting, we had new shoes in our resupply box, and we were already almost out of Wyoming, which had been a surprisingly pleasant state.

We also knew we were in bear country, which had us a bit more aware than normal. While we'd hiked in black bear country on every trail we'd ever hiked, this was our first time in grizzly bear territory. After hearing stories from hikers and locals, black bears suddenly seemed more like pesky critters compared to the grizz, and these big bears began to consume much of our talking time on the trail.

After Julie had purchased bear spray for me while in Steamboat Springs, I subsequently threw it in my pack where it was not at all accessible. However, upon leaving the Lodge and heading toward Yellowstone National Park, our next resupply point, the sixty dollar bear spray with its fancy little holster was latched onto my hip belt and ready for use. I hadn't actually practiced with it because I didn't want to deplete it (it was only good for about nine seconds worth of spraying) but mentally, carrying the spray was now part of my hiking routine.

Carrying the spray did come at a cost as it weighed close to twelve ounces and with a total pack weight of only around ten pounds minus food and water, nearly an extra pound of bear protection felt like a fairly significant addition. However, the spray was somehow empowering and I felt a bit more confident in the face of any potential aggressors, even frisky cattle.

Along with carrying the spray, we were also now much more vigilant in hanging our food at night. For the majority of the trail we simply slept with our food in our tent. To anyone other than PCT and CDT thru-hikers, this may sound downright stupid, but it is a way of life on these trails and a large percentage of long distance hikers do the same without major consequence. We generally kept our food in odor proof sacks that fit inside of a larger plastic bag placed inside of our backpacks, under our feet, and inside our tent, but with big grizzly bears, we weren't willing to take the same risks.

The challenge was that good bear bagging trees to hang our food were often difficult to come by. In order to be effective, the tree branch typically needed to be at least ten feet high and at least four feet out from the trunk, and even when we were once again back in forested land after the Basin, the trees tended to be the type that grew straight up like a pole with little wimpy branches sticking off their tall trunks, leaving nothing to hang food on. It was easy to say that we needed to hang our food, but in practice it was often much more challenging. As we headed north from Brooks Lake Lodge, good bear bagging trees often dictated where we would set up camp each evening.

While the calendar now showed late July, the temperatures were definitely indicative of how far north we were actually getting on our hike. The nights were often cold and our thirty degree quilts with extra down fill were barely scraping by for comfortable warmth on many of the nights. If not for the one-person tent Julie and I shared, and the subsequent snuggle factor, I think it would have been downright too cold on many of those nights.

On our first full morning out from the Lodge we were reminded of just how much colder it was in northern Wyoming as we neared the Buffalo River crossing. We had had plenty of river crossings up to that point and usually they were welcomed opportunities to drink up, clean up, and cool off. They weren't always as welcomed early in the morning, as was the case on this particular day, and as we carried our shoes and socks in hand, not wanting to have wet feet all day, the cold rushing water forced panic-filled thoughts into both our heads simultaneously.

I was midway across the gushing river that was knee to mid-thigh depth when the numbing pain and sensation really kicked in. At first it was funny just how cold the water was and we hooted and hollered in our solitary wilderness morning. But a little over half way across I had a sudden and real thought, "What if I can't actually make it across?"

I had this thought because the pain was getting to be very real and the water really, really cold. I thought, "If I don't make it, do I simply fall down and allow the cold, strong current to drag me down?"

My focus sharpened and I pushed faster, moving my feet less cautiously along the slippery rock bottom of the river, my toes slipping and jamming into big river bottom rocks, as I pushed for the river bank another twenty yards away.

By the time I got to shore and lay down on dry land I winced and whined in agonizing pain as my feet began to thaw out. Julie was still in the water and driving with the same focused determination I'd just experienced. When we got to hiking again, pushing the uphill from the river bank in an effort to warm ourselves, we both talked about how the cold water had made us think about not being able to move and how horrible it must be to actually get hypothermia in water, as it seemingly made our minds want to stop and shut down.

The day moved along slowly and though we were making miles, we both felt sluggish. Around lunchtime we came to a small creek and found a spot a few feet off the trail to take a rest and to rinse our clothes. Our personal hygiene standards had been slipping of late and the reality of not having had a shower since Rawlins was becoming more evident. The trail was now wide and dusty, and as a result, our legs were an unnatural shade of tan, desperately crying out for a bath.

After eating some food I was first to make the move for the creek to wash my clothes and body. I had our Dr. Bronner's liquid soap and a gallon Ziploc bag to wash and rinse in. I was stripped down to a pair of shorty running shorts and bare feet as I went about cleaning everything else. I was down to rinsing my last socks when the first mule train passed through.

It must have included fifteen mules heavily weighed down, following a cowboy on a horse directing the rope connecting all the mules. He didn't seem too amused to see me down at the creek and the mules each looked at me skittishly as they passed close by me and headed up the trail.

Julie then went down and did her laundry and was subsequently passed by two mule trains during her work.

As we waited for our laundry to dry in the afternoon breeze and continued to snack on dehydrated trail food, a couple of hikers came our way. They were not thru-hikers as only the woman carried a pack, but they carried an air of experience and comfort in the backcountry that immediately prompted questions. The man also had a good mustache and facial hair, was dressed like a cowboy, and even had a pistol strapped to his belt.

Seth and Beth explained that they worked for an outfitter in the area and that they had the afternoon off, so they were out getting in some hiking. They worked on trips that lead hunters, fishermen, horsemen, and other adventurers through the mountains south of Yellowstone throughout the fall and summer. They would set up base camps for their clients, cook them food, and provide a safe and entertaining experience for them. Wearing the cowboy outfit and carrying the gun was all part of the experience.

We also learned a good deal about the outdoorsman life from them, similar to how we learned about raising cattle from Mark and Cody down in New Mexico and about sheep-herding in the mountains from Ron. Seth carried his gun, part for show, but primarily in the event that he had to put down a horse. While it seemed that it may have been for protection from bears, he said that if a horse went lame out in the woods, their only option was to put it down. He said there were Forest Service rules for them on how to do this too. They had to lead the horse at least a quarter mile off-trail before killing the horse and leaving it.

He also told us about the mule trains and how they carried supplies in and out for the outfitter companies. He said we probably got the stink eye from the cowboys leading the mules because we didn't get far enough off the trail. The reason this was important was because if one of the mules got spooked by us, which apparently was a very real and likely possibility, the mule would throw off the entire train since they're all connected and they all tended to move as one. So if we hikers didn't get far enough off the trail and a mule got riled up, a huge mess for the cowboy was likely to ensue, and hence, the stink eye.

We had learned similar things from the cattle and sheep herders and we were amazed with how little we knew of the lives of the other trail users. It was similar with hunters. We were usually more concerned about being shot at or being attacked by their dogs than about getting to know them or how we could all get along better.

We talked for over an hour before we felt the pull of the trail to get moving again. We crossed a beautiful meadow where we could see their base camp set up before we began our climb up and out of the valley. I knew from our datasheet that there were some small mountain lakes up around 10,000' and I pushed for those for the evening, thinking it'd be better to be up high.

The push took us right up until dark. We were slightly disappointed that our high mountain lakes were no more than drying cow ponds and we were a bit concerned that bears may actually be just as interested in the cooler temperatures at higher altitudes as we were. There were also very few trees. It was shortly after dark when we found a tree worth taking a chance on. It wasn't very tall, the branch didn't stick out as far as we needed, and it was one of only a few trees in the entire open mountain-top landscape. It was our best option though so we hung the food, we set up camp out of the wind and out of sight of our food bag, and we went to sleep.

It was a windy night and we both slept lightly thinking about our food bag hanging from a not-so-high tree, blowing in the wind all night. We didn't need to push the next day due to Yellowstone camping permit issues but we both awoke early the next day with an urge to check on our food.

Thankfully it was all there, just as we'd left it. We both realized how reassuring it was to have our food under our feet every night and not hanging like a big banner in the wind each night from a tree. But we'd seen the large paw prints of the grizzly bear and we'd seen their scat to know that we didn't want to take any chances with them.

This day of hiking was dictated by the National Park Service. Each national park we hiked through, whether it was on the AT, PCT, or CDT, had its own unique set of rules that we were required to follow. This was often a big change from the vast freedom of movement we experienced throughout the remainder of our trails. In the case of Yellowstone National Park, we had planned and received permits back in May, reserving campsites to get us through the park. As expected though, we didn't arrive on the day we had planned, and as a result, we were at the whim of the park regarding preciously few available back country campsite permits.

Yellowstone National Park has a series of campsites that are established along the trail system running throughout the park. Backcountry camp permits can be obtained, but all overnight camping in the park must be at these designated sites. We had called from Brooks Lake Lodge, one of three places in the entire state where we had a cell signal, and were told there was only one spot available the night we were planning on entering the park. That meant one short day of twenty-three miles, followed by a long day of thirty-eight miles in order to reach Old Faithful Village in time to meet with friends that were making the trip to visit us. It was out of our hands so we got ourselves pumped up for a short day.

The trail was generally easy to follow and our anticipation was that as we got closer and closer to the major landmarks of the park, that the trail would get nicer and nicer.

We entered the park from what seemed to be the back door as there was no check-in point and there were no rangers present. It was obviously not very highly used, despite being one of the most popular parks in the country. The scenery was fairly non-descript other than signs of a past forest fire.

Much of our time in the park was characterized by the remains of a fire that had burned all the way back in 1988. We learned that the park had largely let the blaze burn, allowing nature to take its course. We were amazed to learn how long it often takes for a forest to grow back after big burns. So much of our time in Yellowstone ended up being through these open sections where young trees were only now finally starting to spring up.

The terrain was beautiful in its own way. Wildflowers were everywhere. Yellows, purples, reds, and whites dotted the hillsides. There weren't many places for breaks though because without shade trees, ground brush tended to dominate, and land covered completely by plants was not a place to sit down to rest while on the trail. As a result, we walked straight through most of the day.

We got to our designated campsite by around 4:00pm and we were quick to eat, drink water, and get cleaned up. The spot was right on a river that was pleasantly warm, as it was an outflow from a bigger lake. I proceeded to submerge myself in the warm water to wash up, while Julie opted to wait for town the next day.

Despite having the company of another hiker at camp that night, we were both ready to call it an early evening. The idea of going to sleep really early after a couple weeks of hiking until dark every night was very appealing, so by 7:00pm we were in our tent and quickly asleep.

We set our alarm that night for the first time since Julie had gotten back on the trail because we were supposed to meet Zippers and her partner Amy at the Village at 6:00pm the next day, thirty-eight miles up the trail. We met Zippers while hiking the AT back in 2011, and have been friends ever since. She and her partner Amy lived nearby and seemed thrilled by the opportunity to provide trail magic. We were not only excited to see them for the sheer joy of seeing good friends, but also because we knew Zippers knew how to cook. She knew what hiker hunger was all about and we were salivating simply thinking about what may be awaiting us. While we expected fast miles on the well groomed trails of Yellowstone, we still knew thirty-eight miles was likely a minimum of thirteen hours of hiking, so we set the watch for 3:00am.

It was a bright full moon when we woke to the alarm and we both looked at each other and immediately knew what the other was thinking. We were not night hiking. We were enjoying the extra sleep too much to get up and push that early. We reset the alarm for 5:30am and were out on the trail by 6:00am.

The extra sleep was wonderful. We were both recharged and oddly excited for the big day. Our packs were light with only a day's worth of food remaining and water was plentiful.

We started the day in an abnormal fashion by hiking over twelve miles without stopping. We didn't talk much but neither of us showed signs of needing to stop, so we just walked. While we hadn't begun running, our hiking was smooth, efficient, and in the moment as we made our way through the park that morning.

In fact, we kept putting off running almost the entire day. Instead, we opted for very few breaks to the point that it became a game. After covering more than twelve miles before our first break, we proceeded to go another twelve miles before stopping again, leaving us with only thirteen miles remaining and a little less than three hours to do it.

It was now game time. Sure, we could have been late to meet our friends, but didn't want to worry them. Plus, we loved the challenge. When we were both fresh, well-fed, and focused, one of our favorite things to do on the trail was to find ways to push ourselves physically and mentally, and today we were ready.

We began to shuffle-run the flat sections. We were shuffling down hills as we passed along Shoshone Lake from above. We walked right through big water crossings without taking our shoes off, and we even jogged right on by our own tour of geysers as the hours ticked by.

We did slow down in order to snap some photos and to take in the peculiarity of this unique trail wonder. Unlike the areas around Old Faithful that are accessible by car and built up with wooden walkways and railings, this section of geysers on the Geyser Basin Trail seemed to be just for us. No one was out there, few if any people probably ever went there because it was a few miles from any road. There were no fences or railings as the trail went within feet of deep, hot, bubbling pools of varying spectacular colors. It was a jog through another planet that afternoon and it proved to be the highlight of Yellowstone for us.

For our final thirteen mile section, we even opted to not carry any water in order to make it easier to run. Instead, we had our emergency straws ready and twice along the last section, we made quick stops to dip our bottles and quickly chug through our straws before running on.

I began to tire before Julie. She was leading and pushing every possible section. While I was usually the positive force driving us up the trail, she was at the helm now, and I was doing my best to keep up. She even began singing. She made it all the way through Don Maclean's "American Pie," along with many other classics she knew by heart. I was simply amazed by her positive attitude and at her ability to not dwell on the challenges of the day as she so often did. She managed to stay positive and slightly distracted, while still being focused on what needed to be done in order to meet our goal.

Shortly before 6:00pm we looked down upon Old Faithful Village and could see the Disneyland of the National Park system below. We ran down the hill knowing we'd be a few minutes late but as we shuffled into the parking lot that evening at 6:15pm, we felt an enormous sense of accomplishment and joy.

The next challenge was to actually find Zippers and Amy amidst the chaos of Old Faithful. We hadn't agreed upon a meeting spot, at least we hadn't received a phone signal recently enough to confirm one. We first set about looking in what seemed like common meeting places, but we were unsuccessful in locating them.

After such a focused and steady push for the day we were both getting a little frazzled. By 7:00pm, we finally found a place to get on a wifi network and we were able to email and text with Zippers. They'd booked us a room at the employee dorms for the night, and laundry machines and hot showers awaited us.

We quickly made our way to the dorms, showered up, and just as we were finishing getting cleaned up, there they were with smiles, hugs, and congratulations. It was a momentous occasion and the smiles left our faces only between bites of vegan treats and chocolate cake.

5
Stopwatch

We did it! We walked thirty-eight miles in twelve hours and I was downright giddy for the last few hours of the day. I liked the type of hiker I was becoming: Positive, even in the face of pressure.

All the day's underlying tension was relieved the moment our feet hit the parking lot pavement at Old Faithful Village and our heads swiveled around in search of Zippers. There were many more people there than we had expected and I had a feeling we should have picked a meeting point other than just Old Faithful Village.

By the time we were able to check email it was already 7:00pm, time had melted away and the day's events were starting to frazzle us. In our inbox were detailed instructions from Zippers about a free room in an employee dorm, where she and her partner, Amy, would bring coolers of food.

We made our way to the dorm and I took a hot shower while Matt emailed Zippers of our whereabouts. I got out of the shower just as Zippers and Amy were carrying in a cooler and several bags of food, all home-cooked vegan food, including fresh bread, roasted vegetables, salad, and a double-layer chocolate cake, complete with chocolate frosting. I squealed as I opened the cooler of food and saw my favorite town beverage, the one thing I craved the most on the trail, a Sunkist soda. Zippers had remembered it and I had tears in my eyes because I felt so lucky to have such good, supportive friends. She even brought us laundry detergent so we could wash our clothes in the free laundry machines in the dorm. Zippers really left no detail unnoticed and we were so grateful.

As we sat there and ate, hashing over the last two months of hiking stories and reliving some of our AT stories with Zippers, Amy sat quietly, taking it all in. It was our first time meeting her and she was a reserved person to begin with, so she didn't say much. One of the first things she said as she sat back and observed us scooping seconds and thirds onto our plates was, "You're much more civilized than I imagined!"

Though Matt and I felt like we were tearing into the food like starving savages, we must have been holding back our crazy, hungry-hiker tendencies. We all burst out laughing as we recalled one of Zippers' AT feats, sharing an entire birthday sheet cake with another hiker.

After dinner we all sat in the dorm room together until 11:00pm, talking so boisterously that an employee in the room next door knocked on our door to warn us about quiet hours. I didn't want the night to end.

All the chocolate cake energized us both and once Zippers and Amy left, we found it hard to fall asleep. We stayed up until 3:00am, writing blog stories and catching up on our real life to-do list. I finally went to sleep, excited for the next morning's breakfast, leftover cake and coffee.

Our goal for the next day was to leave Yellowstone. That sounds a bit harsh, but it was for legitimate reasons that we needed to hike at least eighteen and a half miles that day to cross the park border. We no longer had a permit to camp in the park and had no intention of breaking the rules, so we started our morning early with an 8:00am run to the post office. When it came to national parks in general, there were often many more rules to follow, thru-hiker or not, and for good reason because of the vast amount of users in the parks.

As we packed up our next leg of food, Matt Skyped with our friend, Alex, whose trail name was Stagg, who was southbounding the CDT at that moment and who was currently in Lima, Montana, our next town. They picked a meeting spot in between our two locations to camp together. He was a good friend of ours from Portland, Oregon, so we were excited for the extra motivation to cover the miles so we could maximize our time with him.

Our packs were stupid heavy leaving Old Faithful, which was all the more noticeable on the climb up to Summit Lake. We could tell we'd just spent a section being hungry and now we were making up for it. I had at least three pounds of chocolate cake in a gallon-sized Ziploc on the top of my pack, while Matt packed out pasta salad and vegetables, along with extra chips and candy from the general store at Old Faithful. We took several breaks that day just to sit and eat so we could lower our pack weight.

A few miles before the park border, we officially completed the state of Wyoming and entered into Idaho. Nearly a thousand miles still remained until Canada, much of which was in Montana. Looking back on our time in Wyoming, we realized how much we loved the state. It had been incredibly diverse in its scenery, from the dusty bowl of the Basin to the lush meadows in the Winds, to the popular trails of Yellowstone. We had great weather throughout the entire state and though we'd been warned that there was little official tread in the state, we felt like the combination of dirt roads and existing tread made for enjoyable hiking.

Looking forward to Montana, we simply knew that it was long, comprising nearly a third of the trail, and that it culminated in Glacier National Park, which was rumored to be one of the most scenic parts of the trail. Glacier National Park was almost all we'd heard about Montana, which made us wonder what the other ninety percent of the state offered.

We made it to the park border by 7:30pm after a day of fairly ugly scenery, given we were in a national park. Much of the day was spent walking through a recovering burn section, so it was dusty, charred and desolate with little greenery and lots of gray. Just a half-mile past the border we chose a campsite, both of us tired from staying up so late the night before. We were ready to call it a day, hang our food, eat some food from Zippers, and go to sleep.

Our batteries were recharged by the next morning and we got an early start in the cool morning. The clouds showed signs of rain, which was oddly exciting to us. We'd been uncomfortably warm the last few days, especially in some of the exposed post-burn sections of Yellowstone. Within five minutes of walking, we ran into a southbounder who must have camped within a half-mile of us. Before we even exchanged names, he asked us, "Do you have enough water?"

Neither of us was expecting the question, nor did we fully understand what he was getting at, wondering if he was asking for some of our water, so we both looked at each other and answered, "Um, we each have about a liter."

"Well, most of the upcoming sources are dry so there's no water until Reas Creek, which is twenty-six miles away, and you have to go off-trail to find it," he explained.

It wasn't even 6:30am yet, I was barely awake enough to be walking, and I hadn't eaten breakfast. I wasn't exactly ready to talk water sources, but this guy was adamant.

"Well, I guess that's what we'll do then," Matt answered. In reality, it was good information to know that we were coming up on a dry section so we could ration our water. I considered it another blessing that it was chilly and showing signs of rain.

The southbounder was correct and every water source we passed that day was dry. Much of the trail we walked that morning was on dirt roads, with very few trees to offer shade and very few signs of life. Birds weren't even flying overhead so it was an eerily quiet section and we guessed it was because there was little water. We were frustrated that no one had put up a water report on that section on Facebook, but then we realized we were at the front of the pack. Not only were there few people that knew about the water shortage, but many people also took a shorter alternate around that section, which had water.

The clouds never lifted but it also never rained beyond a short misting and since we walked a lot of flat roads, we were able to get in some fast, comfortable miles. As we walked on one of the roads in the early afternoon, each of us with just sips of water left after walking almost twenty-six miles on one liter, a lime green Forest Service truck pulled up beside us and stopped.

"You guys ok? You need anything?" the driver asked us.

I wasn't shy in asking, "Do you have any water?"

Within seconds three men popped out of the vehicle and handed us each a liter and they all had two more in their hands. We both drank one and a half liters right there as we stood talking to them and each took another one and a half liters with us to make it to the next water source. They seemed happy to help and it was fun talking with them about the area we had just hiked through and the area we were coming up on.

I had a completely illogical philosophy that if one half of the day, such as the morning, was easy, then the other half would be hard, like the afternoon, and vice versa. There was no reason for the philosophy other than it was how I felt the trail often went, and that day the afternoon was harder than the morning. The route took us up on the Divide and we relied on the sporadic rock cairns and our GPS to navigate much of the section before again dropping down into the woods, onto a more established path.

Our campsite that evening was slanted and sandwiched between clumps of grass, but we were tired from a thirty-five mile day and after hanging our bear bag as a precaution, we were fast asleep, excited about meeting up with Alex the next evening.

We still had nearly twenty-seven miles before our rendezvous point with Alex, so it was an early start to the day with a 2,000' climb before breakfast. In the short time between the creation of our maps and that moment, new tread had been laid, new signage was up, and we were torn on which way to go. We decided to blindly follow the new tread, putting faith in the signage. The old route had been on a snowmobile route that went around the mountain, while the new route quickly gained elevation and then rode the Divide. It was a chilly, windy morning on the bare, rocky Divide and we did our best to follow the route without GPS waypoints to guide us. Much of the morning was spent climbing while much of the afternoon was a descent that allowed us to move quickly towards our pre-determined campsite.

As we approached our meeting point with Alex, Anthill Spring, I saw a red jacket in the distance, running towards us on the dirt road we'd been walking for the last few miles. Alex reached us just as we made it to the spring and we all exchanged excited hugs, followed by a bit of silence. It was almost as if we didn't know where to begin in our conversation because there was so much to talk about. It was also such a unique situation we were all in, as thru-hikers on such a remote, challenging trail in a random location in the backcountry of Montana.

Alex had started from the Canadian border with another hiker, but had been alone for the last couple of weeks. I didn't know how he did it. On the CDT, hiking alone meant absolute alone time, risk of not running into another soul for days, and inevitably, loneliness.

Being alone meant being really, really, *really* alone. We all seemed equally eager for some time among friends.

We quickly set up our tent near Alex's and we sat and talked with him for the entire evening. It was comforting to see a friend from home because we had so much more to talk about than just the trail; we had a history and we had a future, which was a lot more than most of our relationships with other hikers. We also discussed upcoming water, terrain, and animals. For the most part, Alex was fairly tame in his descriptions. It didn't sound like there were crazy dry sections like New Mexico, or exhausting changes in elevations like Colorado, or days of dirt road-walking like Wyoming, but rather just a steady progression north. He did say that some of the terrain was dry, exposed, and up on the Divide, which surprised me. So far I had pictured Montana as a lush green forest with plenty of coverage overhead, though I had no legitimate reason to back up that idea.

We finally had to call it a night when it got dark and cold and we were all getting tired. Just like with Zippers, I didn't want the night to end. That night thunderstorms rolled in and it rained heavily throughout the night for one of the first times on the trail. Alex had said his time in Montana had been relatively dry so I hoped the storms weren't a sign for weather to come.

There was some sadness in the air the next morning. We and Alex would be going our opposite ways and it was doubtful we'd cross paths again on the trail. There was a slight possibility that we'd see him in Colorado when we went back to finish up the section that was originally on fire, but that was so far away that it felt like a waste of energy to focus on making it happen. Yet, Alex seemed in better spirits that morning than he had been the prior afternoon. Goodbye hugs were given and as we started walking again, it was hard not to look back. It wasn't that I felt sorry for Alex that he had to hike so much alone; I just felt sad about it. I wanted companionship for him. It made me think of Matt being out there alone and I was again reminded of how happy I was with my decision to get back on the trail.

We looked at the rest of the miles into Lima, our next destination, and saw we had sixty-seven miles left. Sixty-seven miles was very doable in two days, considering a bed and a hot shower were the reward, but we could never depend on good tread, so instead of aiming for Lima, we both agreed to put in a good day's effort for the next two days and see where that took us.

Most of the day was spent on rolling terrain over the Divide. Another aspect of hiking on the Divide, besides the usual route-finding and elevation changes over exposed, windswept, often scrubby landscape, was the lack of water. There were very few streams, creeks, or lakes on the Divide; we needed to drop down in elevation to get water. By late afternoon we'd been on the Divide for quite some time, maneuvering over terrain that looked smooth in the distance but was rocky and ankle-rolling up close, and we finally dropped down to a creek by the end of the day. We'd covered just over thirty-three miles, leaving thirty-four to town. Neither of us was sure we could cover that mileage the next day, but we both promised to put in another full day. We camped about a half-mile after the creek, setting up our tent just as a lightning storm started off in the distance; it was a good thing we dropped down off the Divide.

The late morning and early afternoon miles were high and sun-drenched yet again and offered views for miles out into a flat valley. As we stopped at one point to admire the view, I found it hard to believe that we might be in civilization that very night, given how far away we felt from any form of normal human life.

That day we also passed a trail journal at a trailhead, a rare occurrence, especially compared to the large amounts of journals on the AT and PCT. We saw that Rob Steady and Why Wait signed in recently; they were significant to Matt because he met them in Colorado on his first day without me. Matt said he was such a mess when he met them that he had to leave after he started talking to them because he started crying. We also saw that Aquaman signed in a couple days ahead of us, so we assumed we wouldn't see him again, knowing the fast pace he kept.

Shortly after maneuvering through tricky blow downs strewn all over the trail, the skies opened up. Thunder boomed and lightning cracked overhead as a drizzle quickly morphed into a heavy downpour. Within minutes of the first drizzle we both stopped to put on our rain jackets, our wind pants, and our rain mittens. The temperature dropped at least ten degrees in a matter of minutes and we were glad that most of the high up, exposed ridges were behind us. My solace as we walked through the pouring rain was that we'd probably make it to town that night. I didn't care how wet my gear got, a hot shower and a dry room awaited me if I kept up the pace.

With seven miles to go and clear skies overhead, we turned onto a dirt road and were immediately set free of route-finding and cross-country walking. I started running the flats and the downhills, and while Matt wasn't in the mood to run, he had no option but to run to keep up. He was confident we'd make it to town even with walking, but I wasn't taking any chances. In the final miles, as we could see I-15 in the distance from the dirt road we were running, I had a little scare when one of the cows we passed started running behind me. I was literally being chased by a cow, which weighed hundreds of pounds more than me, and I was a little scared. Matt was standing at the ready with his bear spray, in case the cow made a move against me, but just at the last second it ran ahead of me and veered towards a herd of cows in the distance. Apparently it was so freaked out about being separated from the herd that it was running behind me in order to make its way back to the other cows.

It was 8:00pm when we made it to I-15 and we barely had a signal to call the motel to get a ride into Lima, a tiny town that was over twelve miles up the highway. Once in town, we dined on the only vegan food available in a town so small, whatever was available at the Exxon gas station and whatever we could cook in our room's microwave. We ate a bag of chips, a box of spaghetti and a jar of Prego, and candy. We were so accustomed to the lack of good vegan food on the trail that at that point, that caliber of food was actually quite pleasing and we no longer snuffed our noses at its quality. Straight calories were all that mattered after a thirty-four mile push to town.

6
Optimist

We had been burning the candle at both ends and the motel stop in Lima was no exception. The people there were great, we had a nice room with a wifi signal, and we had microwavable food from the convenience store to munch on. Sleep was sacrificed.

Plus, this town experience was notably different than any other on the CDT thus far. We got our first clue that Lima would be different on our ride into town, which we shared with a couple of southbound CDT hikers. They said they were part of a larger group and the motel owner confirmed that there were indeed, quite a few hikers at the motel currently. For us having not seen many hikers over our nearly 2,000 miles, the prospect of multiple hikers in one place was all-together new.

Due to our late arrival and long to-do list, we kept to ourselves that evening, preferring to get clean, fed, and organized. But the next morning, by the time I had picked up our packages at the post office, Aquaman was in our room chatting it up. We'd hiked with him briefly in Wyoming and had run into him again at Yellowstone. He had been hiking binge style where he'd do multiple forty-plus mile days, but then take chunks of time off. He had already been in Lima for three days.

Aquaman had been staying with Beacon, another northbound hiker, and he said there was a good chance that more northbound hikers would likely be arriving later that day. We were intrigued. While we'd been in close proximity to other hikers ever since skipping the fires back in Colorado, we hadn't actually met a whole lot of them, having passed each other while in towns or on different routes.

On the other hand, we were also eager to get back to the trail. As fate would have it, we were once again dealing with a time crunch to get to our next resupply town of Leadore, Idaho, for yet another Saturday post office deadline. So we chatted with Aquaman as we went through our resupply box, ditching some food we had tired of and supplementing with food from the convenience store. As we packed up our bags we looked out the window only to realize that we'd missed the 10:00am shuttle back to the trail.

While initially kicking ourselves for missing the first ride back to the trail and thus making our next deadline all the more challenging, we happened into a unique CDT experience that was well worth the delayed start out of Lima. After checking out of our room, we sat out on the lawn in front of the motel in the shade of some trees. We were out there only a few minutes before more hikers popped out. We first met six southbound hikers and then Beacon. Beacon had hiked the CDT once already and was out doing a "gentleman's hike," as he called it, skipping crappier sections and road walks, while hitting some of the trail highlights. He also was the one who had put together the datasheet based on the Bear Creek waypoints that we'd been using from the beginning of the hike. He loved the trail and he made us feel good about our choice of sticking to the official route, saying we were only two of four people he knew that were attempting the route, with us likely to be the first to actually finish it.

As we were sitting around talking with Beacon, Aquaman, and the southbounders, a truckload of fresh hikers arrived. As they all jumped out we were finally able to put faces to names we'd heard of for much of the trail. We met Bloodbath and his girlfriend Rampage, Wired, Sweet As, Dain, Gnar and Pod, along with Norm and his girlfriend Amanda who showed up a little later.

It was a full-on hiker fest at the Lima motel and everyone was sharing stories, trail updates, and gossip. We had heard of them, they had heard of us, and we were all finally together. It was thru-hiker camaraderie at its best and we were glad to have been stuck a little while longer in Lima than planned.

A little after noon we were offered a ride, so along with Gnar and Pod, another couple hiking the trail together, we headed back to the mountains. Once dropped off we had a flat eight mile dirt road walk, which the four of us walked together in the afternoon sun. We'd heard stories about them from Softwalker and we were happy to finally spend a few hours with them. While we had different backgrounds, we felt like there were plenty of commonalities, and we were sad to say goodbye when we got to a trail junction which took us up on the Divide while they stayed down low.

We looked up at the climb which our friend Alex had labeled, "The Dragon's Tail," and knew that town time was over and that it was time to get back to the trail. As we traversed the steep, often unmaintained trail we really began to question the idea of the CDT as a corridor hike. We had committed ourselves to the idea of hiking the official route as marked by our maps, but when we set out, we also thought that each route was as official as the next. As we hiked out of the valley and up along the Divide that afternoon, following CDT signs the entire way, we recalled many of the other sections we'd been through thus far that were "official" but rarely used, and many of those were also marked with the official CDT trail signs and logos. They may not have been marked well or maintained well, but there was obvious intention that this was the trail. We by no means were putting others down or saying their hikes weren't challenging hikes, but the idea of there being an actual official CDT route was becoming more official in our minds.

After the busy social morning we were alone again on the vast, windy Divide. We knew we had a long twenty-one mile waterless section coming out of Lima and that the trail would likely be challenging, but the terrain along the Montana and Idaho border continued to surprise us. We were now in the mountains again, but at this point the mountains rarely had any trees. We walked along the tops of the mountains and looked out upon the valleys below. Up high, the terrain was covered with short, golden grass and rough, rocky, rutted terrain, while down in the valleys there was occasional green and forest. It was no wonder we had a waterless stretch as the ridges we were tracking were void of anything green.

It was pretty though, unique from anything else we'd hiked before. We both knew it as we were hiking it, but at the same time, the degree of difficulty associated with steep climbs of a few hundred feet, followed by knee pounding descents, only to climb right back up, began to wear on us that day. It was just like a dragon's tail as Alex had warned. We had started at the end of the tail, meaning that we had a small climb followed by a small descent, though the descent was not as large as the first climb. This was followed by another climb to a new high, and then followed by another descent, though again, not as much a drop as the gain we'd just had. In this repeated fashion, we reached higher and higher elevations while working our tails off.

We felt very exposed on the ridges as well, and this was punctuated by the multitude of storm clouds constantly in sight throughout the afternoon. Though they'd been on different ridges than the one we had been following, we knew we could get one at any time. Around 4:00pm we finally got ours, and with the speed the storm came rolling in with, we were only able and willing to drop about twenty yards from the ridge. We quickly got out our mats, put on our rain jackets, and got in lightning pose, crouching low to the ground with as little surface area actually touching the ground as possible, all just before the first serious rains came pounding down on us.

Lightning lit up the sky and thunder cracked and boomed around us. We were suddenly in the thick of the storm and getting drilled by it. We were both down as low to the ground as possible due to the lightning and doing all we could to keep ourselves warm and dry at the same time. We stayed like this for half an hour before finally feeling safe enough to stand up again. We fetched our metal hiking poles, which we'd thrown twenty yards away from us, and we got moving. We were cold and a bit shaken from the experience. Our objective for the remainder of the day was to finish that ridge and to get down.

The skies quickly cleared and we had a beautiful cold and windy sunset as we hurried along the slow terrain of the mountaintops. We met some more southbounders, the trio of Greta, Charlie, and Chris, and we stopped to snack and chat with them shortly before dark. They too were following the official route. We each talked about our reasons for doing so and both agreed that it was in some ways a less complicated hike because we always knew the route we were following. While other hikers often debated which routes to take, our choice had been made long ago so it was something we rarely thought about. While we had camaraderie in Lima with all the hikers earlier that day, we felt a real kinship with this trio.

As we walked into the night, determined to get off the ridge and down to water, we struggled. Our nerves had been frazzled by the storm and the hiking had been difficult. Plus, we hadn't gotten water all day. We simply wanted down and we wanted to finish what we'd set out to do for the day. Oftentimes, we were satisfied with lower mileage days but on this day, there were no good places to stop up on the ridge, and as we finally started coming down, struggling to find our way in the dark, there also were no good places to call home for the night.

Finally, around 10:30pm we were in among some bushes and as the cow pies multiplied, we knew water was close. We walked on a few minutes more and came across Shineberger Creek and called it a night. I filled up water for the morning, Julie set up the tent, and within fifteen minutes we were both sound asleep.

The next morning we woke with the sun. We packed up, ate some granola bars and were walking within twenty-five minutes of waking. Ever since Julie had been back on the trail we'd been hiking big miles, and we'd been enjoying it. Our low mileage days were still in the twenties, and our usual hiking day was in the low thirties. We did this by waking with the sun and hiking until the sun went down. As this particular morning dragged on though, we were both dragging with it. We hadn't taken a day off since she'd been back on the trail, and we hadn't had a big recharge sleep night since our 7:00pm bedtime in Yellowstone.

In the early afternoon, with little talking required, we both agreed to stop and rest. There was a spot off the side of the trail under the shade of some trees, and within two minutes of stopping, we were on our mats, in our bags, and snuggled up for an afternoon nap. It was splendid. While the sleep wasn't totally deep, the simple act of chilling out for the afternoon recharged our batteries and gave us some good mental rest. We even had sex, which, while still part of the trail life, did not keep up the frequency or quality it had in regular life.

After our nap we got going again, but with a new acceptance that we may not make our deadline this time around. We had known for some time that we were somehow on this continual Saturday town schedule and that if we messed up one of them, then we may well mess up more because it kept working out that with our normal hiking mileage, nearly every Saturday had us getting to another town. However, at this point, the miles and the town deadlines were taking their toll. We were worn out and the terrain, while challenging, seemed more challenging than normal.

We found a small section of trees later in the day and stopped well before dark. We went to bed at 8:00pm that Thursday night knowing we still had sixty miles left to cover before Leadore. If we woke up feeling great from the extra rest, and the terrain eased up a bit, then maybe we'd night hike to get in on Saturday morning. But we were also prepared to get in late on Saturday, being forced to take a zero day in town to wait for the post office on Monday.

We worked steadily the next day. Some stretches traversed rough mountain jeep roads, while others were downright confusing as we'd be following trail one moment, only to have it open to a meadow with no visible sign of a trail the next. We had sections on roads that were up on the Divide but the roads were so overgrown with bushes and ground cover that walking was slow and ankle-rolling-treacherous. The late afternoon had us climbing up to some really exposed high desert grasslands with the wind blowing and no trail visible. There were occasional cairns along the way and maybe a sign post, but in general, we were out there alone, walking in the wilderness. It is a romantic and powerful image to recall, seeing us high in the Montana mountains, far from civilization with no trail and no real signs of human interference. The reality of the moment was often that this terrain made for really difficult walking. We kept a positive perspective most of the time though and would often add to the drama by listening to dramatic music, singing out loud to the hillsides, Julie Andrews style.

I had been doing all the GPS work ever since Julie had left the trail and I proudly navigated us through our cross-country adventure that afternoon. I had been going waypoint to waypoint until we were suddenly faced with a steep drop off. We spent a few minutes walking all along the steep slopes leading down from the open ridge but we could not find an obvious route down. We eventually just went for it taking the best line we could find, bushwhacking through brush, hopping over downed trees, and making our best effort to hike in the direction of the next waypoint. And then, as we neared the bottom, we spotted a sign telling us we were indeed on trail. In fact, new, clear-to-see trail was waiting for us for the walk down to Coyote Creek.

While we'd hiked the majority of the day still thinking we might hike through the night in order to make the post office deadline, we decided late Friday afternoon that for the first time on the trail, we were not making town on time. Acceptance was actually pretty easy as we were both tired, we both knew we'd been putting in a solid effort, and the fact was, we simply weren't making it to Leadore.

The next day was filled with a sense of relief. We still had thirty miles to town, so while relieved, we still kept on the accelerator to make sure that we still made it to Leadore. Also, the road to town was a fourteen mile dirt road that we needed to hitchhike; it was known to be one of the toughest hitches on the entire trail because there were so few cars.

The morning was fairly easy as we were on manageable dirt roads. We stopped in surprise as we were climbing up the dirt road from Morrison Lake as I thought I saw a black bear drinking from the lake. Julie, who I often referred to as Hawkeye, confirmed it was two large black cows.

We'd heard from nearly every southbounder we'd passed that we were quickly gaining on a couple, Rob Steady and Why Wait. They were significant to me because they were the two I'd met while hiking alone in Colorado just outside of Breckenridge. I had begun talking with them only to break down in tears. So I hadn't spoken with them for very long. I was interested to see if they remembered me and excited for them to see Julie back on the trail.

The afternoon featured one last big climb up Elk Mountain, taking us up to 10,000' for the last time in Montana. We then began a steady descent down to Bannock Pass where we would meet the road to town. In those last few miles we met a couple young guys that brought me back to my early hiking days. They were energetic and excited to be on the trail. My guess was that they were in their early to mid-twenties and that this was their first thru-hike. They were eager to learn and just happy to be out there in the wilderness. Upon learning their names, Matt and Dan, they forged a special place in my heart, as my first hike back in 2000 was with my buddy Dan; we were spitting images of these two, ready for anything the trail may throw at us.

From there we hit rocky dirt roads that rode the Divide toward the pass. There was more down than up this time and we ran at every opportunity. Julie was amazingly positive and focused. Relative to her attitude over our first 6,000 miles of hiking together, the past 600 miles she seemed to be enjoying herself and the experience immensely more than I could ever recall.

As we neared the final push to the pass I could see a car kicking up dust on the dirt road, bound for Leadore. We looked at each other and yelled, "Run!" We both barreled down the last hill to the road and I made it just as the car was cresting the hill. With my thumb out and my smile fully showing, the woman driver looked at me, then at Julie, who had just made it down the hill, and then at the two older hikers sitting off the side of the road with their packs. She asked what we needed and though her car was already stuffed with random things, she made room in her Subaru for all four of us.

The two other hikers were Rob Steady and Why Wait, and along with Candy, the geologist driver that had so kindly picked us up, we all chatted away the miles to town. She dropped us off at the Leadore Inn, a mom and pops type of place with only four rooms. The owners lived across the street and were well-versed in helping hikers. For Saturday night we got one of the rooms without the kitchenette but the owners were willing to switch us the next day so we could cook on our day off. They also showed us the laundry room which we used freely, and invited Julie into their home so we could use their computer to upload some of our photos to our website.

Before we did all this though, they called the one restaurant in town, the Silver Dollar, and told them to stay open for us. The restaurant was known on the trail for not having reliable hours, often open when they felt like it or when they had customers, as well as being known for not always having menu items available. Basically, they cooked what they wanted, when they wanted.

I went for the social time while Julie, Why Wait, and Rob Steady ordered food. We were talking trail when I noticed the locals at the table behind us eavesdropping on our conversation. I was talking about the challenges of being vegan on the trail and joked loudly enough so the locals could hear me, "I was surprised they didn't have any nori, you know, seaweed, back at the Exxon station back in Lima".

The folks at the table next to us burst out laughing. It was the icebreaker we needed. They said they knew that store well as it was one of the only stores within miles for them and the idea of buying seaweed sounded downright absurd to them.

We learned about the ranching life and they told us all about how the ATV had revolutionized things for them, saying they were able to work so much more efficiently now. They talked about the cycle of raising cattle and what life was like out in these remote parts. They encouraged us to come back for the Fourth of July celebration, claiming that the town grew by close to ten times its normal size for all the festivities. The town had maybe 100 residents total.

After our meal, we headed back to our room, cleaned up, and we went to bed early, knowing we had the entire day ahead of us with no walking.

7
Stopwatch

Try as I might, I couldn't sleep past sunrise. We had made a to-do list the night before in order to take advantage of a full day off and my mind was racing the moment I woke up. Our room in Leadore was so comfortable that I was bubbling over with excitement over our decision to stay there two nights, with a thick, colorful quilt on the welcoming bed, soft carpeting underfoot, and one of the hottest showers on the trail. It was glorious to spend time indoors being barefoot and clean. I started my day with a hot shower, warming me up before we stepped outside into the crisp morning air.

As soon as the store opened we were inside, perusing its contents for vegan food to cook that day. I couldn't keep my eyes off the freshly baked cinnamon rolls, the white icing melting and oozing atop the hot rolls and the intoxicating scent of baked goods filling the entire one-roomed store. We picked up pasta, frozen potatoes, chips and canned vegetables, and I left with a hot cup of coffee in one hand and a cinnamon roll in the other. I was nearly drooling as I left the store and headed back to our room.

The rest of the morning we took turns calling home and writing blog stories. By late morning, the crowd of hikers that we'd left in Lima showed up, including Wired, Rampage and Bloodbath, Aquaman, Dain, and Sweet As. All the guys were now sporting a mohawk, a new look since Lima, Bloodbath's being the best since his hair was naturally spiky. Since the Inn only had four rooms and we and Rob Steady and Why Wait had taken two of the rooms, that didn't leave much room for the rest. Aquaman and his crew had already made reservations at another hotel down the street (we were shocked that a town so small had so many lodging options) and that left Wired, Rampage and Bloodbath to take the other two rooms at the Inn.

By the time they showed up we were nearly done with our town chores, including laundry, blog updates, calling home, and buying food, so it was easy to be social for the rest of the day. Our room became the hiker hub since it had a kitchenette, so everyone who bought food at the general store that needed cooking headed into our room to eat. We loved it. The hikers came to us and we spent the rest of the day swapping trail stories and life stories with the rest of the hikers as they came in to heat up food, a frozen burrito being the most popular item from the general store. We also had plates and silverware, so we truly were the one-stop shop for people in need of food and company.

We shared the most time with Rampage and Bloodbath, a couple in their early twenties, full of youth and excitement. The CDT was Rampage's first thru-hike, an impressive feat, and Bloodbath's second after the PCT. They met during Peace Corp work in Ethiopia, a country dear to our hearts. We spent six months living in Addis Ababa in 2005 and the memories from that trip were deeply engrained into our memories, so we were thrilled to swap stories with them about Ethiopia, surprised to meet others who had spent such a long time living there.

By early evening everyone retreated to their rooms and we called it an early night, going to bed at nearly the same time as that on the trail. We wanted to get an early start the next day after such a long break in town so we went to sleep, hoping to catch up on the rest we'd been craving for so long.

The next morning, my motivation to wake up early once again was the fact that cinnamon rolls and freshly brewed coffee were awaiting me at the general store. The cinnamon roll from the previous day felt like such a teaser and I knew I wanted another one before leaving. Ever since the town of Damascus, Virginia, on the Appalachian Trail, where I only ate one cinnamon roll and regretted not getting seconds for the rest of the trail, I had promised myself I would eat at least two if I ever came across such good rolls ever again. Yes, I thought about food that much.

I walked outside into clear, cool skies and it felt like most of the town was already stirring with wakeup calls for the Monday morning routine, the day significant to me because it meant the post office was open. After grabbing breakfast, this time two cinnamon rolls just for me, absolutely gluttonous, I swung by the post office for our resupply boxes and toted everything the hundred yards back to our room. I opened the door to see that Matt was already cooking up the rest of his spaghetti and frozen potatoes.

By noon we were back on the trail. Bloodbath and Rampage walked ahead with a naturally faster hiking pace while Matt and I stuck with Wired, who hiked surprisingly fast, considering her small stature. She set the pace and led our train of three, her shiny brown hair pulled back in a tight, bouncy pony tail and her small feet adjusting with each step of the ever-changing terrain. Since I walked behind her, I couldn't help but stare at her calves and feet, watching the dust settle around her stretchy gaiters with each quick step.

Nearly the rest of the day rolled on as we hiked with Wired and learned about her life, including her blog that had a strong following, her life as an identical twin, her PCT adventure in a high snow year, and her story of moving from Chicago to Portland for a change of pace. Talking with Wired made the time pass quickly as we spanned all sorts of subjects about life both on and off the trail. While she admitted she didn't reach the level of anxiety I often did on trails, she assured me that she understood what kind of stressed-out, negative places my mind often went to, something Matt didn't always understand, and I felt a strong connection to her because of that.

The trail took us on a long, gradual climb over the first fourteen miles, most of which had a legitimate path, yet a fair amount of exposure, void of many trees. At one point the winds picked up so forcefully that we had to lean into the wind just to stay upright, our feet slipping around on loose rocks. The winds brought a thunderstorm in and out so fast that by the time we put on rain jackets, it had already passed overhead.

Around 7:30pm, Wired stopped so she could write her daily blog story and still get plenty of rest, a routine she'd kept up for much of the trail. Even though we enjoyed hiking with her, it was earlier than we wanted to stop. We all agreed we'd probably see her again the next day since she often started earlier than most other hikers.

Two miles later we caught up with Bloodbath and Rampage; they were cowboy camping under their two-person sleeping quilt off the side of the trail. We dined on refried beans as we sat on the ground and talked with them until dark, taking full advantage of having company along the trail.

Bloodbath and Rampage were up early so we packed up quickly in order to hike with them. As Wired had requested, we left a note on the trail with details of what time we left, so she could know how much of a head start we had, and we were off at a quick pace for the next several miles until the next water source at Lemhi Pass, an intersection of dirt roads. From that point on we leap-frogged with all three of them that entire day.

Much of the day was a long, gradual uphill with periods of flatter, faster miles. All of us had assumed there would be water at Kennedy Creek, fifteen miles from the spring at Lemhi Pass, but when we arrived there, just as the day was bordering on uncomfortably warm, we saw a note on the trail from Wired that indicated there wasn't water anywhere in the vicinity. While we weren't in serious trouble, we were both down to a half-liter and the next reliable water source was at least eleven miles away. We started to doubt the upcoming water sources because the entire day had been so hot and dry.

It was often the case that when we were suddenly faced with a lack of water, my thirst somehow increased and all I could think about was water. The feeling of desperation started creeping in as we continued hiking and I became more worried when our trail transitioned from a shaded, tree-lined path to exposed, windblown, ridge-top walking over loose rocks.

By 5:00pm, we still hadn't gotten water since the two liters we started with that morning. We were downright shocked to be faced with such a dry section. As we sat down for a break to take our final sips, Bloodbath and Rampage showed up. They had found a steep side trail to water and didn't hesitate to share their water with us, saying they had more than they needed. It was an incredibly kind, selfless gesture. We gave them food in exchange, chocolate covered espresso beans and dried mango. They continued hiking while we waited for Wired to show up so we could hike the late afternoon miles with her.

From that point the trail had smooth, easy-to-follow tread and we kept up a strong pace. Yet, it was still very dry without any signs of water. As we made our way down dusty switchbacks, I eyed a thick patch of trees at the bottom of the hill, and I hoped for water. While I was following Wired on the switchbacks, I heard Matt say his attention-grabbing bird call behind me in a quick, quiet voice, "Caw!"

Both Wired and I looked up at the switchback above us at the same moment, only to see Matt's little white butt hanging over the edge as he mooned us. I shook my head and laughed as I continued walking, knowing how much Matt liked surprising people with the shock of his bare behind.

"Oh my gosh!" Wired yelled out. She too laughed, but I guessed that was a first for her.

Within a mile we finally reached water, two liters and twenty-six miles since the last source. Wired continued walking while we sat and drank a liter and a half with our emergency straws.

We walked until we reached the crew of Wired, Rampage and Bloodbath at another creek crossing around 8:00pm. We knew we were close to them when we heard cows mooing in the distance and soon saw fresh cow poop splattered all over the trail, signs that they'd been riled up by someone.

As we sat around camp, all of us were shocked to look at the maps and see that we'd easily covered over thirty-six miles on a regular day, and we were stopping well before dark. There wasn't much conversation among us before we all retreated to our tents for the evening.

Wired had already packed up and left by the time I got up for my morning poop, the flattened patch of grass evidence of her campsite from the night before. I didn't even hear her stirring!

All of us seemed a little sluggish that morning. Just a few miles into the day, all of us completely missed a well-marked right turn. We had stepped over a log that was blocking the wrong path and walked the wrong way for a half-mile before realizing it. Bloodbath was quick to turn around and walk back to the missed turn, Rampage following closely behind. We hung back, taking our time because our GPS was slow in finding a satellite. That was the last time we saw them. It wasn't the normal way to say goodbye, but that's often how it went on the trail. Nothing was ever certain or ceremonial.

Once we were back on track, within thick tree cover, we stopped for our morning granola break at a creek. Eating food and sitting down was our solution for going the wrong way, so we tried to collect ourselves and start fresh with a morning food break. As I faced the trail from which we'd just come, I saw Wired running towards us. I'd completely forgotten that she was supposedly ahead of us. When I saw her I immediately knew she had also gone the wrong way and judging by the time of day, I could tell she had walked in the wrong direction for a long time. She stopped to say hello to us, nearly in tears and winded as she confirmed she had walked for three miles in the wrong direction, only to figure it out and run backwards to catch up with us. All that effort she'd made to get up early and put some miles on us was negated. I felt terrible for her, knowing how upsetting that was to realize she'd gone the wrong way, and for three miles! She only paused briefly to say hi and was quickly off and running to catch Rampage and Bloodbath.

After that kind of start to the morning, Matt and I agreed to put in a relaxed, steady effort all day, paying close attention to the trail once again. That morning we'd been within sixty-six miles of town so our goal was to reach Sula by the end of the next day, Thursday evening, so we could pick up our resupply boxes once the Sula Country Store opened on Friday morning.

Maybe it was because of our laid back approach or maybe the terrain was just easier, but the hiking was fairly fast, with ample signage and much of it on double track, jeep roads. Later that afternoon we had a short, steep climb up to a pass whose view on the other side was of a bowl of bare, craggy mountains, all sweeping down into trees, fields and water sources. We were concerned as we looked out into the bowl and saw a heavy haze sitting over it, like a wildfire was nearby. I wondered if the possibility of wildfires would ever stop chasing us up the trail.

After we made our way down into the bowl, it was a bit more challenging than we expected, with lots of small elevation changes and false summits over faint tread, which oftentimes led us over clumpy grass. We felt worn down, having covered almost thirty-four miles, and at 8:00pm, we heard a voice from off the side of the trail interject into our conversation.

"Optimist and Stopwatch!" Wired yelled from inside her tent.

While we still had another half hour of daylight to hike, it didn't take long for us to decide to stay with Wired that evening. We liked her company and we could tell she wanted us to camp together, given that she'd already scouted out a campsite for us. Wired had told us multiple times over the course of the last few days that she didn't like camping alone, even though she knew it was inevitable on the CDT. I couldn't fault her for it, knowing that I'd never camped alone and never planned on doing so.

It was too chilly of an evening to sit outside, so we all lay in our sleeping bags in our respective tents, conversing through the thin tent walls, and all agreed we'd push to reach town the next day.

Wired was up first, her alarm going off in the dark, and I turned over and listened to the rustle of her gear as she packed up, like the snooze of an alarm. She normally took an hour to get ready, while we needed about twenty minutes.

It was a cold morning, cold enough to start with gloves on, and the skies had cleared from the haze of the evening before as we walked on the inside edge of the bowl over a trail comprised of loose rock. The trail eventually took us over the lip of the bowl, only to drop down a few thousand feet into the 5,000' range, an elevation we hadn't seen since New Mexico. Wired hiked with us for much of the morning as we dropped in elevation, the scenery changing dramatically. We went from exposed, dry conditions down to a damp, humid, weed-choked trail that needed serious maintenance. Much of our clothing was damp from walking through so much brush, and we crossed over several wide creeks of rushing water.

The trail then climbed shortly, bringing us out of the wet, thick brush for a brief moment, and we came to a flat overlook. It was eight miles into the day and Matt and I hadn't eaten more than a Luna bar, so we were ready for breakfast. Wired was much more successful at eating while she walked so we decided to part ways as she continued hiking alone. We gave hugs goodbye, knowing this was probably the last time we'd see each other. She planned on going into Darby, a different town from us, and was taking different zero days in the upcoming weeks, while we still needed to make up some time to return to Colorado. It was difficult and sad to say goodbye to another trail friend.

After pumping ourselves full of calories, we headed downhill yet again, into even thicker brush that towered above our heads and blocked much of our view of the trail. The real challenge of the day, which we could tell would be difficult by the looks of the maps, was the middle nine miles of the day. In looking at the maps the night before, we saw that the trail rode the Divide, which in itself was a challenge. In this particular section, riding the Divide was all the more challenging because it attacked the hills "AT style," as we called it. The Appalachian Trail is known for being hard because the trail goes right up and over the mountains, as opposed to using switchbacks to gain or lose elevation, just as the PCT does. This section of the CDT went straight up and straight down over every hump in the Divide, without a forgiving switchback in sight. To add to the difficulty, it had terrible footing that oftentimes disappeared or took us over faint, cross-country tread on lumpy grass or rooted footing. It was the old-school way of hiking and it kicked our butts.

At that point, getting to town wasn't entirely a given, so I was a little worried about slowing down so much, but I had faith that we'd get through the section and somehow make up the time later in the day.

I hoped and the trail gods didn't let me down. The last six miles of the day were on smooth dirt roads and we made up time jogging the flat and downhill sections of the road, arriving at the highway junction to town at 6:15pm.

An hour after reaching the road, a woman driving a large SUV pulled over. She had two dogs and two kids in the car, and was quick to offer us not only a ride, but also their uneaten KFC food. Since Matt was still strict vegan and since I was only practicing vegetarian, I gladly took anything they were willing to offer and shoveled in a biscuit before I even buckled in.

It was a twenty-mile ride to the Sula Country Store and Resort, nothing more than a store, a gas station, and some cabins and campsites just off the highway, and when we arrived, it was all closed up. Still, there were campsites and bathrooms so we thanked our ride and said goodbye as I stood in the store's parking lot with a box of buttery biscuits, mashed potatoes, macaroni and cheese, and a bag of chips.

We set up our tent in one of the flat patches of dirt as the sun went down and as ominous clouds rolled in, with thunder and lightning nearby. The best part about the "resort" was the free, scolding hot shower in the bathroom. As long as I had a hot shower, I didn't care about a bed, so I stood in that shower for twenty minutes, letting all the previous days' efforts roll off me with the hot water and pink, floral-scented hand soap.

Without the electricity of a hotel room in town, we went to sleep in our tent at a normal time, having no trouble falling asleep after three days in a row of thirty-plus mile hiking days.

8
Optimist

I woke up early with hopes of a better mood to start the new day at the Sula Country Store. I'd gone to bed sort of a grump. I blamed it on the long, hard day capped off by uncertainty regarding our camp spot, along with my lack of special food for dinner. While I had no qualms with Julie dropping the vegan diet on the trail while I maintained it, after a challenging day, it took some extra self-control to be in a good mood as she ate macaroni and cheese, biscuits, mashed potatoes, and cheesy potato chips, while I ate our remaining dehydrated refried beans out of a peanut butter jar.

I also woke up early knowing we hadn't paid for our campsite. I'd tried to call the night before but our phone kept cutting out so we had picked a camp spot at the little campground with a plan to pay the next morning. Thankfully, I'd talked to someone at the campground and obtained the code for the showers so we were able to get cleaned up before bed.

When I walked into the store a little after 7:00am, still a little sleepy, I told the woman our story and our names so we could pick up our resupply boxes. She immediately lit up and said she knew our names and that her cook at the restaurant, Lori, followed our blog. I went over and met Lori and she seemed quite excited to meet me. I quickly perked up, checked out the breakfast menu, and told her we'd be back shortly for breakfast.

I hurried down to Julie at the campground; we quickly packed up our stuff and were up at the restaurant for food within fifteen minutes. Lori was ready to cook and ready for trail stories. She made us feel special and it was refreshing to feel human connection and appreciation for what we were doing. As Lori asked about our trip and talked about following our adventure online, I could fully appreciate how and why Wired spent so much time and energy keeping up her blog.

Julie ordered pancakes, eggs, and hash browns. However, there was nothing vegan on the menu for me. Lori was quick with solutions though and offered to cook me up some hash browns with all the vegetables she had on hand, cooked on the griddle with vegetable oil. I was so appreciative as I'd had hardly any hot restaurant food over the course of over 2,000 miles of walking. Midway through my first heaping plate I ordered another.

We hitched a ride back to the trailhead and just as we were preparing to head back into the woods, a couple with a big trailer pulled over and got out to chat. They were fellow travelers and they were quick to share snacks and beverages with us while we chatted. However, when the topic turned to grizzly bears, they were flabbergasted to learn that we didn't carry a gun. The woman, while otherwise very complimentary of us and our lifestyle, said we were "downright stupid" for not carrying a gun. No matter how much we attempted to explain our position or how much we tried to casually deflect her well-intended advice, she was clear that she felt that in bear country, one needed to be packing more than bear spray.

At noon we were back on the trail, a good start time for us, especially given all our conversations that morning. Our packs were heavy with 162 miles' worth of food but we were reasonably refreshed after our Sula stop. We knew that at this point in the trail we were likely ahead of almost all the other northbound hikers on the trail except for a few random travelers that were moving really fast or had started really early. Otherwise, the pack was behind us.

It was a little strange knowing there was no one to catch and that if we wanted to think in terms of others on the trail relative to us, it was more a matter of whether others would catch us. While in the larger picture of our hike, we didn't mind one way or the other if people were faster or slower than us, it was fun to think of our position relative to others as a game. We knew Joe and Raisins had been trailing us by anywhere from two to four days ever since we'd jumped up in Colorado due to the fires, and while we looked forward to seeing them again, we also liked hiking fast enough that they had a difficult time catching us.

The trail was thankfully quite flat heading out of the pass to start our day. We were surrounded by pine trees but were not shaded by them. We were hiking on trails that in wintertime were most likely used for cross-country skiing, and as a result, the paths were wider, and since the trees seemed to be a bit young, they weren't high enough to shade us from the afternoon sun.

The sun didn't stay out for long though as threatening clouds moved in. The threat of afternoon storms was still nearly a daily occurrence and as the trail made its way from tree-lined paths to a burned out section that exposed us to greater wrath from the weather, we felt the surge of intensity and anxiety that lightning storms carried with them.

The rains eventually came but we saw little advantage in stopping as we were not well covered by the dead, burnt trees. We put on our rain gear and just kept walking. As the winds picked up we realized that possibly more dangerous, but not as obviously so, was the serious likelihood of dead trees being blown over and landing on us. The trees were the tall, skinny type with few branches. They were obviously dead and though many weren't down on the ground yet, it was apparent that it wouldn't take much to take them down. As the winds howled, we began to hear falling trees come crashing down.

We eventually made it through the scary section, pushing the pace throughout, as the rains and wind gradually died down. We also started getting a little higher up into the mountains as we approached the Anaconda-Pintler Wilderness. We'd heard about the Pintlers from numerous southbounders as they told us the section was one of their favorites of their entire trip.

After hiking through more burn sections the next morning, we headed into some denser forest and we continued climbing. Over the next couple of days the scenery changed dramatically and the hiking was characterized by repeated climbs and descents of anywhere from 800' to 1,800'. It looked somewhat daunting on paper but the trails were well-maintained and graded so it was actually pleasant hiking and the views were very rewarding.

Thus far, Montana and Idaho had been way more exposed than we'd imagined. We figured we'd be in deep mountain forests much of the time and we now totally understood why Alex had told us about getting sun burnt while walking much of Montana. Somehow, he'd managed to avoid the afternoon storms though.

The Pintlers, while still high in elevation, were forested, and the Divide was no longer simply the top of rolling, treeless hills. Instead, the terrain was now highlighted with huge slabs of rock jutting up into the sky with colorful rock patterns decorating the massive rock walls. The trail climbed up and over these mountains, cutting through passes to the other side, rather than attempting to stay up high on the Divide the entire time. Upon descending from passes we'd find ourselves in deep, dark, luscious valleys with huge old growth trees. Water was abundant and we knew wildlife must be just as abundant.

The next morning was a typical day on the trail. We woke up with the sun on day eighty, packed up our stuff, and were walking within twenty-five minutes as we so often did. We were a fine-tuned machine together. The majority of the time there wasn't even conversation, but we both knew how to live this life and function well together, no words required. Julie had already been back on the trail for over a month and she seemed like a new hiker. No longer was I worried about her complaining, whining, or quitting the trail. She seemed to be genuinely enjoying herself given the circumstances.

We did an early climb and descent that morning before meeting a couple and their dog camped down by a lake. They were surprised to see us so early in the morning. After asking us about our trip and our mileage, the man said that they were taking their time and were focused on enjoying the outdoors. He said it in a manner that implied that somehow we must not be enjoying the outdoors due to how fast we were hiking. For a long time, these types of comments would get under our skin because so often, when people learned about our hiking style, they assumed many negative things about how it must be to hike like we did. Many would assume that we didn't appreciate nature because we covered so many miles, or that it must be drudgery to walk all day. There were many variations, but no matter what we'd say, there always seemed to be people that thought we were weren't doing it correctly.

After many thousands of miles, we were smiling in the face of criticism because we knew we enjoyed our version of the trail life, regardless of what others may have thought about it. While I could understand the critic's point of view, I also knew my experiences. We smiled now because we felt confident that much of the "enjoying it" part of hiking was a matter of perspective and attitude, and we believed that we could enjoy ourselves and still hike thirty miles per day.

That morning we proceeded to climb a long steady path up to Cutaway Pass. As we neared the top I looked back and could see magnificent rock formations reaching up to the sky. The morning sun was shining on them just right, illuminating them in a splendid manner. We stopped there at the pass and enjoyed an extra long breakfast and soaked it all in.

The passes continued as we hiked through the late morning until we reached an area called Goat Flats. It was here that one of the main alternate routes split from the Bear Creek route we were following. The alternate headed in a more direct route northeast toward the town of Anaconda, while our route stayed up in the mountains, making its way farther east and around the city of Butte before heading north again. The cutoff route knocked off nearly ninety miles compared to our route, so while we were ahead of the main pack, we figured there was a good chance that by the time we reached Helena a week to the north, we may be with hikers again or even chasing some of our friends.

After a section of route-finding and the frustration that inevitably came with it, we reached a meadow. Amazingly, we had a signal with our iPad. I called my mom, and for the first time on this trip Julie and I could both hear genuine sadness in her voice. She stressed tremendously while we were out on the trail, and understandably so. The trail was a foreign world to her and when she imagined our outdoor life, she imagined all the things she feared.

At the same time, now eighty-one days into our adventure, we were starting to feel the urge to get back to the regular world. While we looked forward to fresh food and showers again, we mostly missed the regular contact with our family and friends. My younger brother had been going through major life events with graduating college, moving to a new city, finding a new job, all the while getting more serious with his girlfriend. As the big brother, I knew I was missing out, wanting to be there to share in these big life events.

We finally began a long descent out of the Pintlers and not at all too soon as the afternoon storms rolled in again. This time though, we were deep down in the trees which provided us with a sense of security from the wind and the lightning. We hiked on under the canopy of large, sturdy old trees until we reached a dirt road. From there it was another few miles down to an actual paved road to connect us with a wildlife refuge area.

We had known from looking ahead at our maps that we may have some trouble with private land issues if we went too far for the day so at 8:00pm, after seeing multiple private driveways and seeing some houses and ranches in both directions, we found a spot tucked off the road, back in some trees just before a sign that said, "Leaving Public Lands."

From our camp spot we could see houses and could hear their dogs barking. We set up our tent quietly, quickly ate some food, and snuck into our tent. We felt like stealth campers doing something illegal, even though we'd double-checked the signs to be sure we were on public land. We felt a bit safer knowing our tent was at least an olive green color and relatively camouflaged back in the trees.

The next morning, August 12th, we took off early to leave our camp spot that felt slightly like camping in someone's backyard, and we quickly hit the road.

The skies were clear and it was really cold. We had on all our jackets, our hats, and our gloves. My hands were still cold holding my poles that morning, even with both my fleece gloves and my glove shells. We followed a highway for a couple miles before heading onto dirt roads again and back to public lands. We were happy to have stopped early the night before because we would have had to hike well into the night to get to any place resembling safe, public camping lands again.

We took a break shortly after 9:00am and though the sun was shining, we were still freezing. However, within the next couple hours, the sun got higher overhead and we switched from freezing to sweating. The temperature swings were amazing in Montana at this time of year.

We were back to exposed land again with plenty of cows present. We walked through herd after herd of cattle and as we came upon a flowing stream, we startled a few cows. They were drinking and pooping right next to the spot we were looking to drink from. At this point, we were well accustomed to the presence of cattle and though we weren't too keen on drinking from these types of sources, we'd done so without consequence and were quick to dip our bottles.

We were following old dirt roads that seemed to be rarely used by motorized vehicles and somehow, we still managed to get lost. We were over a half-mile past a supposed turn when we realized it and in looking back at our maps, we realized that the turn was a right, taken sharply off the road at no particular good junction with no particular path. The route was literally just a turn off the road across open land with no trail. We did our best to find our way back but managed to do so by sticking to the dirt road until we reunited a little ways up the trail.

From there the path made its way back into trees and we began a long climb; 2,200' later we were cresting the last of the hills. We hopped on some old mountain jeep roads and again managed to get twisted around. We turned too soon this time and were running down a hill only to turn around and head back up. It was simply that kind of day and we did our best to keep our cool, and to keep moving.

Afternoon storms rolled in to add to the tension. Thankfully though, the trail became much easier to navigate for the remainder of the day and our focus, combined with the storms, meant that we got in good mileage for the day. When it was raining and cold, there was rarely a good place to stop to rest because we would inevitably get cold. So we walked all afternoon. The rains cleared up in the early evening, we hiked until nearly dark, and we eventually stopped in a patch of trees overlooking a large valley. We nestled in and even got a cell signal that night as we were nearing I-15 yet again.

The next morning was again freezing cold. We dropped down from the mountains early and were on dirt roads heading toward the highway. One problem with all this road walking surrounded by private land was bathroom breaks. Often, when the urge to poop hit me, it wouldn't wait long and on this morning, despite frozen hands and nowhere to go, I quickly made a hole just off the side of the road and left my remains under a large rock. As we were hurrying off we saw a huge machine which we quickly determined to be a machine to grade mountain back roads. I hoped he wasn't going too far off the road because if so, he was bound to unearth an unpleasant surprise.

We were within thirty-seven miles of the road down to Homestake Lodge, a private cabin that accepted hiker packages, and a place we'd sent a resupply box. We'd hiked over thirty miles a day every day since leaving Sula and we were once again in a nice groove. Thirties were now totally normal and despite some tiring times earlier in Montana, we were cruising once again.

After we finished our morning of road walking we hit trail again shortly before lunchtime. The road ended at a trailhead where we were supposed to find water shortly thereafter. The source was bone dry. This would prove to be a theme throughout the day. However, it was apparent that the trail we were hiking was fairly new. It was easy to find and easy to follow. It also was built in a more modern way such that it didn't simply go up and over the tops of mountains but instead was carved into the sides of the mountains so there was much less elevation gain and loss. This made for faster and more pleasant walking, even if there wasn't much water.

As we hiked into the late afternoon and early evening Julie and I began a conversation that ended with some real insights into our relationship. It centered around her views of thru-hiking and why she'd struggled so much. As she talked through her feelings, which ran the gamut including moments of tears, followed by moments of insight, I realized how fortunate I was to be with such a thoughtful and self-honest woman. She was able to admit her shortcomings while continually thinking about how to improve.

As we talked through her thoughts, we realized how well we actually were complementing each other and how well we worked as a hiking unit. While I tended toward the overly optimistic, to the point of often being unrealistic, she would tend toward the realistic with a dash of pessimism, often seeing problems in her way and threatening the happiness of her day. We were both gradually coming to some sort of middle where we helped each other be more effective. We helped each other be better people and better hikers. I had gradually become more of a realist with a tendency towards optimism while she had gradually moved towards more of a realistic view of the world while still keeping us grounded. Together, we admitted that we were a dynamite hiking team.

We slept well that night and snuggled up in our little one-person tent. We were three miles from the cutoff to the Homestake Lodge where the next morning, I would leave my pack's belongings and go for a three mile run down the mountain in search of our next resupply box.

9
Stopwatch

Sending a resupply box to Homestake Lodge seemed like a good idea back in mid-March when we were sitting in Matt's parents' house in Ohio, choosing our resupply points. It was just three miles off-trail, an itty-bitty amount in a car, but now that we were standing at the junction of the forest road that led to the lodge, it seemed like a poor decision.

It was silly for both of us to carry our packs to the lodge and take the hour each way to walk it, so Matt, being the selfless, character-of-gold person that he was and still is, volunteered to run to the lodge with an empty pack. I wasn't going to argue with him; I'd be slower if I made the trip and I had been feeling a little sluggish.

As Matt made his way to the lodge, I set up our tent off the side of the road, crawled in, and tried to sleep. As I lay there, I had yesterday's conversation with Matt on my mind.

Yesterday gave me insight as to why I often felt like a failure on trails. Matt was so damn successful at thru-hiking, staying positive in the face of challenges, his iron resolve to complete a task never wavering and therefore never leading to quitting. Even if I was the most successful person out there at thru-hiking, which for all I knew I was since we didn't really know many other hikers, I was still second-best to Matt. After a while, that grated on me. It was hard to continually win second place. I imagined it was hard for his two younger siblings to grow up after a person that not only gave every ounce of effort in every attempt, no matter how big or small, from doing the dishes to running a cross-country race, but who was also highly successful in so many facets, like going to state championships for running and running on a Division I university team. I simply couldn't stack up.

It was a relief the night before when the conversation changed from an unproductive one, discussing my penchant for being negative, to a positive one that tried to explore why I often felt like a failure. I finally hit the mark when I realized that all along, I'd been comparing myself to Matt and was nearly destined to fail as a result. It was difficult to simply turn off that comparison though, even if I knew it was unhealthy, because he was by my side 24/7, like a full-length mirror being carried alongside myself. I couldn't help but look at it and see my faults.

Once we both hashed through all those mixed-up feelings of admiration and resentment for all the very same reasons, the air was clear and I felt a burden lifted. It felt like the final weight that had been holding me down and I was truly set free of negative thoughts.

After laying there for about forty-five minutes, deep in thought, I heard the crunch of feet on the dirt road and thought, "There's no way that can be him already."

It was Matt, proud of his quick turnaround, having timed it on his watch, and he brought with him an entire batch of new food, along with a freshly baked chocolate chip scone from the owner of the lodge. I ate the scone as I packed up my food, its chocolate chips beginning to melt in the morning sun that penetrated through the trees.

After packing up we continued on, stopping at the next junction with I-90 to check email and confirm that our friend Zippers would meet us in Helena on Friday night at 8:00pm. It was Wednesday morning and we had 105 miles to Helena, so nearly three full days. It was a tall order but it was a rare evening that worked for Zippers and we really wanted to spend time with her and Amy again.

There was also a chance we would finally reunite with Joe and Raisins again. They were a few days behind us but planned on taking the "Anaconda Route," as it was known, an alternate route that cut off about ninety miles by taking hikers on a more direct route into Helena.

Motivation to reach Helena was high.

While it seems now that we were constantly pushing for the next town up the trail, at the time it was more like self-imposed motivation to keep making forward progress. Knowing we had a deadline no longer stressed me out; deadlines actually added to the excitement for each day's miles. Also, we approached any mileage pushes with the mindset that we would put in a solid, full day's effort each day until one day out from a town, at which point we'd really turn on the burners and focus on the goal at hand. I found myself enjoying each and every day on the trail, while at the same time having an enticing carrot dangling in front of me, continually leading me to the next town.

The first thirteen miles after the lodge were easy, all over smooth dirt roads with nice grades up and down a roller coaster of hills. Our only concern was the rising temperature as we walked completely exposed to the sun, with few trees lining the trail and even fewer offering shade. We pushed through the miles without taking much of a break, knowing we needed to get through the road before it really heated up, and because we needed water.

We finally made it to Big Pipestone Creek, a rushing creek fed by a lake upstream that was a popular recreation spot. Fortunately, it was water that we greatly needed, yet unfortunately it was warm, which was fairly unsatisfying and even a tad gross. Something about drinking warm water from a lake that I knew people recreated in was disgusting to me, but I had no choice but to drink it. Our options had been limited all morning and didn't look much better for the afternoon.

The heat continued to rise. People in town had told us that these were some of the hottest days in Montana, in the nineties, with an extremely high risk of fires. We just couldn't seem to get away from fires.

Later that day we stopped at our next water source, a low-flowing creek that was barely more than a trickle. It was one of the few water sources for the day, which was to become the trend over those few days, causing many more moments of thirst than we had anticipated.

The miles went fast that evening and soon we were faced with a predicament. We were closing in on crossing I-15, a major highway, and as we headed downhill to the trailhead, we saw building lights fairly close to us. We wanted to hike into the night but upon seeing the lights getting closer and fearing being on private property both before and after I-15, we chose to stop just before dark.

Seventy-eight miles still stood between us and Helena, with just two days to go.

Once we started the next morning, we saw that we had camped within about a half-mile of houses, a little too close for comfort. It was a cold morning, considering the heat from the day before, and we started with all our layers on as we made our way down a dirt road to the I-15 crossing, yet another access point to the town of Butte. Looking at the maps showed that we literally circled nearly all of Butte; it was obvious as to why people took the Anaconda cutoff.

Our main focus of the day was to cover at least forty miles. Other than that, the only other aspect that mattered was getting water, of which there wasn't much because much of the trail was up on the Divide. Later in the afternoon, after passing a water tank surrounded by cows, we walked a nicely graded dirt road on top of the Divide, which eventually turned to a rocky, rutted, steep mess. Our pace slowed down and I started getting nervous about making our deadline.

As dusk was fading into night, we dined on refried beans and corn chips yet again, and put on our wind jackets and wind pants. The temperatures dropped significantly once the sun went down and we started up again with our headlamps, willing to walk through the night if that's what it took. At that point, the people who took the Anaconda route now shared our same route again, so we knew Raisins and Joe were somewhere ahead of us. We contemplated hiking until we reached them, but not knowing exactly where that was, especially in the dark, was reason enough to scratch that plan.

Night hiking has never been my favorite task and that night confirmed it, taking us through dense forests, the trail choked by trees and overgrowth. Walking with a headlamp caused tunnel vision and I didn't like that I had no idea what my surroundings looked like or what creatures could be in those surroundings. We walked until 11:30pm, when we reached forty miles. It was a mini goal of ours to hike a forty mile-plus day in each state and that day completed the feat.

We started hiking well before daylight and again started with headlamps. I never minded hiking in the morning with headlamps because there was always the impending sunrise. It was much more hopeful for me to walk with a gradual lightening of the sky versus sunset or complete darkness.

Though we still had thirty-eight miles before town, we were in good spirits. We knew we'd see Zippers that evening and most likely Raisins and Joe. We wondered what they looked like after eighty-five days, knowing time had changed our physical appearance too.

The miles went forgivingly fast that day, enhanced by a section of new tread in the Bison Mountain Loop, which eventually popped out onto a dirt road. When we hit the road, we'd hiked twenty miles. It was 2:00pm and we needed to hike exactly three miles an hour for the next six hours to make it in time. It was doable, but still concerning. The next six miles were on such a well-graded downhill that we ran most of the miles, making up over twenty minutes of time. We would have had no problem making it in time had we stayed on the road, but shortly after getting water at Telegraph Creek, we took a sharp right turn onto a steep, weed-choked trail. I was annoyed that all the time we'd made up would be spent on the unappealing section of trail, but I tried to stay positive, knowing Matt and I both needed to be on top of our game if we were going to make it to Helena on time.

"Be a hero, Julie, be a hero," still ran through my mind, even if that hero briefly quit in the middle of Colorado.

The unpleasant trail eventually leveled out and brought us to another dirt road which seemed to be up on a high plateau, looking out into a valley below. Raisins and Joe's footprints were in the dirt ahead of us; their shoe prints were a welcomed sight after not seeing them since early on in New Mexico.

With about three miles to go, we were cutting it close when we ran into a few mountain bikers going the opposite way. To us, mountain bikers were a good sign, meaning the trails must be decent enough for mountain bikes, so we continued to run the smooth downhills and even made up some time. As we ran the last quarter mile to MacDonald Pass, the road into Helena, we could see an empty parking lot, but we kept running anyway and made it to the pass at 8:00pm on the dot. We were disappointed to see that Zippers wasn't there, but we were so proud to have made it at the exact moment we had promised.

With three percent of the battery remaining on the iPad, we checked our email and saw that Zippers wrote that she may be up to ninety minutes late! Without even a second thought, we stuck out our thumbs for a hitch into town.

It took twenty minutes of standing off the side of the road, but eventually a new BMW pulled up beside us.

"No way," I thought to myself.

I thought it was a joke and that the driver would pull away as we neared the car, but when we approached the car, the passenger window rolled down and we saw a young guy inside with a can of Red Bull in his hand and techno music pumping through the speakers. It was a unique hitch to Helena, to say the least.

Once in town we booked a room at the hiker-friendly motel, where Zippers and Amy and their two dogs showed up shortly thereafter. As we walked to our motel rooms, we heard Raisins' voice from the staircase to our left.

"Optimist and Stopwatch!"

"Raisins!"

We barely recognized him. He was wearing the same long-sleeve technical shirt that started out as white and which was now off-white, and the same navy blue running shorts that he had the first day. He looked about twenty pounds lighter and much more tired and dirty. Being Korean, he already had a naturally light tan, but having been in the sun for the last two months, his skin was much darker, especially on his face and calves.

"Aww, come here guys," Raisins said. We exchanged hugs and stood there talking in the parking lot for the next ten minutes, getting the quick update on the last eighty days of hiking. While we could have talked for hours with Raisins, we knew we were hiking out with him and Joe the next afternoon and would therefore have plenty of time ahead of us to chat. Zippers and Amy had driven almost two hours to come visit us and they had food, so we assured Raisins we'd see him in the morning and headed up to our room with Zippers and Amy to spend the evening with them.

As we had hoped, Zippers' culinary finesse exceeded expectations and she laid out another spread of vegan food, even better than the first time at Old Faithful. We didn't even shower before eating because we were so hungry.

It was nearly midnight by the time we cut off the flow of conversation. We'd been up before dawn, had hiked thirty-eight miles, and knew we'd have to work to keep pace with Joe and Raisins the next day, so we said goodnight with a long list of to-dos for the next day, including a load of laundry, a visit to both the post office and the grocery store, and finally a hike out with everyone.

10
Optimist

Helena was town overload. It was so good, with so many hiker delicacies to offer us, that we simply didn't have enough time to adequately experience them all. We did our best to balance everything but over-stimulation was tough to counter after months in the woods.

First, we had our good friends Zippers and Amy meeting us again. With the twisting and turning route of the CDT through Montana, we were not only able to see them in Yellowstone, a little over an hour's drive from their home, but yet again 500 trail miles later in Helena, a two hour drive for them. They once again came with an amazing spread, Zippers knowing exactly what any thru-hiker would want.

Next, we had Raisins and Joe. We hadn't seen them since day two in New Mexico though we'd been in touch throughout the trail, sending Facebook messages, emails, and voicemails along the way. They'd been leaving notes on the trail in front of us the last thirty miles before Helena, as they'd finally caught and passed us. We were excited to see them and there was an unsaid commitment that the four of us would be hiking out of Helena together.

Helena was also important because it was our first real town stop in a few hundred miles. Our previous two resupply points had been a lodge and a country store, and while both got us resupplied, neither had all the amenities of a town.

We woke early with a long to-do list. We had laundry to do, family to check in with, the website to update, food to pick up at the post office, and packs to get packed for the next section. On top of that, we had all been closely monitoring fire conditions to our north in the Bob Marshall Wilderness. There had been various fires reported over the past few weeks and Helena was our last reliable source for obtaining information. Cell service outside of town was unreliable and we wouldn't be going through another town until we'd passed through the Bob.

We all got to work, Julie going with the other four to the outfitter and post office, while I worked on getting our gear ready, and catching up with family back home. They were gone for way longer than expected, but they came back with loads of packages from the post office. We had letters and cards from friends, along with the biggest care package we'd ever received. Our friends Scott and Anna went above and beyond on their search for vegan treats. Along with all the goodies, Anna had attached funny notes to each item, explaining why they'd chosen each particular item; the vegan soy jerky had to be my favorite.

It'd been a long time since we'd seen Raisins and Joe and as we rode back to the trail, a few immediate observations presented themselves. One, they were both noticeably thinner and stronger looking. They had both looked a little soft at the start of the trail but after nearly three months on the trail they were thin, hiking machines with tans and sinewy legs. They'd also spent a lot of time together. While they hadn't hiked the entire trail together, they were generally around each other most of the way and had spent more than half of their nights camped together. It was largely a matter of inevitability as they both were fast hikers that didn't take much time off. There aren't many like them and when two rare, fast hikers like them start on the same day, with the same agenda, it's likely they are around each other quite a bit.

It showed instantaneously that they had spent a lot of time together. They knew how to push each other's buttons, getting the other riled up with one little side comment or one seemingly innocuous statement that would knowingly put the other on the defensive. It was funny to see and it provided a glimpse of what was to come as we headed back to the trail together, a sight in itself with six of us, two dogs, and all our gear, packed into a little Subaru.

Amy and Zippers hiked the first five miles out from the pass with us. The first few miles were some slightly uninspiring dirt road miles back to the mountains but we had conversation and eventually some nice views as we got higher up from the pass. When we got to the trail we had steady single track with only a little route-finding. It felt rewarding to share our little CDT world with someone else, especially when, near their planned turnaround point, the water source that was supposed to be there was dry. Raisins, Joe, Julie, and I all smiled as this was typical of our experience. Zippers, having hiked the water-plentiful AT said, "No way, not hiking the CDT!"

They gave us their remaining water since they only had five miles back to their car. We hugged and thanked them for all their amazing trail magic and their friendship, and then headed north on the trail, reunited with the guys we had begun this crazy adventure with nearly three months prior.

The terrain from Helena to our next resupply point at Benchmark Ranch wasn't overly memorable to me. It's not to say it wasn't pretty and that it wasn't worth hiking, but it doesn't largely jump out in my mind. The temperatures started to tame a bit from the ninety degree days we'd been experiencing. We spent much of our time up high on the Divide, exposed to the sun and the wind. The ground was often rocky and dry and we had plenty of moments with panoramic views of the vast, remote Montana wilderness.

However amazing this scenery was, this setting had been the backdrop of our day-to-day lives for what felt like significantly longer than eighty-six days, and while we knew it was special, having the camaraderie and friendship with Joe and Raisins again was the most memorable feature.

We talked nonstop that first day back with them out of Helena. We talked about New Mexico and the routes they took that differed from ours. We talked about drinking from cow tanks and other nasty water sources. We talked about Colorado and its tough climbs. We talked about fires and solving the many logistical problems we'd all encountered.

We also talked about people. With all of us starting so late and moving so quickly, between the four of us, we'd met just about every single hiker on the trail for the year, having passed them at some point. We talked about the people we'd hiked with and spent time with, some of which we overlapped with them, and others we had only heard about. Given the small CDT trail community, we were all essentially aware of each other, and the four of us gossiped about who was doing what and how they were doing it.

We hiked until dark that night and nearly every night after that as we all continued north up the trail together. There was a sense of commitment to each other and though we didn't explicitly say it, we all seemed committed to finishing the trail together.

The challenges associated with hiking together started presenting themselves within those first couple days of hiking together. There we were, four accomplished and generally solo hikers – I count Julie and me as one because we always travel together and make decisions as one. We had all figured out our own ways of making our way north over the past few months and we had all developed our trail routines over our many months and years on the trail.

It was also apparent that everyone was making an effort to work together and to adapt to working together as a unit. The mileage aspect of the group hike was probably the easiest because we were all pretty accustomed to walking at least thirty miles per day. I think Joe and Raisins could have done a bit more if they'd wanted to, but they were always fine with stopping after thirty to thirty-five miles each day. Plus, Joe had been struggling with fairly severe knee pain throughout the trail which limited him from really cranking out miles as he often liked to do.

In general, Raisins would stick with us and walk our slower pace. Joe would often hike with us, talking away for hours, but sometimes he'd just take off and walk at a pace that I don't think I could have maintained had I been trying my hardest. He'd be gone for awhile and then we'd stroll past him as he was taking a break. Some days he'd lag behind and be taking pictures or videos, but we all generally stuck together and camped together. They would usually cowboy camp each night or sleep under their little tarps if there was a chance of rain, while we'd sleep in our one-person tent each night.

Navigating was a compromising effort as we each had developed our own methods of staying found on the trail. I continually kept my GPS around my neck and would check it every mile or two to make sure we were staying on track. At times we'd disagree and even go in slightly different directions but we'd always meet up again.

On our third day out from Helena we came upon Joe, taking a break off the side of the trail in the shade. He was excited to see us and to pass along the news that he'd just been talking with Beacon.

We'd last seen Beacon at the motel in Lima and apparently he'd jumped ahead. We all hurried along to catch up with him. Once we caught him we spent the next half hour listening to his stories as we made our way along the Divide.

The afternoon was filled with some tough climbing and we eventually said goodbye to Beacon. We stuck with our usual routine of hiking until dark and that night we were rewarded with a unique spot on top of a mountain that had been burned long ago. The burn left us with no tree cover, and on that clear night we were treated to a full moon and countless stars. It was cold and windy but we managed to find a little dip in the mountain top where we all camped together for the evening.

We were now well on our way to Canada, and for Joe and Raisins, the end of their journey was drawing near. After our upcoming resupply at the remote Benchmark Ranch location just over a day to our north, we then only had the park town of East Glacier remaining between us and the Canadian border. We could feel their excitement. We could also sense some of their concerns.

One very real and understandable worry they had was that they'd made it so far and yet something like a fire or sickness could so quickly derail their thru-hike. They'd narrowly escaped the fires in Colorado and we knew that fires in the Bob Marshall Wilderness to our north were a real possibility. We kept pushing forward though with the excitement of Canada getting closer each hour.

While waterless stretches had again become somewhat of an issue, we learned that Joe had a much bigger concern. He was legitimately fearful of grizzly bears. I don't blame him, we all had this fear, but Joe's fear impacted his behavior more than we'd imagined it would. With all the miles Joe and Raisins had hiked, they definitely had their share of crazy black bear stories – think cowboy camping and being woken up in the middle of the night by a black bear sniffing your face, only to lift your head and smack your forehead on the bear's lower jawbone, hearing its teeth smack together from the impact! Yet on our last full day before Benchmark, we came upon Joe sitting on the side of the trail waiting for us. He had a fearful look on his face and quickly proceeded to tell us about the grizzly bear he had just seen on the upcoming hillside. From then on we all stuck together. We walked as a group and Joe talked all day. He may have talked regardless of bears, but he was making sure we wouldn't be surprising any grizzlies along the way.

By the end of day eighty-nine, after another thirty-four mile day with the guys, we called it a day. We were three miles out from the trailhead to Benchmark Ranch, where we planned to pick up our next resupply box. This resupply was a unique one because it involved sending our resupply boxes to a couple that owned a ranch near the Bob Marshall Wilderness boundary. There usually wasn't anyone at the ranch so hikers would send their food to the couple's city address and then the couple would occasionally bring the food out to the ranch, leaving it in bear proof boxes for hikers to pick up on the honor system. We were a little concerned with the set up because we were putting a lot of faith in these people. But it was the way everyone seemed to do it, and there were very few options in this remote part of Montana.

We'd done all we were told to do, including sending our twenty-five dollar check to the couple for their service, along with an email and phone message telling them when we planned on arriving. Rocket Cop and Jessica had sent our resupply package as planned and we'd received our tracking number confirming receipt.

So on the morning of day ninety, Joe, Raisins, and I ran with empty packs down to the Ranch. It ended up being three miles from the trail, opposed to the one mile we all thought it was going to be, but we eventually found it. The Ranch was quiet and no one was there as we expected. We opened the big food box and began going through the packages. We found Raisin's resupply box and then we found Joe's. We saw food for our friends behind us, but our food wasn't there. We went through each box one by one. We looked all around the ranch for another box. Nothing.

We were in the middle of nowhere and we didn't have any food. Joe and Raisins were quick to offer some of their food, but as we quickly did the math, we realized that even if we went really fast up the trail, their food for two was not going to make it as food for four for four days. Plus, we were being rerouted around fires in the Bob so we had only vague ideas about what the trail ahead may be like.

We walked back to the trailhead, minds brainstorming on how to overcome what seemed to be one of the biggest curveballs the trail had thrown at us yet.

11
Stopwatch

After forty-five minutes of waiting at the trailhead, Matt came back alone, which I took as a bad sign. I was hoping he was alone simply because he was faster than the other two, but I felt an emptiness in my gut when I realized his pack was still empty.

"Is everything ok?" I asked.

"Well, our box wasn't there," Matt started, "but we have a solution, so pack up your stuff. We're going to Augusta."

"Oh no. What happened?" I asked.

"Just pack up quickly and I'll explain it while we walk. It's a few minutes to the parking lot from here," he said as he stuffed all his belongings into his pack.

As we hurried to the trailhead parking lot, Matt clued me in on the details. Our box was nowhere to be found but Joe's and Raisins' boxes were there, among lots of hikers' boxes. Not only did we not have food, but we also didn't have our maps or data book. There was no one at the ranch and no cell service to call anyone. On the three mile walk from the ranch back to the trailhead, a guy in his truck offered Matt, Joe, and Raisins a ride to the trailhead. Matt explained our dire situation to the truck driver, and it really was dire since the nearest town was thirty miles away, down a dirt road, from a dead-end trailhead which few people visited. After Matt told the truck driver our story the guy asked him, "So what are you going to do?"

"I guess I'm going to try to hitch a ride from this trailhead," Matt said.

In response, the guy lifted up his car keys in front of Matt and said, "My sons and I are going to be out for four days; just make sure the truck's back before then."

We reached the trailhead just as Matt finished the story and I met the truck owner, Dave. Joe and Raisins opted to join us for the ride to Augusta, not passing up the chance for town food, and after talking with Dave briefly, thanking him endlessly for such a random act of selfless kindness, we hopped in the truck and were on our way to town. It was quite possibly the quickest, easiest solution we'd ever had to such a logistical nightmare.

The thirty mile trip took ninety minutes to drive, much of it a slow-going, gravel road, with several tight turns. In town, all of us were quick to get food, groceries, and a full tank of gas. Joe got his pulled-pork sandwich that he'd been craving and talking about the last several days and Raisins and I finished off our sandwiches with a thick milkshake.

By the time we were driving back to the trailhead, the magic of driving and town excitement had worn off and we were ready to get back on the trail. This was a major derailment to our mileage by taking almost five hours out of our day to go to town. A mile before the trailhead, we spotted a hiker heading towards us on the road. It was Beacon. Matt slowed down and pulled up next to Beacon and calmly asked, "Want a ride?"

"What the hell?!?" Beacon blurted, confused to see all of us in a truck, with Matt as the driver. He hopped in the back between Raisins and I, Joe tossed him a bacon burger that he'd gotten to-go in town, and we told the story of our windfall while we drove back to the ranch to get Beacon's box.

Matt, Joe, and Beacon all went together to get Beacon's box while I hung back with Raisins. As we stood there waiting, Raisins sighed and quietly said to me, "I don't think his box is there either. I don't remember seeing his last name."

Sure enough, a few minutes later, all of them walked back empty-handed. There was a brief flash of selfishness on my part when I realized that we would have to go back to Augusta again, taking at least another three hours out of our hiking day. I figured we'd be lucky to get back on the trail at all that day. But, we had the ability to help Beacon out, and really, an obligation. There was no way we were going to accept such trail magic and not share it with another hiker who was in the exact same predicament we were in just hours prior. Matt didn't hesitate and said, "Well, it looks like we're going back to Augusta. Who's in?"

Raisins was quick to stick with us but Joe admitted he was worried about making it through without getting stopped by fires. We'd had a conversation with a ranger earlier that morning who confirmed that there were fires blocking the official trail and that we'd be required to take a detour. Upon hearing that, we were all glad we'd bought maps of the area but we were still worried that the fires would spread even farther. Joe was especially shaken and his existing fear of getting stopped by fires was that much greater. We dropped Joe back off at the trailhead and assured him we'd catch him as soon as possible.

In town, Beacon decided to stay in a hotel for the night so we dropped him off, filled up the gas tank yet again, and headed back to the trailhead. It was 6:00pm by the time we started hiking again and all we could do was laugh at the entire situation. I had to admit, I'd been dragging my feet the past couple of days, feeling very physically tired since our push to Helena, so maybe this was a sly way of the trail telling me to take a break. I gave up all anxieties over mileage and just kept on walking, and from what I could tell, so did Matt and Raisins.

I woke up on the ninety-first day on the trail to the sound of leaves crunching and twigs snapping. It sounded like something or someone had walked right by us, as we were camped about twenty feet off the trail. By the time I stuck my head outside of the tent, I didn't see anything in the dim, pre-dawn light. I was a little concerned about bears and our food, as we hadn't hung it that night and we were in the Bob Marshall Wilderness, an area with a high concentration of bears. Raisins wasn't even carrying a rope and slept in the open air, without his tarp set up, which I felt was a bit extreme given the risks. After that we all stirred and started packing up in the chilly, early-morning air.

The moment we started walking, we saw fresh bear prints on the trail, on top of Joe's shoe prints. The paws were longer than my feet and at least twice the width, and I wore a size ten and a half. That was convincing enough for me to start hanging our food from then on. Within a mile, we saw a sign posted on a tree that said the area was closed to camping due to bear danger, specifically stating,

"Campsites north of river from this point to Reef Creek closed due to bear activity on horse remains."

We had camped within a mile of a bear magnet and that crunching I heard in the early morning was most likely a frequent visitor to the horse remains just past our campsite. All of us wondered where Joe had camped after he saw such a sign, knowing his fear of grizzly bears.

Two hours into the morning, we heard a voice call out to us, "Hey, are those the hikers I lent my truck to?"

We all stopped walking and looked around for the source. To our left, about a hundred feet off the trail, we could barely see three people through the high, thick brush.

"Yes, it is!" Matt called back. "We'll come say hi!"

We pushed through the brush and popped out into a clearing, located just off the side of the Sun River, and saw Dave and his two sons. Joe had camped with them the night before and had updated them on our whirlwind of a day, including two visits to Augusta. We could tell Dave wasn't thrilled we went to town twice, but when we explained that we didn't feel right leaving Beacon in a bind when we had been helped out and had a way to help him, he seemed to understand the situation better and agreed with our decision.

As we sat and talked with them, I tried eating one of my newest experiments in soaking meals in a peanut butter jar. I had soaked a Lipton Noodle dish overnight and had my first taste of it at breakfast. It was disgustingly inedible. The noodles had turned into cold, wet, mushy dough and I could barely swallow such a texture. I added Chex Mix to give it more flavor and crunch, but it didn't do much. Big, big mistake on my part.

Two hours later at the top of a long, steady climb up to a pass, we saw a note sitting in the middle of the trail. It was from Joe, saying the time that he arrived at the pass, at 10:00am. It was 10:45am for us so we were surprised to see that we weren't too far behind.

On the way down, Matt was leading with me behind and Raisins behind me. It was quiet and I looked up and saw Matt' shorts pulled down around his little butt cheeks, completely mooning Raisins and me. Raisins and I laughed when we saw it, but laughed even harder when Matt rounded a turn in a switchback and slid onto his side. The turn had been tighter than he realized, over slick, loose gravel, and his feet slipped right out from under him. He popped up quickly, pulled up his pants, and continued walking, only looking a little embarrassed. I wanted to make sure he was ok but I couldn't stop laughing because the mooning of us had gone completely wrong.

We stopped and made sure he didn't hurt himself, having only a small scratch on his left hip from where he hit the gravel, and he walked on, looking dejected while Raisins and I tried to stop giggling behind him.

All at once, Matt stopped and huffed like a kid and said, "Raisins, I'm a hugger and I haven't had a hug from Julie in days and I just fell. I need a hug."

I nearly cried as I gave Matt a hug, not fully realizing how deflated he felt. Then we each gave Raisins a hug, because we believed hugs were something to be shared, so it was hugs all around for us all to feel better.

That afternoon we met two southbounders who described the terrain coming up in the detour, saying it was relatively flat, marked well, low in elevation, through thick brush, and not very scenic but also not very difficult hiking. The news was surprisingly good for us; as long as it was easy to follow, we didn't care what kind of views there were. We knew Glacier National Park was to follow and we'd heard nothing but good things about the scenery in the park, so we had no doubt our days of good views in Montana were still to come.

As we continued walking we noticed an increase in smoke. It burned our noses, throats and eyes, and we were all nervous. We knew a new fire had popped up on part of the trail that was originally open, but we were shocked that it was so close that the smoke was that heavy. By late afternoon, the smoke cleared and we finally reached the detour junction, taking a left where the trail normally took a right to head towards the famously beautiful Chinese Wall. It was one of the most scenic parts of the trail and we would be forced to miss it.

We caught up to Joe by dusk, his tarp set up off the side of the trail and his food bag already hung. Even after spending just a day apart, we had plenty of new stories to share among us.

The next morning, we all moved slowly and couldn't seem to pack up as fast as normal. I credited it to the detour because we were walking blindly. No one was sure if the detour was longer or shorter than the original route, and therefore none of us had a good estimate as to when we might arrive in East Glacier. It was Friday morning at the time and because of the Benchmark Ranch debacle, I guessed Sunday was a realistic arrival time.

Joe left camp before us and Matt and I walked with Raisins again. Though we walked together a lot, we didn't always talk. It seemed like all three of us knew when it was appropriate to have a conversation and when we all just wanted to be within our own heads, even when we walked together. He reminded me of our days with Rumblestrip on the Appalachian Trail, an eighteen-year-old Mennonite from Ohio who we walked all of Maine with. I appreciated the fact that we all gave each other space, even when we were walking just feet from each other for ten hours a day.

On the flipside, Joe was a talker, which was also welcome at times. He was like a real-life iPod, his stream of life stories like a podcast in my ears as I listened to stories from his youth, his previous hikes, and all the other crazy adventures he'd been a part of. He certainly brought diversity to our crew of thru-hikers; I still smile when I picture our little train of four moving up the trail together.

Just a few miles into the day, I stopped mid-stride as I led in front of Matt and Raisins. Ahead of me was a fresh pool of blood, about three feet long by one foot wide, that hadn't even fully soaked into the ground. All of us looked around into the surrounding foliage, expecting a grizzly to jump out at any moment, but we didn't see or hear anything. Raisins noticed speckles of blood on nearby leaves and rocks and we guessed another animal had just dragged its prey off the trail.

We quickly snapped a few photos and fled the scene. We frantically searched out Joe's footprints, hoping he was still alive and not the source of the blood, and thankfully saw the unmistakable mark of his Brooks Cascadia trail-running shoes. Seeing the blood reminded us of the ever-present fear of a grizzly bear encounter. Most of all, it confirmed our often misguided, Hollywood-influenced conception of the circle of life. The circle of life was no longer a cartoon about a cute lion, but rather a very real, shockingly raw, and disturbingly rough reality on the CDT. It truly was survival of the fittest and we didn't exactly feel like the fittest, so we stuck together the rest of the day and increased our respect for the wildness of wildlife yet again.

That pool of blood had a lasting impression on me in a unique way. In the past, I've taken some criticism for not being enough of a "nature lover" on the trail. Now that I've been removed from the trail to really think about how I feel about nature, I realize that I have a problem with the term, nature lover, because I don't think it's about love. For me, it's about the difference between being an observer of nature and a participant in nature. As an observer, nature is seen from a distance and though there might be threatening factors present, nothing is actually a threat. It's like "Jurassic Park" *before* everything goes wrong. As a participant, nature is experienced first-hand and one is part of that circle of life, that very real, very threatening circle of life. It's like "Jurassic Park" *after* everything goes wrong. A real T-Rex isn't so fascinating once there's no longer an electric fence to keep it from being a threat.

On the CDT and as a thru-hiker, I was technically a participant in the circle of life. Nature on the trail was unforgiving and rough. It may have been beautiful but it still included life and death, rather than love and hate, and it wasn't touchy-feely. While being a participant as a thru-hiker, there weren't many moments where I could sit back and observe because I had to constantly worry about my own well-being and defense against the other predators in the wild. I never felt love or hate for nature; I felt that I lived in it and therefore played by its rules, which were life or death.

Coming across a fresh pool of blood on the trail certainly ratcheted up the intensity we felt in grizzly country in Montana and made us all the more aware of our participation in nature.

Much of the rest of the day, after we caught up with Joe and folded him into our hiking crew, was through a recent burn area. A large portion of the Bob Marshall Wilderness had been plagued by fires in the past and that day we walked through very dry, desolate, charred sections. Many trees still stood but all of their trunks were blackened and none had leaves to cover us from the hot, draining afternoon sun.

Around early evening Matt started falling behind, which was strange. He never fell behind, never hiked slower than me, and rarely felt physically bad or injured. I stopped and waited for him to catch up and learned that he was fighting sudden, sharp pains in his groin. The pain increased quickly and within fifteen minutes he needed to stop. I'd just started feeling some shin pain so I was ready to stop too, along with the rest of the crew. It was 8:00pm and we were still in the thick of a fresh burn section as we set up camp on ashy, charred ground.

The next morning there was new energy among us. If all went normal, we'd meet up with the original trail again and finally know what sort of mileage we had left to East Glacier.

Matt's mystery pain in his groin seemed to have healed overnight but my shin pain unfortunately felt worse. I started popping pain killers from the start but no increase of dosage or frequency was helping the increasing pain. I'd had shin splints before from running too much, too hard, too soon, but I'd been hiking high mileage for ninety-three days. Raisins guessed that it was because I was wearing such old shoes and I had to agree that he had a valid point. My shoes had over 1,000 miles on them and I knew they needed to go another 150 miles before being replaced.

By the end of the day, stabbing pains radiated up and down the front of my shins and I was nearly in tears, hoping the upcoming town stop would somehow magically heal me. I was in so much pain that my concern over having enough time for Colorado became concern over just making it to Canada.

We walked on a rolling dirt road for the latter part of the day and agreed to sleep off the side of it once dusk approached. Joe was hesitant to sleep that close to the road but there was such thick, lumpy brush alongside it that we finally gave up on finding a spot off the road and took our chances sleeping very close to it.

Joe must have been so nervous about being on the road that in the middle of the night, he woke us up when he yelled, "There's a car coming! I see headlights! There's a car!"

All of us popped up, only to see darkness and to realize Joe was dreaming. No one said a word and we all went back to sleep.

The next day represented our last town day in Montana. Matt and I were looking forward to getting out of the grizzly country of Montana, looking forward to familiar Colorado territory, where black bears seemed downright docile in comparison to a grizzly.

Unfortunately, my shins were in more pain than the day before and I took two pain pills every two hours. Every time we took a break, no matter how short, I sat down and massaged my shins, trying to rub out the pain with pressure. Downhills were most painful because I had to point my toes, which shot deep, throbbing pains into my shins; I relied heavily on my hiking poles to bear my weight.

While on a small downhill in the early afternoon, my legs were in so much pain that I started crying. I could barely point my toes or flex my feet without extreme pain in my calves. I fell behind the group and Matt waited for me while Joe and Raisins went ahead. Not fifty feet later, they stopped and got out their cameras.

Matt and I soon arrived, only to be faced with a half-eaten moose carcass lying in a creek. Great, I looked like the weakest link, falling behind as I limped along on the trail, and we'd been in a grizzly hotspot, visited so frequently by bears that the area was surrounded by big piles of bear poop that we literally had to tip-toe around. I wanted to take a break so badly but I couldn't take one there, right next to a rotting moose carcass, a magnet for every bear within a few mile radius because of the pungent smells it was emitting. We walked another mile before I stopped to massage my legs again.

Raisins and Joe were then ahead of us and a few minutes later we ran into a couple that was out for a day-hike. I couldn't help but mention my leg pain because it was at the front of my mind. My calves were visibly swollen and the couple gave me hefty pain killers from their pack that I was quick to take. Looking back, it seems abnormally unsafe that I'd take unmarked pills from strangers in the woods, but I was so desperate for relief from the pain that I didn't even question my decision.

From then on the pain in my legs diminished greatly and we caught up with Raisins and Joe again. Much of the trail that afternoon was severely under-maintained, bushes choking the trail so badly that we couldn't even see our feet below us as we moved blindly through branches and weeds covering the trail. We hoped the upcoming border of Glacier National Park would be a gateway to better-maintained trail.

It was an exciting moment to reach the park's border because we'd already heard so much about Glacier. The park was most hikers' favorite part of all of Montana.

Our hopes for clear trails were delayed when we crossed the border and found the trail to be just as weed-choked and full of overgrowth as the Bob Marshall Wilderness had been. We walked through five-foot tall bushes that reached over the trail like they were holding hands with the bushes across the trail, making it harder to make quick progress.

With fifteen miles to go to East Glacier, Matt brightened up our spirits when he realized he had a strong signal on the iPad. He turned on the REO Speedwagon station on Pandora and stuck the iPad in the outside of his pack. All of us sang out loud in unison, Raisins excluded because he was so young he didn't know "Dad Rock," as he called it.

We made it to town by 6:00pm on that Sunday evening, tired yet excited for one final section in Montana. I started to feel a little sad, knowing that while it was the end in Canada for Raisins and Joe, we still had miles left to complete in Colorado. I let myself get excited over the fact that it was the end of Montana, not necessarily the end of the trail.

Before getting a hotel room, we stopped at the general store to pick up our resupply boxes and my heart nearly skipped a beat when I saw what box had been sent. We originally had two shipments ready to mail to East Glacier, one with food and passports, and one with clothing to wear after Canada. I had told our friends to mail only the one with food and passports. The passports were absolutely necessary in order to get back into the US after we crossed the Canadian border. I knew when I saw the box that it had the clothing in it and I had to admit, it was my fault. I hadn't done a great job in discerning the two boxes for our friends in Seattle, forgetting how similar they looked, and our friends had sent the wrong box. I prayed I was wrong as I walked out to the front porch to meet Matt, but deep down I knew the truth. Matt knew it too as soon as he saw the box.

As I opened up the box outside the general store, Matt's face in shock as he ran the logistical nightmare through his mind, I felt sick. Inside was our clothing and not our passports or food. We would not be going to Canada if we didn't figure out a way to get our passports in the next three days.

12
Optimist

"Here we go again," I thought as the CDT trail logistics seemingly never ended. Julie knew as she opened the box that we had the wrong package and that our passports would not be inside. This was an issue because the route we'd so meticulously followed the entire journey thus far, of which we had 105 miles remaining to Canada, required that we have our passports in order to reenter the US upon finishing the trail in Waterton, Canada. There was an alternate route that finished at a border crossing to the east, and one could argue that it was just as official as the Waterton finish, but I'd done the work to stay on route the entire journey and I was determined to finish.

Figuring out this logistical mess felt like it was all on me to solve. Julie's shins had been hurting her to the point of tears and she was not in the mood to problem-solve. She, along with the other guys, weren't too concerned which route they took so long as it was a continuous walk that could connect their footsteps from end to end.

I got to work using Joe's cell phone. I first contacted an inn located in the park town of Many Glacier. This seemed like the one potential place we could send an express package, and despite being told by a few locals that what I was trying to accomplish couldn't be done, the inn at Many Glacier offered to accept our overnight package. I then called Rocketcop and Jessica, our resupply friends in Seattle. They were quick as always to offer their help. They found the box with our passports and Rocketcop assured us that he'd send them via overnight delivery first thing the next morning. I was cautiously optimistic that yet another CDT roadblock had been overcome.

We'd chosen to get a nice room for the night rather than the nearby hostel. One, as a couple, a hotel room cost nearly as much as two hostel beds, and the difference in price was well worth the privacy, space, and amenities we received. Plus, we'd been hiking with two guys for over a week straight. It had been great, but we needed some couple time after having them camped out within a few feet of our tent each night.

Another logistical issue that we went to bed with that night was the thirty-seven mile day hanging over our head for the day out of town. Joe had called the park the day before in order to set up our camping permits for Glacier National Park, and similar to our Yellowstone experience, we had to reserve specific spots, carry a permit, and have our itinerary approved based on availability. Our options were limited and a thirty-seven mile day seemed like the best deal we could get from the rangers.

The morning started off with a hefty to-do list including a trip to the post office to mail things home. Joe didn't need to wait for the post office so he got out earlier, aiming for the ranger station eleven miles to our north in order to secure our park permits. We were going to be following quickly behind, knowing that we'd likely have a long day of hiking ahead of us.

As we were heading out of town we had another Beacon sighting. He had just gotten into town after skipping the burnt out Bob Marshall Wilderness section on his gentleman's hike. He was all smiles as usual under his big white beard. He was with Kathleen, the mother of a thru-hiker that was a few days behind us. She had recently retired from work and midway through the trail began meeting her son Dain along the way. We'd heard about her from other hikers as her presence and generosity along the trail was becoming legendary. We stopped to chat at her minivan before heading out and we saw how fabulous it must have been to actually have a support person along the way. Julie told her about her aching shins and Kathleen was quick with a solution. She had strong pain meds and she gave Julie some Icy Hot to numb the pain.

Once on the trail our hopes for beautiful scenery and clear trails were realized as we climbed out of East Glacier. The path was wide and smooth, obviously well-maintained and well-traveled. We worked our way up a large climb to an exposed ridge, offering us our first stunning views of the park. As we crested the top we could see Two Medicine Lake and the campground down below. The shimmering lake filled up much of the valley, carved out between massive rock formations jutting into the sky.

We were all excited to be in Glacier National Park. Julie and I were doing our best to see this as only part of our trail since we were now committed to not only going back to finish the fire section in Colorado, but to also potentially finishing the parts she'd missed from her week off the trail. Regardless of remaining miles, we all soaked in our first spectacular views of the park.

We hurried down the other side toward the lake. We were at least a couple hours behind Joe and we knew that once we got our permits, we still had twenty-six miles to reach our first campsite.

Upon reaching the ranger station, we were immediately told that our previous permit plan was no longer available. Stunned and feeling a little betrayed, we sat outside the station with a map and began coming up with a new plan. Joe spotted us and joined in the brainstorming. We eventually accepted that our day was finished after only eleven miles. Once we got over the initial shock of being forced to stop, we looked around at the pristine lake and well-provisioned camp area and realized that if we were being forced to stop, at least it was in an absolutely gorgeous location.

In the end, we were simply happy to have a reasonable park permit plan going forward. We'd heard of another hiker a couple weeks ahead of us who had been forced to wait three days for his permit because there was no available camping. As we were receiving our permits the ranger read through all the rules and regulations of the park and insisted that we watch a ten minute video on how to live in the backcountry. To top it off, the ranger read the official party line, "Though you will probably revel in this, the United States Government does not recommend your planned itinerary." While our itinerary was a bit below our normal mileage, it was a boost to our egos to know that lower mileage for us was still considered abnormally high compared to normal park itineraries.

That afternoon we made ourselves comfortable at the camp store along the lake. It was a beautiful wood structure lodge with a front deck overlooking the shimmering lake. The wind picked up as the day went on and brought with it some colder temperatures. We eventually retreated inside the lodge and continued eating. We struck up a conversation with an older couple on vacation. After being peppered with pointed questions by the man about why we did what we did and how we paid for such things, he eventually lightened up, even intimating an air of respect for what we were doing. We found out he was a retired US Congressman and that he'd worked on a committee that dealt with stock market regulation. I had a wonderful afternoon asking him questions and learning about the world through his unique eyes.

We went to bed early and as we hiked out the next morning, the rest had done some obvious good for Julie's shins. In searching for the root of the problem, she and Raisins had concluded that it was likely her old shoes. We had less than 100 miles remaining and as we set out on a twenty-six mile day, we hoped the extra rest and shorter days would do her some good.

Joe was out in front early as we climbed 2,400' to Pitamakan Pass over the first eight miles of the day. Up top we were exposed again with gorgeous views. We came across a herd of mountain goats sitting alongside the trail, snacking on grass. They didn't appear too concerned with us, seemingly quite familiar with posing for photos by passing hikers.

As we started down from the pass we could see Joe maneuvering the switchbacks down below. Thankfully he was walking in an area with scrub bushes because upon further inspection, brought on by his hooting and hollering, we realized he was waving his shorts above his head, swinging them round and round. He was getting in on the mooning act now too. After I'd been sneakily flashing hikers on switchbacks, it was catching on and Joe was returning the favor.

As we finished the descent down to some alpine lakes we found Joe washing himself and his clothes (without soap per park regulations) in the cold mountain lake. He encouraged the rest of us to join in and as was typical for our group, I joined Joe in the cold mountain water while Julie and Raisins stood like cats, far from the water's edge. Neither of them had much desire to do anything with the cold water other than drink it and it became somewhat of a running joke with us that our two kittens would avoid getting wet at all cost.

We had another 2,000' climb up to Triple Divide Pass in the

afternoon. We all knew we were very fortunate, as we'd had great weather of late and as a result, the crystal clear skies provided stunning views of the park. We also knew that while we were treated to breathtaking views, if storms rolled in, these same mountain passes could be downright treacherous. We made our way down that afternoon past bright blue glacier melt lakes and through alpine scrub that gradually turned to trees as we made our way to lower elevation.

As the day wore on the scenery changed and we followed the trail into an old forest fire burn section. Like the many burned sections of forest we'd hiked through already, there was no shade and everything was dusty and charred. As the miles of burn walking continued through the late afternoon, it became clear that our campsite would not be atop a mountain but instead, down in the dusty burn.

We did have a lake though and Julie and I went down to it so she could ice her shins in the cold water. They had become increasingly painful for her as the day wore on, especially with the two major descents down from the passes we'd climbed. Thankfully it was a shorter day. We set up camp by 7:30pm that evening and got some quality rest.

The next day was a planned thirty mile day to the campground at Many Glacier. This was exciting for us because Many Glacier had a big campground with a restaurant and a camp store. It was also the location of the inn we were shipping our passports to.

The day started as usual with Joe taking off early. We actually didn't see him the entire day but heard he warded off the bears by playing music on his iPhone at full blast while he hiked.

The trail was mainly flat for the first eleven miles as we made our way along the backside of St. Mary's Lake. We were quite surprised at how badly the trail was maintained through this section as we all got soaked from the wet brush that covered the trail. At times the plants on either side of the trail were taller than we were such that we couldn't see much more than a few feet in front of us. This was made more interesting by the large amount of bear scat littering the trail. We knew bears were around and we knew we probably wouldn't see them until we were all quite close.

As we rounded the lake and joined up with another more popular trail, we ran into a ranger. He was immediately excited to see us and to tell us about his past thru-hike of the PCT. He confirmed that the section we'd just hiked was only hiked by thru-hikers and was therefore very low on the park's priority list for maintenance.

It had also started raining. We snacked in the rain with all our rain gear on and then crossed the Road to the Sun, a major artery through the park, before beginning our 1,900' climb up to Piegan Pass The rains gradually cleared and as we neared the pass the skies transitioned from gray to a gorgeous blue with the sun again shining brightly. Over the course of four miles the weather had made a dramatic turn for the better and it did so at one of the most opportune times of the entire trip, as Piegan Pass offered some of the best views in the entire park. We met some women out for the day and they took our pictures with the jagged rock walls piercing the blue sky background.

From there it was a steady downhill for the remainder of the day to Many Glacier. We eventually made it down to Swiftcurrent Lake, past a hotel, and onto the road toward the campground. We quickly claimed our spot at the hike and bike campground and then, with our fingers crossed, headed over to the inn and camp store with hopes of finding our passports waiting.

We saw Joe out front and before we made it inside, he said he'd seen a UPS envelope sitting at the front desk with our names on it. A big smile came across my face as that meant we could walk the Highline Route into Canada and complete the trail the way I'd hoped to. It also meant that another logistical challenge had been overcome.

We picked up some goodies from the restaurant and camp store and then headed back to our campsite for our last night camping with Joe. He hadn't brought his passport, and based on everything we'd been told by park officials regarding reentering the US after walking into Canada, he had decided to hike to the alternate finishing point.

As a group we'd covered a few hundred miles together, hiking well over thirty miles a day the entire way. Much to Joe's liking we hadn't had any grizzly bear encounters. As we sat around the picnic table in the dark, Joe and Raisins had a celebratory beer and we all shared trail stories.

The next morning Joe was out early. He had plans of pushing to the finish and then trying to hitch back to East Glacier, where he would catch a train to Seattle and then fly home to California. Julie, Raisins, and I had another thirty mile day ahead of us, followed by a short nine mile day the following morning into Canada. We would then be going separate ways, with Raisins heading back to New York and us down to Colorado.

We walked out with the rising sun along the lake and toward Swiftcurrent Pass. The campground was largely still asleep and we smiled as we felt how different our Glacier experience was compared to nearly everyone else in the park. We also smiled because this amazing adventure was coming to an end soon, which meant that we had almost made it to Canada.

As expected, within an hour of leaving Joe, we had our first bear encounter. It was early morning and I heard rustling off the side of the trail. I yelled back to Raisins, telling him to get up with us because there may be trouble. As we walked past some tall brush, bear spray in hand, out popped a young grizzly, maybe three years old. It had the distinct ears, face, and shoulder hump of a grizzly bear. It wasn't a huge, full grown bear, but it was big enough to be independent from its mother. It casually looked at us and then walked off into the trees.

"Whew!" we thought, crisis averted. We continued cautiously up the trail but the entire time we could all hear the bear in the nearby trees no more than thirty yards to our right off the trail. We were still on alert and adrenaline was still pumping through our veins when out popped the bear again from the trees. The intensity of the moment increased as we astonishingly watched as the bear began trotting alongside us, parallel to the trail, jumping and bounding through tall grass. At this point we all stopped in our tracks. I had our bear spray ready to go with the safety removed while Raisins had his bear spray in one hand and his camera in the other.

I was focused but at the same time practically awestruck by the situation. Here we were in Glacier National Park, on our second to last day before Canada with a grizzly bear running alongside us. It was intense yet amazing at the same time. Then the bear turned and began running straight towards me. "I might actually use this sixty dollar can of bear spray I've been lugging around for the past two months," I thought.

I was steady and ready, scared but also so in the moment that I felt slightly outside of myself as the bear ran toward us. At the last moment the bear veered to the right, just as it reached the trail a few yards ahead of us. The grizzly continued up the trail away from us, apparently not at all concerned about our presence. We all stood frozen for a moment and soaked in the experience. We didn't want to follow the bear too closely, since we were traveling in the same direction. Looking back on the situation, the bear didn't have an aggressive look on its face and it didn't seem to be very interested in us at all, but in the moment, we were all ready for anything.

After about ten minutes of waiting we continued north on the trail but now with all of our sensory alarms significantly amplified. Julie said she was ready to be finished with Montana and to be finished with grizzly country. I totally understood where she was coming from, while at the same time thinking that that had been the perfect grizzly bear experience. It was scary and intense, but in the end, not at all harmful. However, I was ready to not have to be so bear aware and I was happy to be losing the twelve ounce bear spray soon.

We continued up toward the pass and as we climbed, we were able to look back on the glacier carved valley we'd just traversed. The sun was up now but not hot, and it cast a shimmer on all the lakes. As we looked down we were treated to still more wildlife, as at one point we spotted two moose grazing in the marshy grass below, and then later, Raisins spotted another grizzly bear on the trail, this time casually walking across a bridge down in the valley.

We took a lunch break at the pass and then headed down toward the Highline Trail. On the way we were treated to our first plentiful huckleberry patch. We all stopped and ate like machines, picking and grabbing with speed and voraciousness, our hands, lips, and tongues stained purple with the tart, yet sweet berries.

We spent the afternoon exposed to the elements on the Highline Trail. While we'd had spectacular weather thus far, we were watching the skies closely because it looked like storms were coming in. We stayed dry all the way until we could see the trees again and as we hurried down into the forest the storm blew in. It was a violent storm with powerful winds, frequent lightning, and loud, crashing thunder. We were now under cover of trees though and we would continue to be so for the remainder of our trip to Canada, so we hiked right through the storm. Raisins wore his rain skirt, a garbage bag with the bottom cut out, and Julie and I jealously watched as his shorts stayed dry while we got soaked walking through all the wet brush. Even after the rains stopped, we were still getting wet from the waist down as we were in dense forest, brushing up against saturated plants for the remainder of the day.

We got into camp shortly before dark. The campsite was nearly full but the other campers made room for us by the fire. We ate our last dinner together with Raisins and chatted with the other campers by the fire. This was one of my favorite times because to most people, the life of a thru-hiker was so foreign, yet often so fascinating. I loved the trail life and therefore, I ate it up whenever someone had any interest in it. The other campers were amazed and impressed as Raisins told stories about his hiking experiences, so vast for someone so young, and we chimed in answering the typical questions about gear, resupplies, and miles as we so often enjoyed doing.

We dried off a bit by the fire that night as we talked well into the night. It was actually the first fire we'd sat next to on the entire journey. We eventually found a spot to throw down the tent and we called it a night, our last on this part of our CDT journey.

We were up and out at our normal hour, shortly after it was light enough to move about without a headlamp. As we got our food from the bear bagging poles and packed up, the rest of the camp calmly began stirring to life. We were out and on the trail before most were fully awake to know we had even left. We had five miles to the Canadian border and another four miles after that to the town of Waterton, Canada, where our hiking with Raisins would end.

Julie and I had made an effort not to get too caught up in the Canada finish because we were now fully committed to going back to Colorado for more hiking. But that morning we basked in the excitement of the northern terminus of the Continental Divide Trail. It was easy walking along Waterton Lake and within an hour and a half we were at the obelisk defining the border between the United States and Canada. There was no border guard, no checkpoint, and we simply walked in. Actually, we stopped and celebrated first.

Raisins had been working on his finishing photo idea in his head for some time now and we helped him capture the perfect picture as he jumped high into the air, arms and legs spread wide, with the obelisk beside him and the mountain lake behind him. We were so glad to be there with him. We thought about Joe and hoped he'd had a good finish too.

I am generally not one to get very emotional or too excited at a journey's finish or from accomplishing a goal. This day was no different as I sat down for my breakfast of cold oatmeal, like I did most every other day on the trail. However, I did so with a constant smile on my face on this particular morning. It felt so good to get to Canada and though the journey really was the major reward for such adventures, there was an undeniable pleasure in actually getting to the finish.

We finished up the last four miles, smiling and joking the entire way. The skies started clearing out with strong winds blowing along the lake, and by the time we reached town the sun had come out. We knew we needed to check in somehow with Canadian border authorities but in order to make sure we acted rationally, we went and had some restaurant food first.

We then found our way to the small police station and waited for the ranger to check us in. He photocopied our passports, all the while talking about the trail and all the hiking he hoped to still do in his lifetime. He was one of the few that we met along the CDT that even knew what the CDT was, let alone aspired to hike parts of it.

Just like that, Raisins' trail was finished and a major part of ours was as well. It was a moment to cherish but soon enough it was back to CDT logistics yet again. The big questions now were, how do we get back to the US, followed by, how do we get a rental car in order to drive Raisins to the airport and us back to Colorado?

PART 4

1
Stopwatch

After ninety-nine days on the trail, on August 30th, a day after Matt's birthday, we reached Canada, the northern terminus of the CDT. It was a cloudy morning with cool temperatures and a touch of humidity. The trail kept us close to the Waterton Lake shore and eventually brought us into a clearing where we reached the US/Canada border. Just like on the PCT, there was a metal obelisk and a line cut into the trees to mark the border. We were all smiles as we dropped our packs and pulled out our cameras.

All three of us were surprisingly quiet upon reaching the border, Raisins much less excited than I had expected. I knew Matt and I would be happy to reach Canada, but since we still had remaining miles in Colorado, it really wasn't our finish. Raisins finally showed some emotion when he posed for his photos and jumped ecstatically in the air, yelling out as he did so, leaping three feet off the ground. It was a moment I was proud to witness and we ate a snack at the border in order to soak in the moment a little longer.

Just like on previous trails, there was a mix of happiness and sadness, happiness in the achievement of such a huge feat of mental and physical strength, and sadness in the ending of a chapter of our lives. For us it wasn't the end, but for Raisins, it was the end of the trail and the beginning of life as a student once again in Maine.

While the Canadian border was exciting, it was admittedly anticlimactic and I had already mentally prepared myself for that moment. There was some jealousy as I watched Raisins jump for joy, knowing he was finished walking and going home. I knew Joe had finished the day before and had already started his journey home to Southern California. But all along, ever since I decided to quit back in Colorado, I knew this day would come and I was ready for it.

I was relieved to be finished with Montana. It was such a long state with such a strong grizzly presence that I was ready to be back in Colorado. There was also the feeling of fall in the air, in the clouds overhead, and in the cool breeze that seemed to surprise us with its force. There was even a slight change in the leaves and the general feeling was that time was running out.

After just four tiny more miles, just as rain clouds and strong winds were threatening with a light sprinkle, we reached the Canadian town of Waterton. The trail ended at the edge of town and we made our way to the middle, seeking out food and a ride back to the US.

We tried our luck with hitching a ride to the border, only to stand on the roadside for two hours, putting on our best pity faces, but with no luck. With our heads down and pride a little hurt, we returned to town to sign up for a paid shuttle to the border, where we showed our passports and walked back into the US.

The first car that crossed the border into the US picked us up and we felt our luck turn for the better. The kind, lively couple took us to an intersection within the park and from there we stuck out our thumbs yet again, easily getting picked up by another couple that took us to East Glacier. It was early evening by the time we arrived in East Glacier and within an hour of arriving we had picked up a rental car and started our drive to Durango, Colorado, where the rental car was due back within twenty-four hours. The drive to Durango was estimated to take at least twenty hours.

Raisins was still with us because we had promised to take him to the airport in Great Falls, MT, on our way to Durango. A few hours later we said goodbye to Raisins after nearly two weeks of spending most of our waking and sleeping hours by his side. There wasn't time for tears or for a drawn-out farewell because we were in such a rush to get on the road, but we all gave long hugs goodbye and wished each other well in the next chapters of our lives. I wondered if we'd ever see him again, knowing we were heading back to Seattle after the trail, clear across the country.

Saying goodbye to a fellow thru-hiker is a part of the trail life that never ceases to amaze me. We can spend hours, days, and even weeks with another individual, in very trying circumstances, and then cut the cord between us once the trail is finished. That cord is never really severed because of the bonds developed over a thru-hike, but the physical detachment is so quick and immediate that it's hard not to feel some pain and sadness in parting ways.

And then we drove.

It was the same day as our arrival into Canada but it already seemed like days since we stood at the northern terminus of the CDT. Both of us were equally tired from having started the day before dawn so we agreed that each of us would drive a minimum of ninety minutes in order to give the passenger enough time to sleep.

Throughout the entire night, we switched drivers every two to three hours, both of us snacking on carrots and celery, chips, jelly beans, and water to keep ourselves awake. When it was my turn to sleep, I passed out in the back seat and the hours passed by in seconds.

The next day we arrived in Durango at noon, a full five hours before the car was due back. We breathed easier knowing we had made it with plenty of time to spare. Durango was the only town where we could return our rental car so we needed a ride from there to Cumbres Pass, our next starting point to move up the trail once again. Karla, the trail angel that had given us a ride to Monarch Pass at the time of the fires, was happily willing to help us out again with a ride to the pass. She wasn't scheduled to arrive until late afternoon, so we used the free time to pick up our next leg of resupply food and most importantly, new shoes for me. The pain had subsided over the last couple of days but I was done messing around with old shoes.

Karla picked us up around 4:00pm and from there, we were in her hands. The last time she gave us a ride, I was so anxious about getting back on the trail that it led to my demise just a few days later. This time, I approached the situation differently. I knew Karla was a busy woman with a lot going on and that she had a heart of gold for helping us out in a pinch yet again. I was going to let the situation unfold as it would, without trying to control the clock or force my own initiatives, knowing we'd eventually get back on the trail and would have to just take it from there.

Before heading home, Karla had a few errands to run in nearby cities and I learned just how much some small-town Colorado residents must drive to get their errands accomplished. She drove about forty-five minutes south of Durango to Farmington, NM, to pick up a computer at a Best Buy, only to then drive another few hours home, back to South Fork, CO, stopping at a grocery store along the way for food because they had a foreign exchange student from Germany staying in their home. Her life made my head spin and I was thankful for the simplicity of the trail life.

It was 10:00pm by the time we made it to her home, a beautifully built log-cabin straight out of a dream home catalog, and we were in awe of its craftsmanship and coziness. Her home was so warm and inviting that I wished I was finished hiking just so I could have stayed there for a week, soaking in the views of the mountains just outside the windows. Karla gave us the five-star treatment when we arrived, giving us each fluffy, full-body bathrobes to use after hot showers and bubble baths, and I was nearly comatose by the time I was out of the bath because I was so tired from having driven straight through the night.

We both shoveled in a plate of food as we sat on the couch and talked late into the night with Karla, finally going to bed at midnight. I was so tired I didn't even take off my bathrobe before crawling into bed and passing out.

The sunrise first woke me up, pouring through the large bedroom windows, but I didn't heed the call. I rolled over onto Matt's side of the bed after he got up to make phone calls, and finally got out of bed at 8:30am. It was part of my plan to go with the flow of the day and just be thankful that Karla was so good to us.

The kitchen was full of excitement by the time I came out of our bedroom, coffee already brewed and vegan blueberry pancakes being concocted. A friend of Karla's was in town, staying at a neighbor's house across the street, and was in the kitchen cooking eggs while I made vegan sausage. I still hadn't gotten out of my bathrobe as I stood there gulping coffee.

As I had guessed it would be, it was a slow-moving morning with cooking food, sitting around the table and chatting, and packing up. We got back in Karla's car around noon, with a two-hour drive ahead of us to the pass. The skies looked threatening as the afternoon continued on, my one big beef with Colorado's weather, and yet the trees looked much greener than I had remembered. Karla confirmed that they'd received a lot of much needed rain over the summer and that the rain had yet to let up. That worried me a little, considering the high, lightning-prone sections we were about to hike.

We arrived at Cumbres Pass, a memorable, meaningful place for Matt and me, as it signified the beginning of the end to our normal thru-hike. We took pictures at the pass with Karla, signed into a hiker register, and were on our way yet again by 3:30pm.

That morning, we had confirmed with our friends in Creede that we'd meet them at Spring Creek Pass by that coming Friday, September 6th, at 6:00pm. By the time we started hiking again, we had 187 miles ahead of us with just over five days to accomplish the miles, through the Weminuche Wilderness and the Southern San Juans, some of the most rugged, difficult terrain on the entire trail.

We had some serious work to do.

2
Optimist

It was becoming increasingly apparent with each passing hour that we'd done it again and bitten off more than we could chew. We weren't even starting that late heading out of Cumbres Pass and with the amazing hospitality from Karla and Mark we couldn't have forced ourselves to hurry along any faster if we'd wanted to.

The challenge was now to complete 187 miles from Cumbres Pass north on the trail to Spring Creek Pass, where our friends Lowell and Dottie would pick us up and take us back to their home in Creede for the evening. With it now being 3:30pm, we had a little less than five and a half days until our meeting point on Friday at 6:00pm.

We'd missed Lowell and Dottie our first time through because of the fires. Not only had we been pushed off the trail, but they'd been pushed out of their home. The smoke had been so bad that they evacuated. We knew there were plenty of stories to share and we were eager to see them.

We also had the motivation to push the pace because we still had a realistic, though challenging possibility, of finishing all the miles Julie had missed when she took her week off in Steamboat. I'd been doing the math all along and it wasn't until somewhere in mid-Montana that she voiced her desire to finish her section if at all possible. From Cumbres Pass outside of Chama, we would have to average a little over thirty miles per day in order to make it, and that included a stopover at our friend's home, as well as some additional logistical challenges.

Not only did we have miles to cover, but we learned quickly upon our arrival back in Colorado that we had more hurdles to clear in order to finish our adventure the way we had hoped to. First, it got dark much earlier in Colorado than in Montana. While we'd been able to hike until a little before 9:00pm in Montana, it was getting dark in Colorado before 8:00pm, leaving us with an hour less of hiking time each day. We could also feel the cold of autumn blowing in. It was windy in Colorado, as it was on so much of the CDT, but there was a new chill in the air. We knew we were cutting it close with the impending snow season, but we crossed our fingers hoping that we still had time.

We also had some challenges we'd made for ourselves. Mainly, we'd made the rookie mistake of packing out too much food. We knew this 187 mile stretch would be our longest carry of the entire trail so we didn't want to skimp, but we also had a rental car and were able to go to a Natural Grocer in Durango, where we picked up all kinds of fun vegan treats for the long stretch. We over packed and rather than carrying six days of food, we each had closer to eight.

Lastly, we were back at higher altitudes. We weren't sure how this would impact us as we'd already hiked half of Colorado and hadn't had too many noticeable issues. However, we felt it very quickly this time around as we struggled mightily out of the gate, leaving the pass on a sunny Sunday afternoon.

The trail was very navigable our first day out and thankfully so because this was the first full section we were hiking without our maps or our datasheet. By this point though, after having walked over 2,800 miles, I was feeling confident in my navigation capabilities.

Though we had a big 2,000' climb that first day out, we were both in good spirits. We felt refreshed and rejuvenated to be back on the trail in Colorado. We would often state in amazement to each other that we were actually back in Colorado, hiking the big burn section after being in Waterton just one day prior. The whole thing was pretty amazing and we felt like we were really going to make it, though there was an underlying pressure knowing we had to make Creede in just over five days.

At this point in the trail, we were both focused on finishing. We both felt we'd grown as individuals and as a couple over the past few months on the trail. We'd experienced so much of the outdoors and nature, and though we knew there was plenty of beauty and experiences ahead of us, we also wanted to finish what we'd started, and that meant hiking big miles and pushing the pace the rest of the way. We were mentally ready for it and we assumed we were physically ready as well.

We got in thirteen miles that day, leaving us with 174 miles to go with not quite five full days to do it in. We began our second day with optimism but also urgency knowing we needed to average thirty-five miles per day for the next five days.

We were doing our best to find the rhythm that'd carried us through the latter half of Montana but we continually felt sluggish all day. Our packs were way too heavy and we both acknowledged our mistake early on. We wanted to make up for our mistake by cramming calories to lighten our load but Julie was having a hard time eating, feeling nauseous almost every time she ate, which was such a shame because we had such good food to eat. While I wasn't feeling sick, I had a headache and was just generally tired.

We didn't have tons of climbing that second day out but we were up high all day, getting as high as 12,300', while not dropping below 11,200' all day. We were reluctant to believe it but our heavy packs coupled with the vast change in elevation were taking their toll.

On top of our physical issues, the trail was often tough to follow that day with sections of minimal to no tread. We tried to hike into the night, having both agreed that we needed the hours from 8:00pm to 10:00pm each day for hiking, even if the sun was no longer with us. However, as the day turned to dusk and we continued climbing out of a deep valley up toward a ridgeline, we lost our way. It was dark, we were above tree line, everything was damp around us, and as we walked through the tall grass, we had a mini panic moment. I had been doing my best to follow the GPS waypoints but for some odd reason, I was struggling to get any closer to the next point. It was like we were in the Bermuda Triangle of trail, and we were doing it in the dark.

We trudged through Manzanita bushes that roughly scratched and tore at our legs. They also got our shoes and socks more wet. At least Julie had her new homemade garbage bag rain skirt she'd made at Karla's, so her shorts were dry.

We resigned ourselves to stopping as soon as we could find a relatively flat spot to throw down our tent for the night. I was in total grump mode as I sometimes got when I felt lost. Somehow Julie managed to find the trail again. We spotted some ground not covered by bushes, and though it was wet and slanted, we set up and went to sleep, determined to push on the next morning. However, we'd only gotten in thirty miles for the day, which increased our already high required number of miles per day to an even higher number.

Determined, though dragging, we got going with the sun on our third day out. With the daylight we could see that we were high up and going higher. We crested the ridge with the sun warming us in the cold, clear morning air. We were well above tree line as we walked up on the Divide before heading down to Elwood Pass. We were both making our best effort to be positive and to keep doing what we'd been doing ever since Julie had gotten back on the trail, now nearly two months back. We were working steadily throughout the day, taking short food breaks, and doing our best to keep smiling and to keep moving.

After an extra long lunch break, we put on our music and kept hiking. It then proceeded to rain, forcing our mp3 players back into our packs, but we kept walking. The miles actually began clicking off quickly as the afternoon progressed and our hopes picked up. The trail was very walkable again and as we made our way toward Wolf Creek Pass, we thought about checking for a cell signal to call Lowell and Dottie to push back our meeting date. However, by the time we got there late on Tuesday, we both felt a new sense of confidence and we chose to push on with the big challenge.

That evening we continued to have good trail without too much climbing. We were in and out of tree cover much of the way and as a result, we were able to hike until shortly after 10:00pm. We also found a wonderful campsite a little off the trail with a perfectly flat spot to call home for the evening. We'd hiked thirty-five miles for the day, leaving us with 110 miles and three days to do it in. We felt like things were looking up.

On our fourth day out, we began seeing the effects of the massive fires that had closed such a huge section of the trail and burned thousands of acres of forest land. We climbed early in the day up to the Divide and for much of the day we were above tree line. While we weren't directly in the burn section, we could see it on both sides of the trail as we looked down to see entire valleys charred. There were swaths of green forest still mixed in but due to all the dead trees from the beetle kill, much of the forest had been quick to burn.

The short sections of burn we did walk through were strange and otherworldly. It was a cloudy, misty morning, sometimes with low visibility, and I can clearly picture the gnarled, charred remains of trees twisting up toward the sky. They were miniature versions because most of the trunks had been burnt but some parts still remained. Amazingly, much of the ground was already showing signs of green growth due to all the rain and sunshine.

Regardless of our effort, we knew we'd been moving slowly. As had been the case with almost the entire trail since we'd gotten back on in Colorado, if we were high up in elevation and near the Divide, it was likely to be difficult hiking, and as a result, slow going.

We debated that evening what to do. We had checked for a cell signal and hadn't gotten anything. We thought that we'd be fine with falling short of our goal of making it to Creede by Friday at 6:00pm, but we were concerned about what would happen if we didn't show up. As with our time in the Black Range in New Mexico when we didn't show up when expected, we nearly had Search and Rescue called to look for us. We again considered the likelihood that Lowell and Dottie would react similarly. We didn't blame them and we would have very well done the same thing had someone we were waiting for not shown up as planned. But we were running out of time.

After hiking into the night, down from an exposed pass surrounded by whistling marmots and squeaking pikas, we found a spot in some rough, patchy grass to sleep for the night. The trail had seemingly disappeared again in the treeless expanse of the San Juan Mountains and rather than struggle in the dark for slow and uncertain miles, we decided to call it a day after another grueling thirty mile day.

We now had roughly eighty miles remaining to our meet up point and we calculated that if we maintained a similar pace to what we'd been able to do thus far, we would likely have to hike straight through the next two days to make it. We somehow still had hope though. We knew we were closing in on where the CDT left the remote Weminuche Wilderness and rejoined the Colorado Trail. We'd hiked this section the year before and knew that even though it was high and exposed with much of the trail above 12,000', it also had very navigable trail. Our hope was that if we could make it to the CT, we could make it to Creede.

We woke up a bit later than normal but felt like we needed the sleep knowing what was ahead. The trail, which we could not locate in the dark, was literally ten feet from where we slept. The challenge was that the trail was usually a narrow slit of hard ground with tough, mountain grass growing all around it, hanging over the edges and hiding the trail from sight. In the dark, it was exceedingly difficult to follow.

The first part of the day worked us. We were positive and ready for our ultra challenge but a descent down to 11,200', followed by a climb to 12,500', followed by a drop down to 10,500' capped off with another climb back up to 12,300' was chipping away at our spirit, and this was all in the first twenty-three miles of the day. The rain clouds moved in and out, occasionally dropping rain, sometimes hail, and just as quickly, they cleared out to reveal sun for awhile.

We eventually dropped down to a valley, which we crossed before climbing up the other side. It had an eerie stillness to it. We knew it was the beginning of hunting season and we had seen camps set up off-trail, but we'd yet to actually see any hunters. We had a feeling they were around, looking for an elk, deer, or bear to kill, but the silences we experienced as a result were often unpleasant and uncomfortable.

The climb started well and as was usually the case, it wasn't until we were closer to 12,000' and climbing that we could really feel the effects of the altitude on our performance, and this time, we were climbing to 12,647'. On the way up we saw one of Dottie's favorite places on the trail. She'd talked about it in the past and though we'd never seen it until now, we knew as soon as we saw it that this was the spot she so frequently talked about. The Window is a section of a mountain ridge that looks as if a perfectly square piece has been knocked out of the ridge, exposing a big open window to the sky, looking almost like a missing tooth.

The trail worked its way up and around the Window and kept us up high for much of the remaining afternoon. With mountain lakes and wet terrain surrounding us, and a massive mountain wall a hundred yards or so off to our left, Julie and I were pulled from our afternoon quiet by the sound of loose rock falling from the rock wall. We quickly peered over to our left in search of the source of the sound. My eye sight was terrible at far distances but Julie had proven to have the eyes of a hawk. She said first that it appeared to be a big rabbit scrambling up the cliff. We both immediately questioned that, considering how far away the rocky scramble was occurring. It then clicked for Julie, "It's a mountain lion!" Whether we were hiking slow or fast, there was no mistaking a mountain lion as it scaled an amazing rock wall right in front of us. Julie spotted its silhouette as the cat reached the top and stared down at us, its ears perked up as it eyed us. We walked for the next few hours knowing we were likely being tracked by a mountain lion that we would probably never see again.

After our minds gradually left the big cat, we shifted back to what had been occupying our minds the rest of the day: running numbers and determining if we'd still be able to make it and if there'd be any possibility for a break. We'd thought about stopping at some point after dark, but as we sat for a quick snack break with daylight fading, we determined that we had simply been moving too slowly to have any reason to believe that we could afford to take any extended breaks. We put on our hats and gloves, along with our wind pants and jackets, and headed off into the night.

We were high up on a pass at this point as we made our way down to a river. It was really cold and we decided that our strategy would be to walk a minimum of ninety minutes at a time with ten minute breaks in between. We'd take turns leading the way so the other person didn't have to think too much about navigating in the dark.

As we finished our descent down to the river we passed a sign saying we were leaving the Weminuche Wilderness area; it felt like we were making progress. The novelty and excitement of the challenge was still carrying us forward as we attacked yet another climb.

It was steep going and shortly after midnight we finally made it to the junction with the Colorado Trail. We both vividly remembered this spot, as we'd taken pictures there the year before, knowing we'd be back to that very spot someday on the CDT. We didn't think it'd be at midnight on a cold September night though.

From there we knew we had a good long stretch of rolling terrain all up around 12,000'. The stars shone magnificently on that cold night. Most importantly, it was dry with no rain.

Our system of leading and breaking, switching roles every ninety to 120 minutes, was working really well. We floated through the night along rocky, though well-traveled trail. At one point we woke a pack of dogs off to our right. We first thought they were with campers but later convinced ourselves they were sheep dogs protecting their flock. They barked at us for a good ten minutes before we were finally a safe distance from them. We never saw them but they had our adrenaline rushing.

Closer to 3:00am we began a bigger climb and we had to make more of a concerted effort to stay on trail. After making our way up and over the climb and past Stony Pass, we followed trail cut into the side of a mountain. Down in the valley we both simultaneously noticed three large sets of eyes looking back up at us. We instinctively stopped in our tracks for a moment. Just as quickly, we both got walking again while continually looking down into the canyon to be sure we weren't being followed. We didn't know what those eyes belonged to, but they were big, and we made an effort to keep moving.

It was at this point in the night that we began to lose it a little. I was definitely struggling and when shortly after 4:00am Julie suggested that we take a forty-five minute nap, I was quick to agree. We put some distance between us and the big eyes from the canyon, and shortly after 4:15am we took out our sleeping mats and our quilts and lay down with all our clothes on, off to the side of the trail. I was instantly asleep. It didn't matter that I was literally lying on the ground off the side of the trail in the middle of remote, expansive wilderness; I needed to sleep.

Our alarm went off forty-five minutes later and after snoozing it once for ten minutes, we were up, stuffing our gear back into our packs. We were moving within five minutes. Julie hadn't slept well and she was shivering cold. We tried to walk quickly to warm up but my brain was mush. I felt like I was drunk or hallucinating. I moved my feet and legs but it all seemed separate from my mind. My mind was screaming at me, telling me I needed to stop and sleep. It was still pitch black outside and cold. We didn't talk, we didn't eat – even though we were both hungry, all we did was walk. Eventually the sun came up and we stopped for a break. After pounding some food and drinking water right from the source without bleaching or using my straw, I started feeling a little more normal.

Thankfully, we were both committed to giving our best effort that day and neither complained. We were on familiar turf and Julie was quick to recall our previous hike on the CT. She knew everything that was coming up and we passed the time talking about who we'd met and how our hike had been the last time through.

We hit a pass with an elevation at just under 13,000', a little over twenty miles out from Spring Creek Pass in the late morning. We knew we needed to average close to three miles per hour the rest of the way in order to make it, but there was no way we were running any of these climbs or descents at our current altitude.

We continued the up and down day as we walked down a long meadow to a steep dirt road up to Carson Saddle. From there we had a couple more big climbs, taking us over 13,000' before dropping us down toward Spring Creek Pass.

We were both tired, physically and mentally. We needed showers and we needed to brush our teeth. Yet we were compelled forward with the task of making it to the pass on time, and we pushed on. We took few breaks, only stopping for water once over the final six hours, and by the time we got back into the trees again we were able to start shuffling some of the downs and the flats.

Within an hour of our cutoff we were pummeled by rain. We kept pushing and with a couple miles to go our trail joined up with a dirt forest road. We ran for it. We knew it'd be fine if we were a little late but at this point, we were so close to our 6:00pm goal that we wanted to make it simply because it'd been driving us for the past thirty-five hours. We saw the parking lot from above and ran down the hill to Lowell and Dottie's truck. It was 6:00pm on the nose.

Lowell and Dottie emerged from the truck and were quick to inform us that they had a surprise for us, and out of the car popped Alex. We hadn't seen him since Montana and though we'd hoped to see him again as he continued his trip south, we weren't sure if it'd work out.

We'd made it. It was probably the toughest push we'd ever done, and one we were by no means looking forward to repeating, but bottom line was that we'd finished what we'd set out to do and now it was time to relax, get cleaned up, and enjoy the evening with our friends.

3
Stopwatch

I was both shocked and elated to look at my watch and see that we had made it to Spring Creek Pass by 6:00pm. I knew Lowell and Dottie's SUV from the year prior when we visited them on the Colorado Trail, and I knew they were punctual, so I breathed easy when I saw their car in the parking lot, just at the mouth of the trailhead. It was sprinkling rain as we ran in, my rain skirt blowing sideways in the wind.

I was more shocked when I saw Alex pop out of the backseat of the car after Lowell said they had a surprise for us. We guessed we'd see him somewhere up the trail, not knowing what sort of progress he was making, but we told him we'd be reaching Creede on this day just to give him an idea of our location. Once he knew we were getting there, he also pushed his pace to meet up with us in town. He reached the pass a half hour before us, asked Lowell and Dottie if they "knew the Urbanskis," and hung out in their car, awaiting our arrival as we ran those last few rain-soaked miles. We were thrilled to see him.

Time seemed to pause briefly, just for a moment as we stood there in the rain with our friends after walking over eighty miles straight through the San Juan Mountains of Colorado, and I savored that first sense of satisfaction in making it.

Dottie had freshly baked cookies and bottled water in the car and I used all the self-restraint I could muster by limiting myself to four cookies on the drive back to their home, over twenty-five miles away.

On the drive home they pointed out some of the recent burn area, hundreds of acres of black scars all over the mountainsides.

Lowell and Dottie were quick to make room for Alex to stay the night with us, a complete change in plans and yet a welcome surprise. We were treated to a deliciously filling dinner of pasta, salad, and bread. Warm food represented an entirely new level of luxury at that point. Alex seemed so happy and grateful to have so much good company and food surrounding him. He'd hiked alone since we last saw him in early Montana and over a month had passed since then.

All of us were yawning by 11:00pm and my eyelids were heavy with white wine, compounding my existing lack of sleep, so we called it a night. Not thirty seconds after curling up under a homemade quilt in a soft bed, we were asleep.

The following morning, more than anything, I wanted sleep. I wanted thirteen hours of comatose, black-out, catch-up sleep. But that day, I would not get it. We needed to keep moving up the trail if we were going to have time to complete the one last section that I had originally skipped.

The plan was to get on the road by 8:00am and I knew Lowell and Dottie would be ready. They ran a tight ship if given a schedule and I didn't want to be the one that messed with the plans, so after another home cooked meal by Dottie, including eggs, cinnamon rolls, and toast, we all piled into their SUV once again.

Before heading back to the trailhead, Lowell and Dottie drove us around Creede to show us some of the old mining memorabilia around town. It really was an incredible sight to see old wooden buildings literally built into the rock, hundreds of feet off the ground. From there we drove around the surrounding area to see some of the damage the summer's wildfires had done to the trees and vegetation. I was surprised to see how much of the area had burned, yet signs of life were already popping up in the lime-green colored grass growing back in thick patches on the ground. The burn was on a much, much bigger scale than we had all originally realized and I still couldn't imagine how Joe and other hikers had made it through that area.

Back in the parking lot at Spring Creek Pass, we were left with Alex at the trailhead, with the difficult act of parting ways yet again. We'd all hiked more than a thousand miles since our last meeting in Montana, and here we were again, saying goodbyes and walking the opposite way. I didn't envy any of the miles Alex had ahead of him;

they were tough, exposed, and oftentimes undefined. We talked with Alex for nearly a half hour as we stood in the parking lot.

Our time with Alex felt so short, but it was time to say goodbye. The clock was around noon and I could already see thunderclouds forming above. I knew we had a very exposed section ahead of us on the Snow Mesa, a flat table-top section that had nothing more than small bowls to huddle in, in the event of lightning. I also knew Alex had an equally exposed section coming up, even longer than ours.

We all exchanged hugs before Matt and I headed towards the mesa. Two miles and 1,300' of climbing later, we reached the flat top, where the clouds were dark, there was thunder in the distance, and little hints of rain kept warning us of impending storms. I was scared of the storms rolling in, carrying with them strong gusts of wind that nearly pushed us off the narrow single-track trail, into thick tufts of grass.

We soon passed a spot that we'd camped at just a year before and had a little moment there. I was still so happy to be with Matt for those miles, knowing how sad he would have been had he passed that spot alone.

The exposed miles seemed to last forever but luckily we dodged the thunderstorms around us. We could see them two ridges over, but nothing ever settled on top of us, so we continued a steady push the rest of the day. We again were hiking fairly blind, without maps or the data book, but we felt confident in this section because nearly the entire way was shared with the Colorado Trail.

On that first day out of Creede we hiked a surprising amount of elevation change and yet we both felt amazingly good for having pushed so much the previous two days. I attributed it to eating multiple cinnamon rolls at Lowell and Dottie's. Nineteen miles into the day, at around 9:30pm, we stopped to camp at a saddle, a flat but windy spot. Nothing could have kept me awake with how tired I felt once I lay down under my sleeping quilt.

The next morning, the trail immediately dropped down into a long, downhill meadow and we let gravity help us cover miles as we walked sleepily during the morning miles. It was a beautiful morning but cooler for much longer than I had expected. I was accustomed to temperatures rising fairly quickly in the Colorado mornings once the sun came out, but that morning the sun popped out briefly, only to give way to early morning clouds.

All morning was spent talking about what we remembered about the upcoming miles, what they looked like, any elevation changes, and what we were thinking and feeling the prior year as we passed over those miles. It doesn't sound exciting as I write about it now, but on the 108th day on the trail, the fact that we had something new to talk about was enough to put some excitement and fire in us.

Much of the day was fast, easy hiking. We had good tread and even had some faster miles on a dirt road. I had to admit, I loved the Colorado Trail. It was so much easier than the CDT because of its shorter length of 486 miles, its good tread, and its overall lack of massive elevation changes. Maybe that made me a wimpy hiker who liked easier stuff, but I didn't care. I was a sucker for flatter, well-maintained trails that didn't completely kick my butt.

Though the skies threatened all day, they never rained on us for more than a few minutes. I relaxed once we reached the early evening and the clouds gave way to clearer skies. Just after a section of dirt road we turned onto a wide, smooth trail, like an old carriage road, surrounded by trees on each side and blanketed with pine needles. It was heavenly.

Because we had such easy trail to follow, we walked well into the dark, until 10:00pm. We would have gone farther but we were approaching a highway crossing and a road walk on a popular forest service road. I was scared of possibly passing campers along the road so we stopped before going any farther, calling it a day after thirty-five miles.

As soon as we finished eating dinner and both crawled into the tent, it started pouring rain.

We were up and out early, feeling the push of being so close to both our finishes. Shortly into the forest service road, as we sat and ate breakfast at the only water spot for the next twenty-two miles, a truck passed us on the road. There were two men inside who I guessed to be hunters; it was now hunting season, which scared me and gave me all the more reason to be finished. It also justified my fear in hiking too much into the night, knowing we'd probably pass hunters' camps.

We took a late-morning break and as we sat there, a cold breeze kicked up and it made me nervous. It was much cooler than I had anticipated it would be in mid-September and I wondered about the possibility of snow.

Later that afternoon we ran into a guy who was out surveying the trail for a maintenance crew. He said we were lucky to be finishing at Monarch Pass the next day because a storm front was moving in that would bring a lot of rain and snow to the area, especially in higher elevations. In our next section, from Copper Mountain to Steamboat Springs, we still had the highest point on the entire trail, above 14,000', with many more miles above 10,000'. It was bad news that I had already suspected by looking up at the skies. I feared our time was running out.

We took one final break in the daylight at a creek and as we sat there purifying our water, up walked Greta and Chris, two southbounders we had met on our day out of Lima, Montana. They were down one hiker from before, Charlie, who was battling major health issues with stomach and leg pains, and who had just quit at Monarch Pass. They were noticeably bummed about having lost a companion, hoping that if we caught up to Charlie at the pass that he might be motivated to keep going. That gave us a little fire to keep going that evening.

After that we hiked for several more hours, much of which was covered under trees as we made our way over rolling terrain. We hiked until we were within a mile of a road crossing, just like the night before, and picked a spot on a soft bed of pine needles, tucked into trees. Just as we got in the tent, it started pouring rain yet again. It was so cold that night that I wore all my clothes, including my wind breaker, my down jacket, and my rain jacket. Thankfully I'd bought lightweight tights and a long sleeve shirt in Durango, anticipating some cold Colorado nights.

The next morning, eleven itty-bitty miles stood between Matt and his official finish of the CDT. I was so happy for him because he was about to accomplish what he'd set out to do and because I'd been able to be a part of it after all. And yet, just as I felt with Joe and Raisins, I was sad that I would once again witness someone else's finish without being finished myself. I dreaded the upcoming miles from Copper to Steamboat, especially if storms were moving in.

We popped up energetically to start the day. Much of the upcoming section was very memorable for us because it had been one of our favorite days on the Colorado Trail. The year before, we hiked the section in the early morning sun and it had been a beautiful, clear, warm day. This day was cold and foggy, which was unfortunate because the section normally offered sweeping views of the surrounding area. We couldn't see more than twenty feet ahead of us.

Those miles were very popular with mountain bikers because of the fairly smooth trail, amazing views, and easy accessibility by road. With about a mile to go we met two women out for a ride, two sisters who lived in Salida, the nearest town to Monarch Pass. After talking with them for ten minutes, they offered us a ride to Salida if we were still at Monarch Pass when they returned from their ride.

When we reached the pass, Matt's official finishing point, I started crying. They were tears of joy for Matt. He'd reached the finish of his CDT thru-hike. I was so happy that he had finally finished the trail, despite all the tribulations, and that he was a triple crowner. We took photos of each other with the sign at the pass, then headed inside to the Monarch Pass General Store, getting a brief reprieve from the cold morning amid heavy, dense fog.

At the same time of soaking in Matt's accomplishment, we also started thinking about the next steps to take in order for me to complete every piece of the trail. We needed a ride to Copper Mountain, almost one hundred miles away. Inside the store we borrowed an old piece of cardboard and a thick black marker and made a sign, hoping it would help us hitch up to Copper. The sign read, "CDT Hikers to Salida…Leadville…Copper."

With so many things against us, including time, weather, and the logistical challenge of actually returning to Copper Mountain, the upcoming section all the way to Steamboat Springs seemed like anything but a done deal.

4
Optimist

Despite logistical challenges galore, including the massive fire that had derailed and altered our hike immensely, here we were, back in Colorado at the spot we'd skipped ahead to more than two months back, marking my completion of the 3,000 mile trail. I totally understood the feelings Raisins and Joe had had during their last week before Canada and the relief that came with actually connecting my steps to finish the CDT in a way that I was satisfied with. I also knew the feelings Julie must have been having, knowing that she had miles left to hike.

We'd both known for some time that we were going to attempt to finish her section too. So as we walked into the parking lot at Monarch Pass, I had feelings of accomplishment from completing the hike, as well as anticipation as we began game planning for the next section.

In order to finish Julie's section, we needed to get back to Cooper Mountain where she'd gotten off the trail, and then hike roughly 250 miles to Steamboat Springs, where she'd gotten back on a little over a week later. It was going to be a huge challenge because the miles ahead were tough miles, it had been cold and wet of late, we had less than eight days left to do it in, and we needed to hitchhike nearly 100 miles from Monarch Pass to Copper Mountain before we could even get started.

We hurried into the hiker-friendly store at Monarch Pass to get something warm to drink and to strategize. Julie managed to get us cardboard and a marker to make a sign and within a few minutes, we were back on the road with our thumbs out, trying to get to Copper.

We had a backup plan if no one picked us up and thankfully so because after thirty minutes with no one stopping for us, a couple women we'd met out on the trail had returned to their cars to head home. They offered us a ride and we were quick to latch onto them to take them up on the offer.

What was going to be a twenty mile leg of the journey with our new friend Jill, turned into a nearly seventy-five mile trip with her, taking us all the way to the town of Leadville. She dropped us off at Subway so we could grab lunch, and from there it was only one more road and twenty-five miles to Copper. Luck was still on our side and we caught a ride within ten minutes. In near record fashion, we were standing at the entrance of the Copper Mountain Resort. It was early afternoon and we were now ready to resume our hike, the final leg of our CDT journey.

I think the entrance to the Copper Mountain Resort will forever be an emotionally charged place for us. As we stood there together, looking at the signed archway above the entrance to the resort, there was emotion and there were a few tears as we were whisked back to that sad day, which felt like a lifetime ago, when Julie got off the trail.

I looked at Julie and said, "Are you ready for this?" She nodded her head and off we were, back to the trail for the final leg of the journey.

I felt as if I knew this section like the back of my hand now. This was now my third time in the past twelve months hiking this section of trail and the familiarity was comforting. As had been the case for most of our time in Colorado, the afternoon clouds were threatening as we made our way up Ten Mile Ridge, separating the ski towns of Copper and Breckenridge.

We were confident we could make it to Breckenridge shortly after the sun went down and the debate became whether to stay in town for the night or to get into town, buy food, and get back out. The mileage game had us leaning towards a quick in and out, but our love for Breckenridge and the possibility of being dry for the night were heavy motivators as well.

We hiked on through the afternoon, hardly stopping at all. We did the 2,600' climb in one push, only stopping near the top to put on our rain jackets and to grab an energy bar as we made our way above tree line and along the exposed ridge.

It was a wet, cloudy, and dreary day, but our spirits were high. We were on a mission and at this point we were both fully aware that our success primarily depended on how we were feeling about the mission. Consequently, we were both fine-tuned to staying positive and relaxed while maintaining our constant forward progress up the trail. Looking back, I hardly paused at Monarch Pass to think much about the technical completion of my hike because I was so engrossed in the mission of getting back on the trail to walk with Julie for her remaining miles.

As we began our descent from Ten Mile Ridge and headed down toward Breckenridge, we passed a section before heading back into the trees that will be forever etched in my memory. I remember crying as I listened to the pikas squeaking as I walked alone without Julie two months back. This was the spot she had so happily squeaked to the pikas the year before, the back and forth lasting minutes in my mind. As we walked through this section, this time amidst soft rain, I said to the cheerful pikas, "I brought a friend with me this time." Julie squeaked in her best pika pitch and cried a bit as we both felt the strength of our bond as a couple and as a team stronger than ever before.

The rest of the early evening was downhill hiking as we were in a race with the sun. It was now getting dark well before 8:00pm and with the cloud cover, it felt like our time was running out.

It started raining just as we got to Highway 9. We walked the bike path to the bus stop to town. It was 8:00pm, it was dark, it was raining, we needed food, and it was decided that we were staying in town.

The search for a hotel, which we'd thought would be easy, was anything but, as it was apparently "mud season" in Colorado, a time between summer and ski season, which was the low season for tourists. Eventually, we went with a resort with a free shuttle. It was on the high end of our price range but cost seemed less important than comfort at this point in the journey.

We hurried around town to do our resupply and were picked up shortly before 10:00pm by the resort shuttle. We had bags of food, wet and stinky packs, and we must have looked like quite the sight as we walked up to the hotel clerk to check in. He said that he'd quoted us a price for a basic room but after looking us over, he said he'd upgrade us to a suite for no additional charge.

As we walked into the plush suite with a living room, hot tub, and a full kitchen, we smiled at each other lovingly. This was the trail life. As funny as it sounds, getting to town late at night in the rain with our resupply in hand, and walking into a really nice room was just as much a part of the experience as the desolate walks on the Divide, and the bottom line was that we were so happy to be there experiencing it together.

We got cleaned up, we packed our food for the morning, and a little after midnight we were asleep as soon as the lights were turned off. Our plan was to exert some willpower in order to get up and out early so we could be back on the trail as soon as possible. We had a long way to go and time was running out.

5
Stopwatch

It was raining when we woke up and it took all the willpower we had to pack up and leave our plush hotel suite. There was absolutely no wiggle room in our schedule. We needed to leave as soon as possible to get nearly 230 miles completed in seven days, and we had some of the hardest miles of the trail ahead of us. Matt knew the upcoming section well and warned me about a long, treadless, cairn-less section coming up.

The hotel shuttle driver took us directly back to the trailhead, a few miles out of town, saving us at least an hour of waiting around for the free bus at the edge of town. As we sat in the cold, empty mini-bus, it was spitting rain outside with dense, low clouds, and all I could think about was my desire to be sitting in a warm, dry coffee shop in Breckenridge, sipping a warm beverage and eating sticky pastries. Most of all, I didn't feel good about the upcoming miles, knowing how high in elevation we'd be with all that rain, wondering how cold it was, and knowing how little experience we had in the snow.

The first twenty miles of the day went smoothly considering the persistent rain. There were periods of light rain, lots of clouds, and we still shared the well-maintained Colorado Trail. But, nearly every hiker I met over the last several weeks told me the trail was rough after it split off from the Colorado Trail, and that split was coming up very quickly.

Just before Georgia Pass, we tucked ourselves into trees for a snack break, out of the cold wind. We saw ahead that the trail was above tree line and Matt assured me we had plenty of exposed miles ahead of us. The skies above us looked like water balloons just waiting to burst with that first puncture and I took the opportunity to put on my rain gear, including my rain jacket, my wind pants, and my rain skirt.

Just as we stood up to leave, it started raining sideways and we could no longer see Georgia Pass, just a hundred yards away from us. We both sat down again, waiting for the initial burst of rain to subside. A few minutes later, we were too cold to keep sitting idly so we started walking in the rain.

Thus began some of the wettest, coldest, most rugged, most miserable miles I've ever hiked on a trail, including the eleven straight days of rain we hiked in the state of Pennsylvania on the Appalachian Trail.

Just as others had warned me, the trail was tortuously hard once it split from the Colorado Trail. First, there was no longer a trail, and second, even if there were cairns to follow, it was so foggy that we couldn't see them until we were right on top of them. I had trouble with even the smallest of climbs as we rode the roller coaster of the Divide. The altimeter on my watch was fairly unreliable because we changed elevation so much. It was only until after the trail that I realized we were well over 12,000' for all of that section, and later over 13,000'. Matt had a hard time with route-finding, considering he'd already hiked the section, because it was so foggy and therefore unfamiliar compared to the last time he hiked it, amidst clear, blue skies.

As the daylight started to dim, much earlier because of the fog and rain, I asked Matt how far we'd walked through the tough section. I could tell by the look on his face that he didn't want to share that information.

"Well, I think it was about eleven miles of this tough section of trail...and we've done about four miles of it."

For the first time since I quit the trail at Copper Mountain months back, I felt defeated. It just didn't seem possible to cover that kind of ground in the time we had and the weather wasn't getting any better.

We talked over our options as we continued our slow progress on the Divide, considering hiking through the night. The intermittent tread and difficulty in finding the trail in the daylight scared us too much to seriously consider that option. The last thing we wanted to do was to get lost, and as we talked it over, we decided that if we ran out of time to get to Steamboat Springs, we'd at least try to get as far as possible. That simply had to be enough for us at that point, and I was ok with that.

Just before dark, we found a small flat spot just off the side of the trail, a rare occurrence considering we were hiking on the spine of the mountain. The elevation was right around 13,000', nearly a full 4,000' higher than the town of Breckenridge. Once we crawled inside the tent, it started pouring outside, much heavier than it had the entire day, and for the first time on the trail the tent started leaking. It was only on my side, near the seam above my shoulders. The rain started soaking in, then traveling its way down a seam before beading up and dripping on me, inside the tent. Not good. Really, really not good. I tried not to worry about it, thinking only the shoulder area of my sleeping quilt would get damp, but the thought of a leaky tent in that kind of rain gnawed on my nerves all night. I slept poorly, thinking about that leak and about the challenging miles coming up.

The next day was simply unrelenting.

It started with more miles of cairn-hunting, GPS coordinate searching, and frustration between the two of us for such a slow, grind-it-out-pace that took so much more effort than we wanted to give. At one point I saw a cairn off to the left of the Divide and followed it, soon finding myself and Matt on the side of the mountain, among loose rocks and boulders, with rain pouring down overhead. We had obviously gone the wrong way but I was so angry about a cairn pointing us in that direction that I was determined to find my way over the terrain. Then there was a microscopic moment when we realized the unsafe conditions we were in, chancing a rock slide with so much loose ground and rocks due to heavy rains, and it scared the hell out of us. We both scrambled as deftly and lightly as we could at an angle, up the side of the mountain, until we reached safe ground on the spine yet again. We were out of breath when we reached the top and near the point of exhaustion because the stress of being lost was compounded with every drop of rain and low-lying cloud above us. As much as I tried, I couldn't think of any solutions for dealing with the route-finding or the rain. These were not the final days I had envisioned and yet the factors were so out of my control that I felt numb as I pushed forward.

A brief walk on a dirt road calmed us down, only to lead us to a turn off the road that literally lead to nowhere, off the side of a cliff. We could see our trail down below, where we were headed, but couldn't see any hint of a trail down the side of the mountain to get us there. Not a switchback, not a cairn, nothing. As we picked our way down the side of the cliff, slipping on loose rocks, scooting down on our butts, and nearly holding our breath out of fear the entire time, I thought back to my original decision to quit and realized that had I gone through this section the first time with my negative attitude, it would have certainly driven me over the edge. Not that it helped my current situation in covering the miles, but in a way, my decision felt justified.

Twelve miles into the day, we made it to Peru Creek by late morning. All of the small creeks were swollen, flooding much of the trail, and Peru Creek was rushing with fresh rain water. It started raining hard yet again as we found cover under trees along the bank of the creek. There was no sign of an end to the rain.

As we sat there eating a snack by the creek, a woman pulled up in a Subaru and got out to walk her dog; I was shocked to see people out there and honestly contemplated getting a ride out of there because of the rain. We asked the woman about the rain and she looked a little guilty as she said, "They're calling for a lot of rain until Tuesday and then it's supposed to clear up starting on Wednesday."

It was Thursday morning and we only had until Tuesday to hike because our flight home was on Wednesday. This information hit me in the gut and I started crying after we started walking again. The idea of five more days of this rain crushed every ounce of positive energy I had left and I felt depressed. I truly wanted to give in, but Matt was having none of it.

"You've come so far, with just five days to go! Just finish this!" he yelled at me.

He was right. When the going got really tough, I tended to get going, and I needed to overcome my discomforts and just keep walking. Just ahead of us was the toughest section and highest point yet: Grays Peak.

Part one of the tough section was a 1,300' climb up to Argentine Pass. It was drizzling, our feet were soaked from walking through all the swollen creeks, and we both put on our power songs on our mp3 players to help us push up the mountain. I led our train of two, keeping up a good pace as we hammered it up to the pass. I felt good, I started feeling positive again, and I was ready to keep fighting. Overall, the climb was tough, inevitably so because it was high in elevation heading up to the pass of 13,212', but still very doable. We had a well-defined path the entire way to the pass and I nearly cried tears of gratitude.

Then part two began. From the pass, which was usually the highest point but in this case was just a stepping stone to more high points, we walked a mile on the spine of the Divide. All in all, the six hundred foot gain over this mile was slow but again, doable. We reached Mount Edwards at 13,818' and felt triumphant in reaching this point. Our pace was significantly slower because of so many factors, including the labored breathing at such high elevation, the continuous drizzle of rain and overbearing fog, and the lack of legitimate tread to guide the way. Compared to the day before though, this was the true spine of the mountain, which was actually easier to navigate because there weren't many options on where to go. If we didn't follow the spine, we chanced careening off the side of the mountain, so it made route-finding that much easier.

Part three of this section was what separated the men from the boys. From Mount Edwards we walked one and a half miles to Grays Peak at 14,261'. For nearly two hours we scrambled over loose rocks along the spine of the mountain, oftentimes on steep terrain and sometimes in fairly precarious, scary situations. It was raining sideways, clouds hiding anything more than a twenty-foot radius around us, and we navigated over slanted, slick rocks that were loosening and giving way under so much rain. Red Hot Chili Peppers songs were playing in my ears as we picked our way over the spine. Matt and I didn't talk much, not out of anger but out of concentration, other than to agree on a route as we half-hiked, half-climbed our way up and down the spine, and then up one final ascent to the peak. Looking back, we were in a very dangerous situation given the rain, the visibility, the slickness of the rocks, and the unforgiving terrain, not to mention that there wasn't a soul within a several mile radius of us.

Just before we started the final ascent up to Grays, as we stood on one side of the ridge of the mountain, looking across a small dip in the spine, I paused for a moment to look up. Something in my instincts told me to stop and look out ahead of me and as I stood there, the fog cleared for a brief moment to reveal a herd of fifteen shaggy white mountain goats just ahead of us, standing on the loose rock.

"Shaggy white mountain goats!" I yelled to Matt. He looked up and stopped moving just as I had, stuck in the moment as all the goats turned their heads to stare at us.

It was one of the most magical, surreal moments I've ever had while hiking and I felt happiness nearly burst inside me. My entire hiking history flashed before my eyes as the fog blew over and revealed the stark white goats against a dark gray backdrop, and I couldn't recall any other moment like it, where my hike finally felt complete, no matter what happened. I felt calm, I felt at peace, and most of all, I felt fulfilled. We were in the worst of conditions as we stood there, our rain gear soaked through as we covered slow, rugged terrain, there was no one around for miles, and yet I still had Matt by my side as we stood there locking eyes with shaggy white mountain goats. For one of the few times in my life, I was lost in the moment and all peripheral thoughts momentarily disappeared, just like the fog.

Our magical moment passed as the fog rolled in again, covering the goats from afar, and we climbed to the other side where the goats stood. They let us get within six feet of them before they moved on, effortlessly down the side of the mountain. It would be an understatement to say that I felt ill-equipped for such weather and terrain as I watched then hop up and down the mountainside without so much as a "neh" in response.

Once we passed the goats our focus was on the final climb up to the top of Grays Peak. It was so steep at such high elevation that I stopped every ten steps to catch my breath. Then, out of nowhere, about thirty feet from the peak, I found myself walking on a smooth, clear path. Matt bounded up the new tread and I followed, ecstatic that we were nearing the top.

At the top, it was the same sight we'd seen all day: a cold, wind-blown, foggy landscape that we couldn't see much of beyond twenty feet. But I didn't care; I hadn't come for the view. I came to reach the top and I had my own personal brush with shaggy white mountain goats on an epic day of nasty weather, all with my best friend. I started crying out of overwhelming happiness.

Matt walked over to me, grabbed me by the shoulders as he

choked back tears, and said to me, "That's the hardest thing you'll ever do on this trail, and you did it. I'm so proud of you." I cried even harder because I was so happy and proud that I'd pushed on and made it to the top, and that I had made Matt proud.

We didn't linger long at the top because of the weather and quickly headed down, freezing from being sweaty from the climb and heading downhill. The tread was such a wide, smooth path on the other side that we started running some of the sections. We were giddy as we enjoyed the smooth downhill, both relieved and exhausted.

Just as the rain started to increase from a drizzle to a pour, we reached the trailhead where there were pit toilets, a parking lot, and campsites. It was only 7:30pm but we decided to call it a night. We had barely covered twenty-four miles but we were beaten down, physically and mentally. All of our hiking clothing was soaked, including our rain gear, and I didn't know how we'd get through another five days of rain. I was used to normal Colorado weather where the morning sun allowed for drying time, just in time for the afternoon storms to come in, then making way for clear evening skies. I couldn't fathom a week straight of rain in Colorado, but it was really happening.

As we sat in the doorway of the bathroom, sitting on our mats on the concrete floor, we contemplated sleeping in the bathrooms but decided against it when I nearly threw up my dinner because of the smell. We set up the tent under some trees and settled in for the night, hoping to rest up and stay dry.

The tough day was followed by a difficult night. The tent leaked even worse than the night before, on several more points along the seams, and both of our sleeping quilts got soaked through, particularly the feet, where most of the down tended to concentrate. Even our sleeping clothes got wet, which rounded out my entire wardrobe, so I woke up with just one dry item, a pair of socks.

Upon waking up and assessing the damage the leaky tent had done to our sleeping quilts, one of our most sacred pieces of gear, I knew we had a decision to make. About seven miles into our day we were going to cross I-70, a chance to get out of this rain and call it a best-effort without incurring further damage or risking our safety. As we walked on a dirt road that morning, the creek alongside us was rushing with muddy water and the road was littered with large rocks that had tumbled down from the adjacent hillside. Then we walked on a bike path paralleling I-70 as we talked over our present situation.

At the Herman Gulch Trailhead at I-70, we unpacked our packs to assess the water damage to our gear. There was an inch puddle of water at the bottom of my pack, accumulated in the trash bag liner I used as a rain barrier, which wasn't doing much good being a water bucket. My sleeping quilt, which was packed in that pool of water at the bottom, was so densely wet that when I pulled it out, it dripped water and I squeezed out water like a wet sponge. Everything was heartbreakingly wet.

As we contemplated our options, I looked back on yesterday's events, thinking about those mountain goats and how fulfilling that brief moment had been, and I knew we were finished. We couldn't continue on with so much rain and so much wet gear, and even though it meant I wouldn't have a true thru-hike, I was ok with that. In fact, I was at peace with it. I had the CDT experience I was looking for, one in which I enjoyed nearly every moment on the trail, one in which I finished without an ounce of regret, one in which I was finally at peace with myself, with my relationship with Matt, and with my relationship with the trail. I felt a lot of love for the trail, despite its difficulties, and I had too much respect for it to continue on in such conditions.

It was Friday morning on September 13th and after 113 days on the trail, we both agreed that the highway was the end of the line for us. As we hitched from the highway off-ramp, hoping it was less illegal than hitching from the actual highway, a cop doing his rounds passed us twice before stopping on his third time around to ask if we were ok. Before giving us a ride into town in the name of "desperate hikers risking hypothermia," he frisked us as a precaution and tossed our packs and poles in the trunk.

The ride with the cop definitely topped the BMW into Helena. As we rode in the backseat of the car, the state trooper clued us in as to what had been happening around us while we'd been detached from all forms of communication in the woods. Apparently flooding in the area was rampant, so bad that there was a mud slide on I-70 up ahead on the way to Denver, and nearby towns were being evacuated. It was like walking into Chama all over again, thinking plumes of smoke were oddly-colored clouds that turned out to be signs of one of the largest forest fires in Colorado history.

When we pulled up to the Subway parking lot off the highway, a group of four guys were standing at the back of a car with a map spread out across the trunk.

"What's that a map of?" Matt asked them.

"Rocky Mountain National Park," they said. "It's completely closed because of flooding. We were supposed to go there this weekend."

Had we kept walking, our trail took us right through that park in the next two days and it would have been closed. We weren't even sure if the town of Grand Lake was still functioning, where we were supposed to pick up more food. Another upcoming town near the trail, Estes Park, had already been evacuated. I didn't feel so wimpy after all as we learned about the havoc all the rain was causing in the entire area surrounding the trail.

As we sat in Subway, we felt safe from the weather but we felt stuck. We were in a Subway, off a random interstate exit, without a plan to go anywhere, with a flight that left for home in four days. I walked straight up to a stranger in line and asked him for a ride to Frisco, where I knew we could rent a car. I didn't care who I might offend by asking such a bold question. What in the world could I lose, given that I'd just been through some of the toughest mental and physical battles of my life?

Luckily, the man didn't hesitate and said, "Yes, I'd be happy to. I was going to offer it when I overheard you say that you and your husband were stranded hikers."

Matt hopped up from the Subway booth and our packs were in the back of his truck before we even finished our drinks. It wasn't a half hour later before we were in a rental car office in Frisco, finally getting wheels and our freedom from hitching rides.

With some time left before our flight, we drove our rental car to Steamboat Springs to visit our friend, Eric. It hurt a little to retreat to his home yet again, tail between my legs, this time because of weather pushing us off the trail, but I was over it. We'd made our decision to play it safe and leave some miles on the table and I had to accept that decision.

We stayed with Eric until we flew out of Denver the following Wednesday, when the skies finally cleared. In that time, incredible stories about the flooding poured in, like the flooding in Boulder, the evacuation of Estes Park, and even federal emergency declarations in counties bordering the CDT.

As we spent those final days in Colorado, I thought a lot about the trail. I thought about all the different twists and turns that our adventure took as it evolved into much more than a thru-hike, I thought about all the decisions I had made and therefore had to live with, and I thought about all the things I had learned about myself and about Matt. Lastly, I thought about all the things I was grateful for once I was able to step back from the trail and see life from a broader perspective. While the trail didn't unfold the way we had originally envisioned, I was both happy and proud of my CDT experience. I had an unforgettable, once-in-a-lifetime, incredibly unique, every-cliché-in-the-book journey, and in the end, that mattered more to me than any label could ever encompass.

6
Optimist

We were finally finished. As we walked the wet bike path paralleling I-70 towards the Herman Gulch Trailhead, we both knew the adventure was over. Julie had overcome her fears and anxieties, and we both felt a sense of conclusion alone atop Grays Peak the evening before. Prior to that effort though, Julie had been thinking about quitting, and understandably so. The section of trail from Georgia Pass to Grays Peak, in those conditions, was the most difficult, miserable, and dangerous section of the entire trip. However, I felt like the journey couldn't end with her running away from the challenge. I remember sitting next to her at Peru Creek, telling her how mad she'd be at herself if she were to listen to what she was saying at that moment. While I had done nothing to stop her from leaving the trail back at Copper Mountain the first time, as her best friend, I didn't want her to have any regrets this time around. As we scrambled and clawed our way along the spine of the Divide up to the highest peak on the entire CDT and hugged each other amidst the desolate gray landscape, Julie crying tears of happiness, I felt truly in love. She had made it, she didn't quit, and we were both so proud.

Up until that point I was blindly optimistic to the weather that we were engulfed in. I could sense Julie's desire to run from the challenge and my focus was on helping her stick it out until the end. But after she triumphantly scaled that final peak, we both felt at peace and knew this journey was finished. Any fire I had remaining to keep hiking in the cold, wet, miserable conditions was gone and I too was ready to be finished.

When I think back on the three distinct finishes we experienced on this trail, first with Raisins at Waterton Village in Canada, and then with my official finish at Monarch Pass, and there with Julie at Interstate 70, there is a similar theme to my emotions each time. I have never been one to jump with excitement at the end of the journey and this time was no different. I finished this trail with a sense of calm satisfaction, a small smile on my face, and a mind quickly cataloging the experience while beginning to dream up the next one. I am a doer and while I find value in reminiscing about the past, I tend to find the most joy in thinking about the future. As I finished my CDT hike at Monarch Pass I was thinking about how to get back to Copper Mountain so Julie could finish her hike. When we decided that her trail ended at Grays Peak I began thinking of how to get home in order to start our new life in Seattle.

This is part of why I love the trail life so much. It is a never-ending pursuit. I've now hiked well over 10,000 miles of trail in the United States and I never feel finished. I love long distance hiking and while I don't know when I'll set out again on a long trip, I know it'll always be part of me, as it has ever since I first stepped foot on the Appalachian Trail when I was nineteen years old. There is a simplicity about the life that is freeing. There is a sense of clarity of thought that comes from spending quiet time walking endless hours in the wilderness. There is a strong sense of purpose as we move everyday toward a new destination. There is also both a feeling of significance and insignificance from the trail life that gives my life perspective. It leaves me feeling grounded in who I am and in my place in the world as I return back from the mountains.

The greatest jewel the trail life has given me though is a feeling of love, friendship, and fellowship with other people. Our families live the trail with us from home as they hear about our struggles and our triumphs. Our friends support us and encourage us. Strangers email us words of encouragement and strangers invite us into their homes and take care of us. It is truly amazing what people have done for us. I am still flabbergasted by the kindness of Dave when he handed me the keys to his truck so we could buy food in town when our food was nowhere to be found, and he didn't even know my name. Karla became our personal chauffeur, driving us all around the state of Colorado. She took us into her home and treated us like royalty.

These things happen on the trail and I am so glad they do because they make me feel so good about people that I too want to give to others all the more because of it.

Lastly, the trail has brought me closer than I ever thought possible with my wife. We understand each other so well that we can walk miles on end without talking and still know what the other is thinking. We can function on the trail with speed and dexterity because we have each embraced our roles and we work together like a fine-tuned machine. We are there for each other and I am infinitely grateful that Julie decided to return to the trail to hike the remainder of the CDT with me. I know I could have made it alone and while that experience would no doubt have produced amazing stories and life-altering experiences, I know deep down that life with her is better. I am a hugs kind of guy, and I know that with Julie by my side, it is all the easier for me to be the optimist that I love to be.

7
Stopwatch

My relationship with thru-hiking has typically been love in hindsight rather than love at first sight. I am ashamed yet willing to admit that in the past, I have kicked and screamed while pushing through discomfort and challenges, but I've also finished what I started and have even loved thru-hiking by the end. In my love-hate relationship with thru-hiking, I've had a lot more hate than is healthy and my goal for the CDT was to flip that ratio. I wanted pure joy in a thru-hike and I wanted to experience that joy while hiking on the trail. I didn't want to slog through the miles, only to look back on the hike with fond memories, as I did with previous thru-hikes.

For the first time on any trail, including the Appalachian Trail and Pacific Crest Trail, I have no regrets. When I finished the PCT in 2007, I knew I'd spent a lot of the trail in a ball of misery because the experience was simply so much harder, both physically and mentally, than I had imagined it would be. When I finished the Appalachian Trail in 2011, I was mad at myself yet again for spending so many miserable moments on the trail, again because it was harder than I had originally envisioned, creating an unhappy environment for both Matt and me. Both trails certainly had their bright spots but overall, my biggest takeaway from each one was that I needed to hike another one "correctly." I wanted to tame my anxieties, adapt to changes, find happiness in otherwise dreary situations, and put my best self forward.

Basically, I wanted to conquer myself.

The Continental Divide Trail was anything but a normal thru-hike in so many aspects and yet it is the one I'm most proud of because I truly was my own hero. I saw more wildlife than all other trails combined, I realized I can find my way without a path, and I dealt with ever-changing factors in the weather and terrain. Most of all, I made peace with both myself and the trail.

Looking back, while I still feel a twinge of guilt in leaving Matt for a week on the trail, I have an even greater amount of gratitude for the change in perspective that it gave me. I was able to get back on the trail a week later as a completely different hiker. I was legitimately happy to be out there for the sheer fact that I was with my husband, supporting his dream the only way I knew best, by hiking with him. Once I gave up the pressure of a thru-hike and the allure of the "Triple Crown" label, I embraced those miles as if every single one was one I wanted to walk.

While I still have some unfinished miles in Colorado, I'm proud that I finally took action to alleviate my unhappiness, an action which led to my happiness for the rest of the trail. Part of my acceptance in missing those final miles is because I know none of the previous 2,000 miles would have been possible had I not missed a week in the first place.

I'll always remember my conversation with the four day hikers as I stood outside my rental car in the trailhead parking lot in Grand Lake, waiting for Matt to arrive after his first five days alone on the trail. It was the conversation that lead me to realize that just because a true thru-hike may no longer be possible, that didn't mean I couldn't hike the rest of the way. If it meant I was again with Matt, did a complete thru-hike matter so much that I'd all-together scratch the rest of the trail? No! I'll always remember that "aha" moment, as if a tree was blocking my train of thought by lying on the tracks and someone had just lifted the tree off, allowing for a clearing of the blockage in my brain.

The moment I made that decision to get back on the trail, I always knew it was a possibility that we wouldn't have the time to go back and finish those miles, and I was ok with that. I didn't think it would be flooding that would end up stopping us rather than the clock, but it was the reality that I had to swallow after having completed 2,850 miles.

The question that I think is most important in assessing the CDT as a whole is, "Is it about the journey or the destination?"

Looking back at my hikes on the PCT and AT, it was all about the destination. I wanted to see how quickly we could get from point A to point B, and while I enjoyed some of the events in the middle, my focus was always on that Canadian border or Mt. Katahdin. For the CDT, once I got back on the trail in Steamboat, it was all about the journey. I no longer even had a destination; Canada wasn't my finishing point, nor was Monarch Pass, and I didn't end up making it to Steamboat. I was simply out there to *be* out there, and for me, the fact that I finally lived out that clichéd, over-used yet under-utilized saying, is my true success in hiking the CDT. When I saw those shaggy white mountain goats from across the spine of the mountain as I stood in sideways rain on treacherously wet rocks, with Matt as the only soul near me to witness such a rare, once-in-a-lifetime event, I realized what it meant to be living for the journey, not the destination.

ABOUT THE AUTHORS

Both Ohio natives, Matt and Julie have traveled much of the world together, all the while finding a way to incorporate an adventurous twist. In addition to the Continental Divide Trail, together they have completed the Pacific Crest Trail, the Appalachian Trail, and the Colorado Trail (2007, 2011, 2012). When they are not hiking they are usually running, constantly striving to push the boundaries of distance and time from the mile up to 100 miles. Matt is undoubtedly the impetus and ideas guy behind their adventures, while Julie is the logistical mastermind that keeps them both grounded and prepared to take on every adventure. They currently live in Seattle, Washington. To read more about their past, current, and upcoming adventures, as well as to view pictures from all their thru-hikes, visit their website at urbyville.com.

Julie's other works include *The Trail Life: How I Loved it, Hated it, and Learned from it*, a book about her first long distance hiking experiences on the Pacific Crest Trail, and *Between a Rock and a White Blaze: Searching for Significance on the Appalachian Trail*.

Made in the USA
San Bernardino, CA
02 December 2016